Ecology and Plant Geography

Ecology and Plant Geography

Umesh Kumar

AMIGA PRESS. INC
Delhi -110051

AMIGA
PRESS INC.
AMIGA PRESS INC.
Registered Office:
19 DBS Building, Ansari Road, Darya Ganj, Delhi. 110002, India
Phone: +91-11-23283333 Email: amigapress@gmail.com

This edition is published by Amiga Press.Inc

ISBN : 978-81-929542-4-0

First Published 2018

Reprint 2026

Printed and bound in India by Replika Press Pvt. Ltd.

Preface

The field of plant ecology includes the study of plants and their environment. Rather than just looking at plants in a vacuum, researchers consider how they interact with each other and their environment to create an interconnected system. Plant ecology can include the study of entire ecosystems, such as the rainforest or plateau, or the study of specific areas of interest, like plant populations which manage to survive next to a polluted stream. Plant ecologists also look at animals, soil conditions, and other influences on a plant's environment.

Ecology is a complex and vast field of study which can encompass everything from understanding how natural environments function to how humans interact with the natural world, and how various behaviors can fundamentally alter the natural environment. In plant ecology, people can focus on topics like climate change and its effect on plants, plant evolution, how plants disseminate themselves in nature, symbiotic relationships between plant species, plant diseases, and so forth.

Plant geography as a subject in its own right is relatively modern. It is true that records of plant ranges, as then known, are given by many early authors but they are usually incidental to other studies. For several reasons phytogeography is becoming of increasing importance. The rejuvenation of taxonomy along the lines of the "new systematics" or synthetic taxonomy, the application of data derived from the newer branches of ecology and cytogenetics, the extending realization that man is destroying the natural flora and vegetation of many parts of the world, and, perhaps, one may add, the greater facilities for overseas travel are all stimulating to phytogeographical research.

Ecology is concerned with the relationship between plants and their surroundings and with the grouping of plants into kinds of vegetation. On the whole, plant ecology is intensive while plant geography is extensive in outlook, but both are concerned with plants and, in attempting to correlate observed structure and behaviour with "causes," both refer to the same sum total of environmental factors though the emphasis varies. The purpose of this book is to consolidate all this information and present it in a simple way for the benefit of the students, as well as teachers and researchers.

Plants containing volatile oils, which are readily converted into resins by the action of oxygen, or those containing tannin or other readily oxidizable substances, take up the largest quantity. This is remarkably illustrated by an experiment in which the leaves of the Agave americana, after twenty-four hours' exposure in the dark, were found to have absorbed only 0·3 of their volume of oxygen, while those of the fir, in which volatile oil is abundant, had taken up twice, and those of the oak, containing tannin, eighteen times as much oxygen.

In the flowers, both by day and night, there is a constant absorption of oxygen, and evolution of carbonic acid. In fact, an active oxidation is going on, attended by the evolution of heat, which, in the Arum maculatum and some other plants, is so great as to raise the temperature of the flower 10° or 12° above that of the surrounding air.

The purpose of this book is to consolidate all this information and present it in a simple way for the benefit of the students, as well as teachers and researchers.

—*Editor*

Contents

1

Introduction

The term "geobotany" includes both plant ecology and plant geography. As far as possible it is desirable to refer to ecological "distribution" when describing the habitat conditions and limitations and to phytogeographical "range" when defining the geographical boundaries of taxa, plant communities, etc. It is, however, to be noted that by long usage "distribution" is frequently synonymous with "range." Phytochoria should be defined by their ranges though many other data are included in their descriptions.

The aims of plant geography may be briefly defined as:

1. To find out and to record the occurrences of plants, especially as species, in localities fixed geographically;
2. To determine the units into which the earth can be divided on the basis of similarity of ranges of taxa and to describe these units;
3. To name and classify these units as phytochoria;
4. To determine, as far as possible, the causes which have resulted in the ranges and in the make-up of the phytochoria.

We have noted that plant geography is based on taxonomy and is very closely associated with ecology. From some points of view it can be considered a branch of geography. When "causes" of ranges are under discussion it becomes obvious that it is the most synthetic branch of botany. Not only does the phytogeographer have then to take into account the morphological and physiological particulars of the plants themselves as individuals, as taxa, or as plant communities but he has to obtain data from geology, from archaeology, from history, from meteorology, from pedology, from zoology, and from his botanical colleagues who have specialized in the study of this or that aspect of plant life. Plant geography as a subject in its own right is relatively modern. It is true that records of plant ranges, as then known, are given by many early authors but they are usually incidental to other studies.

Theophrastus, in his *Enquiry into Plants* heads Book IV with "Of the trees and plants special to particular districts and positions" and gives interesting information for many plants of the eastern Mediterranean Region. There is little in the works of the herbalists, or of pre-Linnean authors generally, that can be called plant geography in any proper sense, though there are many references to places whence plants came and some local studies of range and distribution.

Tournefort, in his *Relation d'un voyage du Levant*, 1717, described, somewhat vaguely, altitudinal zonation on Mt. Ararat in Armenia. Linnaeus recognized and described plant communities, mainly for Scandinavia. Albrecht von Haller of Bern for Switzerland and Jean-Louis-Giraud Soulavie for southern France published accounts that include phytogeographical material for the areas with which they were concerned. Carl Ludwig Willdenow, in his *Lehrbuch der Botanik* has a chapter on the history of plants of which he says *"Unter Geschichte der Pflanzen verstehen wir die Einflus des Klimas auf die Vegetation, die Veranderungen, welche die Gewachse wahrscheinlich erlitten haben, wie die Natur fur die Erhaltung derselben sorgt, die Wanderungen der Gewachse und endlich ihre Verbreitung uber den Erdball."*

There is much in Willdenow's chapter relevant to plant geography, but more that is better considered as concerning plant ecology. It is generally held that Alexander von Humboldt was the "father" of plant geography. He published with A. Bonpland an *Essai sur la Geographie des Plantes accompagne d'un tableau physique des regions equinoxiales,* Paris, 1805. In 1817 there appeared his Book *De distributione geographica plantarum secundum coeli temperiem et altitudinem montium Prolegomena.* This is written in Latin and deals with the range and distribution of plants in relation to climate, with the major zones of torrid, temperate, and frigid. Both latitudinal and altitudinal zonation are considered and his coloured diagrams of the latter are famous.

Auguste Pyramus de Candolle, published in 1809, in the *Dictionnaire raisonne et universel d'Agriculture,* an account of "Geographie agricole et botanique," and in 1820, in the *Dictionnaire des sciences naturelles* XVIII his *"Essai elementaire de geographie botanique"* of 64 pages. In these works he deals especially with the relationship between land utilization, botany, and the external factors of the environment.

Joachim Friedrich Schouw, a Dane, published a general textbook of plant geography in Danish in 1822 and in German (*Grundziigen einer allgemeinen Pflanzengeographie*). In the first part of his book he deals with the ecological factors, warmth, moisture, light, etc., and in the second part with the occurrence, range, and distribution of single species, genera, families, and the whole plant kingdom. He first used the ending -etum for plant communities, such as Ericetum, Coryletum, Fagetum, and Quercetum. In the third part he gives a summary of the flora of the earth on the basis of zonations in longitude, latitude, and altitude.

An interesting work that is often overlooked is that of F. J. F. Meyen, *Grundriss der Pflanzengeographie, Berlin, 1836, of which an English translation by M. Johnston was published in 1846 by the Ray Society under the title Outlines of the Geography of Plants. This mainly follows the lines laid down by Humboldt and Schouw but is still well worth reading. It has an extensive "Supplement" dealing with the history of cultivated plants.*

Alphonse de Candolle, in 1855, published two volumes on plant geography. J. D. Hooker has a long essay-review on this work. Its historical importance is that it appeared shortly before the announcement of the theory of natural selection by Darwin and Wallace and the publication of Darwin *Origin of Species*. It is a clear account of the facts of geographical ranges and of ecological relationships as then known and understood but is based on the idea that the majority of species were created such as they now exist. J. D. Hooker was at this time in an "on-the-fence" position regarding the general theory of evolution and his comments on and criticisms of A. de Candolle are extremely illuminating to anyone who tries to understand the mental difficulties of those who were first meeting with the new evolutionary ideas that were so quickly to become biologically orthodox.

THE PLANT ENVIRONMENT

Nutritional problems must be considered in relation to all the conditions in which plants live, and not merely in terms of the amounts of plant nutrients contained in or added to the soil. For example, those who are accustomed to growing plants know that the temperature must not be too low or no growth may result or that if too high the plants may be injured. An optimum temperature is usually recognized and this may vary according as to whether the plant is young or old. Similarly the importance of light is well known and plants may be put in special positions to obtain a maximum supply of light at one stage and may be shaded at another.

The actual duration of the daily period of illumination also affect growth and there are plants which are classified as requiring "long day" conditions to complete their growth cycles and others as needing "short day" conditions. If the special "long" or "short" day periods are not forthcoming for the respective classes of plants requiring these, their growth cycles are abnormal and they may fail entirely to produce flowers, grain or fruit.

The humidity of the atmosphere, as distinct from the water supply in the soil, is of importance in determining the water conditions within the plant, as these are dependent on both water intake by the roots and water loss from the leaves, the latter being largely influenced by the air humidity.

Even the presence of adequate quantities of plant nutrients in the soil is no guarantee that they will be absorbed by the plant roots. It will be shown later how these may be present in forms which are not available to the plants, but even when they would be considered as being present in suitable forms for absorption, other factors may prevent this taking place. An example of this latter condition is afforded in poorly aerated soils where lack of oxygen near the roots may prevent them from actively absorbing mineral nutrients

The problems of such influences in the plant environment as those just mentioned are complicated by the fact that they do not act independently, but their effects are modified by one another. Thus the effects of light intensity or period of daylight may vary with different temperature conditions.

The requirements of plants for different nutrients may be affected by conditions of light, temperature and water supply, and by other factors of the general environment. Thus the need for nitrogen may be less under conditions of relatively low light intensity whereas the need for potash in these circumstances may be greater, these facts being of importance in growing tomatoes under glass. The effect of nitrogen in relation to light may be shown by growing a plant under normal light conditions with insufficient nitrogen, when the leaves will show the well known symptoms of nitrogen deficiency-pale green, yellow, orange and red tints. If such a plant be then shaded, the leaves will turn a darker green and growth may be visibly increased. It can be shown that the lowered light conditions result in an increase of "soluble" a breaking down of proteins, thereby rendering the nitrogen of these available for growth processes.

This interrelationship of environmental factors is well illustrated by an experiment on apple trees at Long Ashton.

Bramley's Seedling trees were grown in compost in large pots and given a small dressing of a nitrogenous fertilizer. Some of the trees were grown in a specially constructed glass house and an equal number in an adjoining wire enclosure. The trees in the enclosure showed severe symptoms of nitrogen deficiency-pale green and yellow leaves, reddish brown barks and highly coloured, red fruits. The condition was corrected by further dressings of nitrogen. In contrast, the trees under glass, where the light was of less intensity and the temperature higher, made vigorous growth, carried large, green leaves and bore large, green fruits.

Iron and zinc deficiency symptoms may be less severe under conditions of low light intensity, whilst boron deficiency effects are less severe and magnesium deficiency effects are more pronounced in wet seasons than in dry ones.

The rate of water absorption is less at lower temperatures than at higher ones and efficient intake is also dependent on good aeration. These facts may result in a water deficit within plants growing in cold, wet soils when the air temperature is high. The raw materials needed for plant growth consist of carbon dioxide, which is obtained from the atmosphere through the stomata of the leaves, and water and the so-called mineral nutrients, which normally enter the plant through the medium of the roots.

The importance of water and carbon dioxide in the nutrition of plants will be apparent from the facts that water often comprises 80 to 90 % of the total weight of growing plants, and carbon and oxygen together may account for over 80% of their dry matter, i.e., the solid matter remaining after water is removed. As against these large amounts, the mineral nutrients, as measured by the ash content of the plants, i.e., the mineral residue obtained when the organic matter is destroyed by heat, often contribute from 5 to 15% of the dry matter.

It has been shown in recent years that certain organic compounds, known as "growth promoting substances" or "hormones", which occur in plants, and some of which are also present in soils and natural manures, are capable of producing marked growth responses, such as increased root growth, shoot and leaf curvatures, stimulation or suppression of buds, increased fruit setting, prevention of fruit abscission etc. They appear to perform important functions in the growth of plants. Examples of substances of this kind which can produce growth responses are 13 indole-acetic acid, 13 indole-butyric acid, phenyl acetic acid, A, naphthalene-acetamide, vitamin B_1

It is not at present clear to what extent growth substances are absorbed by plants from soils, although it has been shown that vitamin B_1, which occurs naturally in soils, can be obtained in this way.

THE MINERAL NUTRIENTS

It has been shown in numerous researches that certain elements are necessary for the healthy growth of plants. They are sometimes spoken of as essential elements and, since some are needed in relatively large quantities and others in very small amounts, the former are referred to as "major" elements and the latter as "minor" or "trace" elements, or as micro nutrients.

The terms "major" and "minor" do not refer to the relative importance of the functions of the elements in plant growth, and for this reason the term "trace" element is preferable for the latter class. Major elements: Nitrogen, phosphorus, calcium, magnesium, potassium, sulfur.

Trace elements: Iron, manganese, boron, copper, zinc and molybdenum. (Iron occupies an intermediate position and is usually included in the major elements group. In dealing with field problems it is more convenient to group it with the trace elements.)

In addition, there are, other elements, such as sodium, chlorine and silicon, which produce beneficial effects on the growth of certain plants but which have not so far been shown to be absolutely essential to growth. The element aluminium is of general occurrence in plants, but seems to be without direct nutritional value, although aluminium sulfate is used, because of its acidifying properties, to change the colour of hydrangeas growing on alkaline soils from pink to blue, and aluminium may also exert indirect influences on nutritional processes.

Other elements often occur in plants but they are not known to serve any useful function and frequently they act as plant poisons or toxins. The nutrient elements can only be absorbed by plants when present in certain forms: nitrogen from nitrates and ammonium salts; phosphorus from phosphates; calcium, magnesium and potassium from their salts; sulfur from sulfates; iron from ferrous or ferric salts (more readily from ferrous salts); manganese from manganous salts; boron from borates; copper and zinc from their salts, and molybdenum from molybdates.

There may appear to be certain exceptions to this statement in practice. For instance, nitrogen may be applied to a soil as "organic" nitrogen, as in hoof meal or urea, and sulfur may be added as the element itself, as in flowers of sulfur, ground sulfur, etc. In such conditions the added materials are, however, converted into the nitrate and sulfate forms respectively by soil organisms before being absorbed by the plants.

Further points of importance in connection with the absorption of the mineral nutrients by plants are as follows:

(a) They must be absorbed from relatively dilute solutions or the plants will be! injured or even killed.

(b) Certain of the elements slow down the absorption of others into the plant, e.g., calcium slows down potassium and vice versa. The phenomenon is known as "antagonism".

(c) Healthy plants result when the nutrients are absorbed in certain relative proportions. When the proportions are suitable the nutrient medium is said to be "balanced". When ratios between nutrients are too wide, deficiency conditions are created. Thus if a high proportion of nitrogen to potassium is absorbed, the plant will suffer from potassium deficiency.

(d) Nutrients, even though present in the nutrient solution in satisfactory amounts and proportions, may not be absorbed by the plant unless the "reaction" of the solution as regards acidity and alkalinity is satisfactory. The reaction is measured in terms of the pH scale, which is merely a convenient notation for stating the conditions of acidity in the solution (strength or intensity of acidity, not total amount). The neutral point is represented by pH 7.0; below this value the solution is acid and above it is alkaline. Many crop plants prefer a reaction slightly on the acid side-pH 6.0 to 6.5 and extreme values are in the neighborhood of 4.0 on the acid side and 9.0 on the alkaline side.

(e) The nutrient medium must contain an adequate supply of oxygen, i.e., aeration must be satisfactory.

THE FUNCTIONS OF THE MINERAL NUTRIENTS

Knowledge of the main functions of the mineral nutrients is useful in helping us to understand the effects produced by deficiencies of any one of them.

Essential Major Elements

Nitrogen. Nitrogen is a major constituent of several of the most important substances, which occur in plants. It is of outstanding importance among the essential elements in that nitrogen compounds comprise from 40 to 50% of the dry matter of protoplasm, the living substance of plant cells. For this reason nitrogen is required in relatively large quantities in connection with all growth processes in plants. It follows directly from this that without an adequate supply of nitrogen appreciable growth cannot take place and that plants must remain stunted and relatively undeveloped when nitrogen is deficient.

Proteins, which are of great importance in many plant organs, e.g., seeds, are compounds of nitrogen whilst chlorophyll, the green colouring matter of the leaves, also contains the element.

From this latter fact it will be apparent that when nitrogen is deficient leaves will contain relatively little chlorophyll, and will thus tend to be pale green in colour.

In addition to the above substances, numerous other organic compounds of importance in plants, such as amino acids, amides, and alkaloids, are compounds of nitrogen.

Certain compounds of nitrogen are very mobile in plants, and this enables them readily to mobilize supplies of the element at vital growing points and to transfer stored supplies to points where they are most required. Such transference is common from old tissues to young growing points when supplies of the element are short. This mobility and re-utilization of nitrogen explains why deficiency symptoms of the element always appear first in the older parts of plants and why growing points are the last to be affected.

Phosphorus: This element, like nitrogen, is closely concerned with the vital growth processes in plants as it is a constituent of nucleic acid, and nuclei in which this occurs are essential parts of all living cells. Hence a deficiency of this element will also be expected to result in greatly restricted growth. Phosphorus is also of importance in seeds and in connection with the metabolism of fats. Compounds of phosphorus are concerned with the processes of respiration and with the efficient functioning and utilization of nitrogen. This relationship to nitrogen probably accounts for the fact that several of the symptoms of phosphorus deficiency are identical or similar to those which result from a deficiency of nitrogen, Phosphorus is also of special importance in the processes concerned in root development and the ripening of seeds and fruits.

Calcium: Calcium occurs in plants chiefly in the leaves and the amounts present in seeds and fruits are relatively low. One of its main functions is as a constituent of the cell wall, the middle lamella of which consists largely of calcium pectate. This function appears to be of fundamental importance since, if calcium is replaced by any other of the essential elements, such as magnesium or potassium, the organic materials and mineral salts in the cells are readily leached through the walls.

Other functions attributed to calcium are as follows: It provides a base for the neutralization of organic acids; it is concerned with activities of growing points (meristems), especially with root tips; it may be of importance in nitrogen absorption.

Although a large proportion of the calcium contained in the plant may be soluble in water-as much as 60% in cabbage calcium does not appear to move freely from the older to the younger parts of plants, and hence young tissues contain lower proportions of calcium than older ones. This may explain why calcium deficiency effects begin at the tips of shoots.

Magnesium: The outstanding fact about magnesium is that it is a constituent of chlorophyll, and is essential to the formation of this pigment. As a result, when magnesium is deficient, one of the symptoms commonly shown by plants is chlorosis. Magnesium is also regarded as a carrier of phosphorus in the plant, particularly in connection with the formation of seeds of high oil content, which contain the compound lecithin.

The element seems to be very mobile within the plant, and when deficient is apparently transferred from older to younger tissues where it can be re-utilized in the growth processes. This agrees with the observation that signs of magnesium deficiency invariably make their appearance first on the oldest leaves and progress systematically from them towards the youngest ones.

Potassium: Unlike all the other major elements, potassium does not enter into the composition of any of the important plant constituents, such as proteins, chlorophyll, fats and carbohydrates, concerned in plant metabolism. For this reason its role is more difficult to determine, and in spite of much study it cannot be said that the functions of potassium are clearly understood.

The element is present in all parts of plants in large or fairly large proportions. It seems to be of special importance in leaves and at growing points, as these are especially rich in potassium. Probably the whole of the potassium in plants is present in soluble form, and most of it seems to be contained in the cell sap and cytoplasm.

It is outstanding among the nutrient elements for its mobility and solubility within the plant tissues, and these properties no doubt account for the ready way in which potassium can be re-utilized by young tissues when the element is in short supply.

Among the functions which have been attributed to potassium and the processes with which it may be concerned, the following may be mentioned: The formation of carbohydrates and proteins; the regulation of water conditions within the plant cell and of water loss by transpiration; as a catalyst and condensing agent of complex substances; as an accelerator of enzyme action; as contributing to photosynthesis through its radioactive properties.

It has been shown in many instances that the potassium content of plants is frequently much higher than is necessary for healthy growth, and it is generally considered that luxury absorption of potassium often takes place.

The great mobility of potassium in plants, its special importance for and its reutilization by young tissues, and its apparent functions as a regulator of plant processes on a large scale are in harmony with the observations that, when potassium is moderately deficient, the effects are seen first in the older tissues and progress from these towards the growing points, but, when the deficiency is acute, growing points are severely affected, and die-back and general collapse of the plants commonly occur.

Sulfur: Sulfur occurs in plants as a constituent of proteins, and of certain volatile compounds such as mustard oil. It seems to be connected with chlorophyll formation, although it is not a constituent of this substance. Its functions in connection with proteins and chlorophyll doubtless account for the similarity of its deficiency effects to those due to deficiency of nitrogen.

Essential Trace Elements

Iron: Iron is closely concerned with chlorophyll formation but is not a constituent of it. Its role appears in this connection to be that of a catalyst. As a result of this function of iron, chlorosis is invariably an outstanding symptom when the element is deficient. Iron may also act as a catalyst, in the role of an oxygen carrier, in respiration.

A point of great importance in connection with iron is its relative immobility in plant tissues. Its mobility seems to be affected by several factors, such as the presence of manganese, potassium deficiency and high light intensity. There is evidence that the amount of chlorophyll is related to "active" iron in plants.

It will thus be seen that so-called iron deficiency in the plant may in fact usually mean iron immobility. Lack of mobility may also account for the fact that iron deficiency is first shown in the younger tissues.

Manganese: The functions of manganese are regarded as being closely associated with those of iron and as being concerned with chlorophyll formation.

Hence, when manganese is deficient, chlorosis is a common symptom.

Manganese may decrease the solubility of iron by oxidation and hence, an abundance of manganese within the plant may lead to iron deficiency and chlorosis.

Manganese is regarded as having the functions of a catalyst; its activities being specially concerned with oxidation and reduction reactions within the plant tissues.

Boron: The exact role of boron is not known, but again the evidence as for the other trace elements, suggests that, its functions are those of a catalyst or reaction regulator. Particular effects attributed to boron are as follows:

It can delay the onset of calcium deficiency effects but cannot replace calcium; it tends to keep calcium soluble; it may act as a regulator of potassium/calcium ratios, and of the absorption of nitrogen; it may be concerned with the oxidation-reduction equilibrium in cells.

Such functions as the above accord with the results which follow from a deficiency of the element, when growth processes show sudden collapse and drastic derangements of metabolism occur.

Zinc and Copper: Although specific functions have not been determined for these elements, here again the evidence points to their roles as catalysts and regulators. Deficiencies of both are associated with chlorosis and a serious general collapse of vital growth processes.

Since catalysts are not used up in the chemical reactions which they promote, we can understand how it comes about that quite small or even minute quantities of the "trace elements", iron, manganese, boron, zinc and copper, may nevertheless be essential to the plant's health and growth.

Elements Sometimes Beneficial

Sodium: As sodium is not strictly an essential element it cannot be expected to have a specific role in the metabolic activities of plants.

Where sodium produces significant effects it is often regarded as a conserver of potassium and as being able partly to replace that element in its role.

In no instance, however, has it been shown that sodium can wholly replace potassium where the latter is acutely deficient. In such circumstances, sodium is ineffective as a substitute for potassium, even for sodium-loving plants, such as sugar beet, mangold and barley.

Sodium seems to affect the water relations of plants and often enables sugar beet and other crops to withstand drought conditions which would otherwise produce severe adverse effects.

Chlorine: The evidence of the role of chlorine in plants is somewhat contradictory, and no general statement can be made. In tobacco it has been shown to increase the water content of the tissues and to affect carbohydrate metabolism, leading to an accumulation of starch in the leaves.

The element is present in plants as chloride, and is wholly soluble.

TOXIC EFFECTS OF MINERAL ELEMENTS

Toxic effects in plants may be produced both by essential nutrient elements and non-essential elements. In the first class, the major nutrients are much less toxic than the trace elements. Indeed, for the major nutrients, there exists a fair safety margin for excess or "luxury" consumption, but for the trace elements the margin is very narrow.

Similar conditions exist in relation to non-essential elements thus some plants will tolerate fairly large amounts of elements such as sodium or chlorine, but are injured by relatively small amounts of elements like arsenic or chromium. Two types of injury may occur: (1) An excess of one element may lead to a deficiency of another which ultimately results in a deranged metabolism, e.g., excess nitrogen or excess phosphorus may result in insufficient potassium and excess potassium may lead to deficiency of magnesium or calcium. This type of injury applies particularly to essential nutrients. (2) The presence of an element may directly injure the protoplasm and bring about the speedy death of the plant.

KNOWLEDGE OF PHYTOGEOGRAPHY

Many other names of botanists who contributed to the knowledge of phytogeography in the first half of the 19th century could be mentioned. One has to remember that from the time of Linnaeus to the time of Darwin there was a tremendous amount of geographical exploration that often included botanical research. It is true that this was very largely systematic and economic but without taxonomy there can be no development of plant geography. Collections poured in from all over the world and were described in "floras" and monographs. Gardens, botanic and horticultural, were enriched and systems of classification were gradually improved.

The work of botanists, whether in taxonomy or in phytogeography, was then essentially descriptive and classificatory. In plant geography, however, there had been some advances on this somewhat static position in that correlations were found between ranges and environmental factors. The theory of evolution was, however, not generally accepted till after the publication of Darwin *Origin of Species* in 1859. The influence of evolutionary theory in explaining the facts of plant geography very speedily became apparent in the writings of botanists.

It is also worth noting that Darwin considered biogeography as of very great importance in supporting his theory of evolution by natural selection. He devotes two chapters to "Geographical Distribution" in the Origin of Species. The development of plant geography was very great during the second half of the 19th century. The flora and vegetation of many countries were explored and described and many of the problems that arise in attempting to explain their origin were often clearly stated.

Only a few outstanding names can be mentioned and that of J. D. Hooker is foremost because of his work "in the field" and his extensive publications in this subject. Hooker, as Assistant Surgeon and Botanist, accompanied James Clark Ross in the *Erebus* and *Terror* expedition to "Antarctica" and collected and studied the flora in Madeira, Cape Verde Islands, St. Helena, Kerguelen Island, Tasmania, The Falklands, Hermite Island, New Zealand, and the Cape. His journey to the eastern Himalaya and botanizing in Sikkim and Assam occupied the whole of 1848 and much of 1849. In 1860, he visited Syria and Palestine, in 1871 Morocco, and in 1877 North America on botanical expeditions. A full account of the phytogeographical researches of Sir Joseph Dalton Hooker was published in 1953.

Partly contemporaneous with J. D. Hooker were the great German botanists – A. Grisebach, A. Engler and O. Drude with their text-books and other comprehensive works on plant geography. The important series of monographs by various authors edited by Engler and Drude under the general title *Die Vegetation der Erde* covered many countries of the world. Karsten und Schenck edited the volumes of *Vegetationsbilder* Jena, 1904 to 1944, 1, 26.

Since 1900 a number of general books on plant geography have been published. The following are given in the bibliography and have been consulted in preparing the accounts of modern methods and results that follow: H. Solms-Laubach, Graebner, Hayek, Campbell, Wulff, Cain, Good, Croizat, and Dansereau.

Special mention must be made of the improvements in plant geography resulting from the rise of ecology and the more recent advances in physiological ecology. The great work of A. F. W. Schimper, *Pflanzengeographie auf physiologischer Grundlage*, Jena 1898, with its English translation *PlantGeography upon a physiological basis*, by W. R. Fisher, revised and edited by P. Groom and I. B. Balfour, Oxford 1903, had a tremendous influence in stimulating interest and research in the subject. Some of Schimper's conclusions, as those on xeromorphism, have been strongly criticized and have to be modified as a result of more evidence though it is interesting to note that more recently still it has been shown that some of the criticisms were too extreme.

A third edition of Schimper *Pflanzengeographie,* by F. C. von Faber, was published at Jena in 1935 in two volumes. A textbook by E. Warming was originally published in Danish, in 1895, under the title *Plantesamfund,* with German editions in 1896 and 1902. What is described as "practically a new work" by E. Warming assisted by M. Vahl, based on *Plantesamfund,* appeared in 1909 as *Oecology of Plants, an introduction to the study of plant-communities,* Oxford. There were later German editions of which the fourth by E. Warming and P. Graebner has the title *Lehrbuch der okologischen Pflanzengeographie,* Berlin 1930- 1933. While Warming's first book quoted above is ecological rather than p hytogeographical, the last edition is wider in its outlook. E. Rubel's scheme for the delimitation and nomenclature of plant communities is also of phytogeographical importance. The full account was published as *Pflanzengesellschaften der Erde,* Bern-Berlin, 1930. Like the works of Schimper and Warming, it has an ecological basis.It is worth recording that the text-books on plant geography and closely related plant ecology mentioned above contain numerous bibliographical references.

The boundary between ecology and phytogeography is frequently passed in many of the papers published in ecological journals such as the *Journal of Ecology, Ecology, Oikos,* and *Vegetationsbilder.* The publication *Pflanzenareale,* with range maps and explanatory text, is more definitely phytogeographical but has apparently ceased publication.The use of palaeobotanical evidence in plant geography can be gauged from Wulff's 1932-1944 publications already noted and from Seward book *Plant-Life through the Ages,* Cambridge, 1931.

There are also the very important works of Reid and Chandler and Chaney, and the publications referred to in Cain Recently there has been the introduction of cytogenetical data into the realm of plant geography. There is no doubt that researches on the cytology and breeding phenomena of plant species will become of increasing importance in tracing the history of their ranges. At present the known facts are meagre relative to the number of species in even poor floras, while cytogenetic investigation of the rich floras of the tropics has been little more than commenced.

POLYPLOIDY AND PLANT GEOGRAPHY

Polyploids are organisms having an increase in the number of chromosome sets above the normal diploid. It is reasonably certain that in any naturally occurring plant series the plants with the lowest chromosome numbers are more primitive than polyploids presumably derived from them. Hagerup, observed a correlation between polyploidy and extreme climates, "those with the higher chromosome numbers are always the ones growing farther north, and thus more exposed to extremes of temperature."

Later correlations were found between increases in percentage of polyploidy and other environmental extremes. The subject has grown considerably and useful summary accounts will be found in Stebbins, Cain, and A. and D. Love. Reese shows that, on available data, polyploidy increases with latitude from North Africa through Europe to the Arctic. He considers that the main correlation is with the age of the flora: the younger the flora the higher the percentage of polyploids.

Those readers particularly interested in the British flora might consult Haskell. Most authors who have written on the ranges and distributions of polyploids conclude that polyploidy confers benefits which enable the species (or other taxon) to extend into less favourable habitats.

This is certainly sometimes true but how far wide conclusions are valid is more doubtful.

The results as presented are frequently statistical and are sometimes open to criticisms: only parts of floras are included, the chromosome numbers used are based on few reliable counts of wild plants of known origin per species, most of the research has been done in Europe in areas heavily glaciated in the Ice Age, tropical and subtropical floras have been very little examined cytogenetically, and so on.

Further, even if it were accepted that polyploidy is, at least on the whole, advantageous in the struggle for existence, there is little or no agreement as to the underlying causes, that is of the nature of the advantages. Structural, physiological, and genetical advantages of various kinds have all been suggested by different authors.

Stebbins said "Perhaps the safest generalization that can be made about polyploids is that they are most numerous in regions that have only recently been open to colonization by plants or that have undergone great changes in their floras in recent times."However, it must also be said that some authors have failed to find such correlations between polyploidy and ranges as indicate that polyploids can withstand less favourable ecological conditions than diploids.

Soo and Heiser and Whitaker are examples and the latter even go so far as to say that generalizations involving polyploidy are probably meaningless. While this last is too sweeping a statement there is no doubt that much more research is needed before the full significance of polyploidy for plant geography is known.

EFFECTS OF HUMIDITY ON PLANT GROWTH

Growth and development are influenced by humidity in and around the plant. Low air humidity creates an environment that enhances the potential for significant plant water loss. At the same time, regulating water loss through stomatal closure causes a reduction in carbon dioxide (CO_2) diffusion that limits growth. High air humidity, on the other hand, promotes environmental conditions favorable for disease development. Humidity refers to the amount of water vapor in the atmosphere. Globally, water vapor levels vary from almost zero in the arctic regions of the world to 4 or 5% of the atmospheric volume in the equatorial regions. The percentage of actual vapor in the atmosphere at any given time in relation to the maximum amount of vapor that can be held is termed relative humidity (RH).

RH = actual vapor pressure saturation vapor pressure

The actual vapor pressure is a measure of the amount of water vapor in a volume of air. As the amount of vapor pressure increases, the actual vapor pressure will increase.

Saturation vapor pressure (also referred to as absolute humidity) is established when the number of water molecules evaporating is equal to the number of water molecules condensing. Relative humidity can change from location to location, day to day, and hour to hour. Relative humidity changes through evaporation and temperature. Water evaporation into the atmosphere changes the amount of vapor in the air. This process is slow, because it takes a considerable time for the water vapor to diffuse into the atmosphere. The amount of moisture held in the atmosphere is determined by temperature. As the air temperature rises, the relative humidity will drop.

Conversely, when the air temperature drops, the relative humidity increases, even though no water vapor has been added. During the night, if temperatures fall, relative humidity will increase, reaching 100%. If the temperature continues to fall, then the water vapor begins to condense and form dew. Relative humidity is not a useful measurement when describing plant transpiration. Transpiration is better described when differences in vapor pressure between the leaf and the atmosphere are used. Water vapor is expressed as either (a) the absolute humidity (mol or g mL"3 ; kg m"3), (b) specific humidity (kg kg"1), or (c) as vapor pressure (kPa). Transpiration occurs because a vapor pressure gradient forms between the leaf surface and the surrounding air. The relative humidity within the leaf or near the leaf surface is considered at or near 100%. Even if the canopy temperature is the same as the ambient temperature, rarely is the atmospheric relative humidity at 100%. Thus a vapor pressure gradient forms between the leaf and the atmosphere, which drives transpiration.

PENMAN EQUATION

Penman defined potential evapotranspiration as "the amount of water transpired in unit time by a short green crop, completely shading the ground, of uniform height and never short of water." Using this definition, he developed the following equation for calculating potential evapotranspiration (2,3): Jn î =1+ LE where Jn = net radiation LE = latent heat es = saturation vapor pressure (absolute humidity) at the surface e = vapor pressure of the air above the surface ea = saturated vapor pressure above the surface î = psychrometric constant (relates wet-bulb and dry-bulb thermometers to vapor pressure) = slope of the saturated vapor pressure versus temperature curve.

The potential evapotranspiration is calculated by measuring net radiation, temperature, vapor pressure, and wind velocity above the crop canopy. Monteith modified the Penman equation to take into account vapor transfer from slightly less than saturated surfaces. This modification, and incorporation of a canopy resistance variable to account for canopy resistance vapor transfer, is known as the Penman-Monteith equation. From these equations a vapor pressure gradient between the plant surface and the surrounding atmosphere is calculated. The greater the deficit between the plant surface, which is at or near 100 relative humidity and the atmospheric relative humidity, the greater the transpiration.

STOMATES

The amount of water being driven from the leaf to the atmosphere, as dictated by the vapor pressure deficit, is governed by stomates. Stomates play a dual role, since they are also the port of entry for CO_2. Stomatal openings are governed by the CO_2 concentrations in the intercellular spaces and not at the leaf surface or in the stomatal pore. If CO_2 concentrations in the leaf are low, stomates will open. Conversely, if CO_2 concentrations in the leaf are high, stomates will close. The dual role of stomates leads to interactions between CO_2 and vapor pressure. Stomatal conductance is a measure of CO_2 and water vapor into and out of the leaf via stomates. Conductance is used instead of resistance because conductance is directly proportional to photosynthesis (CO_2 diffusion) or transpiration. Bunce demonstrated, in a series of short-term studies under controlled and field conditions, that C_4 plants were less sensitive to low humidity than C3 plants even at vapor pressure deficits of 4.5 kPa in the field. Due to the greater CO_2 levels found in the leaf tissue of C4 plants, stomatal conductance had little effect on photosynthesis.

The interaction between CO_2 and vapor pressure deficit depends on the situation. For example, stomatal closures in plant species that grow well in arid regions with adequate soil moisture, like date palm (Phoenix dactylifera), are insensitive to vapor pressure deficit. Under desert conditions, CAM plants open their stomates during the night and close them during the day, which is the opposite of the occurrence for most plants. For CAM plants, the advantage of stomatal closure during the day is that it minimizes water loss, and then closure during the less stressful nighttime open to fix CO_2. Stomatal conductance is governed by other factors, such as light and plant water potentials, besides CO_2 and vapor pressure. Vapor pressure interacts with both light and plant water potentials. In the following sections, stomatal governance by light and leaf water potential is discussed, with attention directed toward the interactions with water vapor.

Stomatal Evolution and Structure

The earliest land plants were astomatous, with thick cuticle around their aerial organs. The lack of stomates, along with a thick cuticle minimized any plant water loss. These plants, however, had a low diffusion rate of carbon dioxide (CO_2). The lack of CO_2 diffusion for photosynthesis probably contributed to the slow growth and development in these early plants. Today, there is a diversity of astomatous plants, which are classified into two groups. The first group contains those species that never possessed stomates, like the gametophytes of bryophytes and lichens. The second group contains plants that were stomatous at one time but developed effective astomatous characteristics. In general, these types of plants are aquatic or parasitic in nature. Many aquatic flowering plants are astomatous when submerged, having little need for gaseous diffusion. Some aquatic flowering plants have dysfunctional stomates that remain permanently open. In some instances, parasitic flowering plants have lost their stomates or have dysfunctional ones. For example, in Neottia nidus-avis, the guard cells have fused shut. Early land plants and stomata most likely evolved during periods of high CO_2 concentrations in the atmosphere. Subsequent periods of low atmospheric CO_2 may have driven evolutionary forces toward high stomatal densities in plants like horsetails, ferns, conifers, and angiosperms. Stomates evolved initially for gaseous diffusion, and then as a mechanism to regulate water loss. Structurally, Esau considers the stomatal area of the leaf to include the guard cells and the stomatal pore. The stomatal area generally accounts for 1% of the leaf surface (<"100 stomates per millimeter). The actual number of stomates per given area varies among species. Green and coworkers calculated the number of stomates, both adaxial and abaxial, for 10 different turfgrass species. The stomatal density was greater on the adaxial than the abaxial leaf sides for most of the grasses. Stomates on the adaxial side ranged from 68 stomates per millimeter for tall fescue (Festuca arundinacea) to 203 stomates per millimeter for hard fescue (Festuca longifolia). No stomates were present on the abaxial side of hard fescue, sheep fescue (Festuca ovina spp. vulgaris), chewings fescue (Festuca rubra spp. commutata), or rough bluegrass (Poa trivialis).

No correlation between stomatal density and the evapotranspiration rate of the grass species was found. This would be expected, given the similar boundary layer among the species. Stomatal size varies depending on whether a plant is grown under optimum moisture levels or under moisture stress. Spence and colleagues studied stomatal size and guard-cell turgor of Vicia faba plants watered twice weekly and plants watered once a week. The plants watered twice weekly never showed wilt symptoms, while those watered once weekly showed wilting symptoms before each watering. The well-watered guard cells were either short and wide or long and thin, with the average size of 40.4 and 46.1 μm, respectively. The water-stressed guard cells were significantly smaller, measuring 37.4 μm. The geometry of the water-stressed guard cell allowed the stomatal pore to remain open at lower guard-cell turgor pressures relative to the surrounding epidermal cells.

Effects of Light on Stomates

Light plays an important role in the governance of stomatal opening. Illumination of the guard cells increases the synthesis of malate and uptake of potassium and chlorine, which results in swelling of the guard cells, thus increasing the pore opening. Blue light is more effective than red light in governing stomatal opening. In grasses, blue light elicits an initial rapid increase in transpiration, followed by a second slower increase. Blue light presumably creates an electrical gradient flux of potassium in the guard cell through hydrogen extrusion and ATP-dependent membrane hyperpolarization. Although red light is not as effective as blue light, continuous background red light enhances the blue light affect.

The magnitude of the blue light effect on stomatal opening is sensitive to CO_2 concentration and vapor pressure. Assmann, working with the plants Paphiopedilum harrisianum and Commelina communis, found that a reduction in intercellular CO_2 concentrations enhanced the blue light response. Assmann found in both plants that increasing vapor pressure deficit, from 0.34 to 0.59 kPA, diminished the stomatal response from blue light. The effects of the vapor pressure deficit were greater than those of the corresponding reduction in intercellular CO_2.

Temporary reduction in light influences stomatal conductance in a plant community. Plants that are continually exposed to short-term reductions in light (passing cloud cover) experience a reduction in photosynthesis and in some cases stomatal closure. Knapp and Smith compared herbaceous and woody plants in a subalpine community with regard to photosynthesis and water loss. The herbaceous species had higher photosynthesis and transpiration rates, lower leaf water potentials, and more rapid stomatal closure during shade than did the woody species. This response would indicate that herbaceous species maximized overall water use efficiency while the woody species with weaker stomatal responses maximized carbon gain. In a later study, Fay and Knapp evaluated the stomatal responses of two tallgrass prairie C3 plants, plains wild indigo (Baptisia bracteata) and annual sunflower (Helianthus annuus).

Although both plants would be expected to perform similarly to the herbaceous plants in their previous study, these two plants inhabit the prairie at different times. Plains wild indigo inhabits the prairie during the cool, wet season while the annual sunflower prefers the hot, dryer season. Wild indigo had no stomatal response to shade and lower photosynthetic capacity, stomatal conductance, and transpiration compared to annual sunflower.

This would be expected given that plains wild indigo experiences little water stress during the time it inhabits the prairie. Annual sunflower, however, had rapid stomatal closure during shade as well as higher photosynthetic capacity, stomatal conductance, and transpiration rates—all characteristics of a plant that experiences some period of water stress. Temporal shade reduces carbon gain and water loss in C3 and C4 plants. In a comparison of two row crops, C4 sorghum and C3 soybean, stomatal movement in response to temporary shade was much more apparent in soybean than sorghum, presumably due to the lower water use rate.

In both species the short-term shade (5 min) at 300 to 400 μmol m"2 s"1 photosynthetic photon flux density reduced photosynthesis, leaf temperature stomatal conductance, transpiration, and water use efficiency. Once the plants were reilluminated, photosynthesis was delayed. When Fay and Knapp compared sorghum with a native C4 grass, eastern gamagrass (Tripsacum dactyloides), responses to temporary shade were similar. Thus, domesticated and native plant responses to temporary shade are similar.

DEFICITS IN VAPOR PRESSURE AND XYLEM CAVITATION

In response to large vapor pressure deficits, many plant species close their stomates. The conditions most favorable for closure are low air humidity and high leaf temperature. In a review article, Grange and Hand point out that humidities between 1.0 and 0.2 kPa have little effect on the physiology and development of horticultural crops. Vapor pressure deficits lower than these lead to water stress, while higher values promote biotic problems like disease. In the studies reviewed here, vapor pressure deficits ranged from 0.5 to 6.0 kPa. Idso et al. reported, under nonirrigated conditions, vapor pressure deficits of 2 to 6 kPa. A number of studies reported vapor pressure deficits greater than

3.0 kPa. Given the range of vapor pressure deficits that a plant faces, rapid water loss due to transpiration can occur. In response to vapor pressure deficits, water moves upward under tension through the plant in conduits collectively known as the xylem. The water tension in the xylem increases as soil moisture decreases and transpiration increases. If the tension increases to a point where the water breaks in the xylem vessels and tracheids, water vapor and air begin to enter the xylem.

This process, whereby water continuity is broken, is termed cavitation. As the xylem vessels and tracheids continue to fill with air and the hydraulic conductivity decreases or ceases, embolism occurs. Cavitation and embolism are often associated with tall, woody materials, where water transport through the xylem travels great distances. Embolism is triggered by air aspirated into the xylem vessel through pores in the wall. Once air is in the vessel, it disrupts water flow. As air fills and embolism occurs, the process can spread to other vessels. Generally larger-diameter vessels and tracheids are most vulnerable to embolism. The pressure necessary to induce embolism varies depending on the species.

Most of the reported threshold values for xylem embolism in woody plants fall between "2.0 and "3.0 MPa. Some plants have xylem embolism at greater or lesser pressures. The importance of stomates in CO_2 diffusion is critical, yet due to the catastrophic nature of embolism, the primary purpose of stomatal closure may be to regulate water loss so as to avoid xylem cavitation. From an evolutionary point of view, stomates would have had to appear first since xylem cavitation would limit how tall a plant could grow. Woodward suggested that increased stomatal density enhanced the evolutionary development of plants by preventing xylem cavitation, resulting in longer xylem pathways in taller and more competitive genotypes.

LEAF WATER POTENTIAL

Moisture deficits in the plant elicit a number of detrimental responses. Hsiao outlined the sequence of events that occurs once moisture stress occurs. Cell growth is the most sensitive to a drop in water potential. A slight decrease in the leaf water potential ("0.1 MPa) causes a reduction in cell growth, resulting in a reduction in shoot and root growth. For this reason, numerous plants have been observed to grow mainly at night, when water loss is minimal. As water potentials become more negative, protein synthesis, nitrate reductase level, growth-regulating substances [abcisic acid (ABA) and cytokinin], CO_2 assimilation, respiration, protein accumulation, and proline accumulation are all affected.

Leaf water potentials in some plants may fluctuate during the day based on vapor pressure deficits and soil moisture, while other plants maintain constant leaf water potentials even under limited soil moisture. Anisohydric behavior is a term used to describe plants that have changing leaf water potential over a given period of time. Plants that exhibit anisohydric behavior include the herbaceous species wheat, sunflower, soybean, subterranean clover, barley, and the woody species of almond and peach. Isohydric plant behavior is the ability to maintain leaf water potentials at a constant value in the presence of changing soil moisture and vapor pressure deficits. Plants that exhibit isohydric behavior include the herbaceous species maize, pea, and sugar cane and the woody species poplar and lupin. Tardieu and Simonneau compared sunflower (anisohydric) and maize (isohydric) behavior during flowering under various irrigation regimes. Predawn leaf water potentials of sunflower were dependent on the moisture treatment.

Higher leaf water potentials were found in the plants under full irrigation compared to the leaf water potentials of the mildly water-stressed plants, which had higher leaf water potentials than the severely water-stressed plants. As the day progresses, stomatal conductance decreases following changes in light energy (photosynthetic photon flux density). Thus, stomatal closure provides control against dehydration, but fluctuation in leaf water potential occurred in response soil moisture and evaporative demand. The response patterns to these fluctuations were similar across the moisture stress treatments. When Tardieu and Simonneau looked at maize, leaf water potentials stabilized during midday for the three water-stress treatments even under high evaporative demand and changing soil moisture. The decrease in stomatal conductance was correlated with ABA levels.

No relationship between ABA and stomatal conductance was found with sunflower. Tradieu and Simonneau postulated that isohydric behavior is linked between hydraulic and chemical information (ABA), while anisohydric behavior lacks this interaction. Interestingly, commonly used classifications of species like monocyte versus dicot or C3 versus C4 were not associated with anisohydric and isohydric plants. Although leaf water potential is often used as an indicator of water stress, stomatal conductance is closely correlated with soil water availability. Naor and coworkers correlated stomatal conductance with stem water potential ($r^2 = 0.90$) as a better indicator of water stress than leaf water potential for apple. This study was followed up with additional field studies with apple, nectarine, and grapevine trees under various irrigation treatments and found similar correlation between stem water potential and stomatal conductance.

NUTRIENT DEFICIENCIES

The major plant nutrients except for calcium are not associated with humidity. Calcium-related disorders have been reported for many fruit and vegetable crops. Common calcium disorders include "tipburn" of strawberry, chicory, and lettuce leaves; "blackheart" of cauliflower, celery, and brussel sprouts; and "blossomend rot" of tomato and bell pepper. Calcium depends almost entirely on the xylem for distribution in the plant. If the water supply is reduced or eliminated to sections of the plant, localized calcium deficiencies occur. Humidity levels around and in the plant influence the likelihood of calcium disorders. Enclosed leaves are usually the most susceptible to calcium deficiencies due to low transpiration rates. Root pressure flow appears to be more important than transpiration in supplying calcium to enclosed leaves. Bradfield and Guttridge, working with tipburn of strawberry, found that nontranspiring leaves depend on water flow from root pressure to supply calcium. High relative humidities at night enhance root pressure, providing calcium to needed areas of the plant.

The presence of guttation is a sign of adequate root pressure. After leaf emergence, calcium movement to the leaves is promoted by dry days, thus indicating that calcium is supplied by transpirational flow. In similar studies, high humidity at night and low humidity during the day was confirmed to alleviate calcium disorders of cabbage and cauliflower. The time of year does not appear to be critical to fruit-associated disorders. Cline and Hanson, working on bitter pit of apple, determined that calcium movement to the fruit was largely due to xylem flow regardless of the season.

Calcium disorders are often independent of the calcium levels in the soil or other portions of the plant. Attempts at alleviating calcium disorders through supplemental calcium [$Ca\ (NO_3)_2$] fertilization have had inconsistent results. In greenhouse studies with blossom-end rot of bell peppers, Schon found that calcium sprays decreased the calcium disorder but also decreased yield. Alexander and Clough treated blossom-end rot of bell peppers with calcium and reported a 50% reduction in yield.

Antitranspirants have had little effect on reducing calcium disorders without also reducing yields. Recently, researchers have looked at combinations of calcium sprays or applications with spun-bonded polypropylene row covers. The row covers reduce solar radiation and lower leaf temperature. Alexander and Clough looked at spunbonded row covers and calcium fertilization on bell peppers grown in the field. They found that sunscald and bottom-end rot were reduced with row covers. Calcium in combination with row covers reduced bottom-end rot.

MANAGING WATER LOSS

Vapor-pressure deficits and stomatal regulation are measures for determining drought-tolerant species. Canopy temperatures are used as an indicator of plant water use and yield. Increases in leaf temperature would indicate decreased transpirational cooling from stomatal closure. Chaudhuri et al. evaluated sorghum genotypes and 42 millet genotypes in a line-source irrigation system. By measuring canopy temperature and air temperature and then regressing these data on the observed vapor pressure deficit, Chaudhuri et al. determined the drought tolerance of the genotypes.

Genotypes with a mean temperature greater than the average mean temperature for all genotypes were considered warm. Warm genotypes and genotypes less sensitive to changes in vapor pressure deficits produced viable heads under the more extreme drought treatments. The concept of warm genotypes being more drought tolerant appears to be species-specific. Warm soybean genotypes were found to be no more droughttolerant than cooler genotypes.

The growth stage of certain plants plays an important role in stomatal sensitivity. Sorghum stomates are quite sensitive to changes in leaf water potentials during vegetative growth and are insensitive during reproductive development.

The regulation of stomatal conductance through management or chemical applications could potentially reduce water loss during periods of high vaporpressure deficits. Agronomic practices like row spacing influence stomatal activity.

Peanuts grown in narrow 30-cm-spacing north-south rows lost less water due to evapotranspiration than peanuts grown 90-cm-spacing north-south rows or 30-cm rows planted in an east-west direction. An explanation for this was provided in work done by McCauley and colleagues, who found that water loss was less in narrow north-south rows because of a reduction in net radiation, and the aerodynamic roughness of the plant canopy reduced the prevailing south wind effect.

In later studies, narrow-row plantings of peanuts were observed to close their stomates earlier in the day than wide-row-planted peanuts. Regarding yield, the closer row plantings produced higher yields for peanuts and sorghum.

Early closing of stomates has been attributed to morphological characteristics of the plants growing in the narrow rows (thinner, smaller leaves and longer internodes). Similar morphological features of high shoot density, low leaf area, and narrow leaf texture are associated with C4 turfgrasses with low evapotranspiration rates. Antitranspirants are chemicals that induce stomatal closure to reduce transpiration. It has been argued that there is no need for antitranspirants because plants close their stomata in response to water stress.

However, given the habit of growing plants outside of their native habitat, antitranspirants have been widely tested. The two major types of antitranspirants are the stomata inhibitors and the film-forming compounds. Stomata inhibitors are synthetic substances that induce stomatal closure by directly affecting the stomatal mechanism.

Many of these types of products are plant-growth regulators, herbicides, and fungicides. Film-forming compounds are products that, when applied to the leaf's surface, act as a physical barrier to water vapor. These compounds form a film that obstructs the stomatal pore and reduces transpiration. Film-forming compounds tend to have a selective permeability to water and carbon dioxide, causing a greater reduction in photosynthesis than transpiration and producing a poorer production ratio. Reductions in production yields are associated with limited antitranspirant use in row crops.

HIGH HUMIDITY AND LEAF WETNESS

Studies looking at the effect of high humidity around the plant are few. Generally, high humidity has little positive effect on many horticultural crops. However, there have been reports on tuber crops that high relatively humidity can increase yield. Wheeler et al. grew three potato cultivars at 20°C at two vapor-pressure deficits, 0.40 kPa (85% relative humidity) and 1.15 kPa (51% relative humidity); they measured dry weights of leaf, stem, total plant, and tuber. No difference was found in total dry weight of the plants between humidity treatments, but plants grown under 0.40 kPa produced higher tuber yields.

Similar results have been required with sweet potato. Additional research has reported on field-grown crops of lettuce, wheat, and sugar beet, stating that increasing humidity created positive growth responses. Free moisture on the leaf causes detrimental growth and yield loss by providing conditions favorable for pathogens to infect the host and establish themselves in it. Rainfall, irrigation, and dew are the major sources of free moisture on the leaf.

Dew is of interest here because of its association with water vapor. Dew forms from condensation of water vapor on the leaf and from guttation water forced out of hydathodes by root pressure. The temperature at which moisture condenses on the leaf is referred to as the dew point.

If the dew point is above 0°C, then dew forms; if the temperature is below 0°C, frost forms. The maximum condensation rates for plants growing under soil—and atmospheric— saturated conditions is approximately 0.07 to 0.09 mm h"1. The amount of dew accumulated is linearly related to the duration. Conditions favorable for guttation are high soil moisture levels with corresponding high humidity (low transpiration).

In most row crops and orchards, condensation would be the primary source of dew. However in short, dense canopies with minimal wind movement, guttation could be a significant component of dew. Williams and coworkers reported that on a short cut (19-mm) creeping bentgrass fairway, guttation could account for 33% of the total dew on the plant canopy. Leaf wetness refers to the period of time where free moisture is present on the leaf blade.

Fungal pathogens vary in their dependence on free moisture for infection and sporulation. Oomycetes and chrtridiales are extremely dependent on free moisture for infection and development, while free moisture plays a minor role with the powdery mildews. Most fungal pathogens fall between these two extremes. In general, spore production requires longer periods of leaf wetness than the duration of free moisture needed for infection. The necessary period for wetting varies depending on the pathogen. In a review article by Huber and Gillespie, they reported that the wetting periods required for several foliar pathogens ranged from 0.5 to 140 hr. In general, increasing periods of leaf wetness increase the severity of infection. From a disease-management perspective, minimizing the period of leaf wetness could reduce spore loads and/or disease severity.

The pathogen downy mildew (Bremia lactucae) sporulates at night; spore release begins at sunrise. If the leaf wetness period continues 3 to 4 hr after sunrise, the spores that were released reinfect lettuce tissue.

Reducing the leaf wetness period after sunrise could potentially minimize the severity of downy mildew of lettuce. The concept of reduced disease through a reduction of the leaf wetness period has been demonstrated.

Early-morning dew removal from a creeping bentgrass golf course fairway by mowing reduced the severity of dollar spot (Sclerotinia homoeocarpa). Interrupting the leaf wetness period may also affect the infection cycle of certain diseases. Alternaria linicola is a pathogen of linseed that is sensitive to interruptions in leaf wetness. Dry interruptions of wet periods, whether short (2 hr) or long (12 hr) in duration, occurring sometime between 2 and 6 hr after inoculation stopped conidia germination.

Monitoring the length of leaf wetness is a practical means of timing fungicide applications. Fungicide applications for downy mildew of lettuce were reduced by 67% relative to a standard calendar-based schedule, with no difference in disease intensity, based on the presence of leaf wetness at 1000 hr.

Dainello and Jones made fungicide applications for the control of white rust (Albugo occidentalis) on spinach based on leaf wetness periods. They found that if they made fungicide applications of metalaxyl based on a 12-hr continuous leaf wetness period—as opposed to a 7-day preventative schedule—they required five fewer sprays and still provided the same level of control. On cantaloup, a delay in fungicide applications until leaf wetness periods were of 8 hr duration gave equivalent control, with a one-third reduction in number of applications compared to applications based on crop phenology.

THE FUTURE OF PHYTOGEOGRAPHY

For several reasons phytogeography is becoming of increasing importance. The rejuvenation of taxonomy along the lines of the "new systematics" or synthetic taxonomy, the application of data derived from the newer branches of ecology and cytogenetics, the extending realization that man is destroying the natural flora and vegetation of many parts of the world, and, perhaps, one may add, the greater facilities for overseas travel are all stimulating to phytogeographical research.

It may, therefore, be worth while to give seriatim some suggestions for extending investigations from which the phytogeographer can reasonably expect new and important data.

1. Exploration, and further botanical exploration, of certain parts of the world, especially of Indo-China, New Guinea, Amazonia, and the Pacific Islands. Though no part of the earth is over-explored.
2. The intensification of research on fossil angiosperms. For many taxa existing ranges are the relicts of past ranges and these can only be inadequately inferred in the absence of palaeobotanical data. The excellent work of pollen analysis, in Europe and North America, and more recently in New Zealand and Australia, should be extended to as many countries and as many kinds of deposits as possible.
3. Cytotaxonomic investigations need to be undertaken in many more phytochoria, with the co-operation of taxonomists and phytogeographers.
4. Concentrated investigation, including controlled experiments, of long distance dispersal of disseminules is required to replace vague but often dogmatic assertions.
5. Much more consideration needs to be given to the study of clines in plant groups.
6. Botany seems out of balance with zoology in the taxonomic and ecological examination of populations over wide geographical areas.
7. The causes of death and extinction of taxa need investigation extensively.
8. There is considerable need for definition or re-definition of terms. Thus the word "alpine" is used in at least two senses: growing at high altitudes or restricted in range to the European Alps.
9. The adequate summarizing of books and papers on phytogeography written in certain languages, especially Russian and Japanese.

2

Ecology

Ecology is the study of the "relationships among living organisms or between them and the physical environment."

Some characteristics of the scientific study of ecology:

- Macro-scale ecologists (global-scale ecology, '60's) have lost political ground to micro-scale ecologists.
- Landscape ecology recognizes human influence on non-human species, yet persist in distinguishing human from natural landscapes.
- Human ecology concentrates on systematic and evolutionary aspects, while social ecology emphasizes behavior. Both study human-environmenal relationships in distant past or present. Sociobiology is a paradigm within human social ecology
- Cultural ecology and cultural geography examine adaptive strategies. Both are cognizant of the role of culture in human adaptation, but not interested in long term change.
- Environmental History is the intellectual history of the environmental movement, including the political and economical implications of environmental interaction.
- Environmental Ethics explores value systems as they relate to human conduct.

None of these fields has truly integrative approach, and many lack an explicit historical component. What is needed is a multi-scalar temporal and spatial frame with an explicit focus on the role of human cognition in the human-environmental dialectic.

HISTORICAL ANALOGS

Global climate change is one of the most pressing event of current times. The anticipated changes demand investigations into patterns of human adaptation to climatic variability and change. However, the global climate change models used by physical scientists to predict climatic changes do not discriminate among biotic zones or anywhere near a human scale. Furthermore, many physical scientists assume that "novel circumstances" render any historical analogy to current anticipated global climatic change irrelevant. This attitude is due to:

(1) The lack of high quality long term (>100 yr.) instrumentally obtained data
(2) Local proxy data (such as tree ring) are only valid at the broadest temporal scales.
(3) Dismay of the comparative messiness of soft social science data
(4) Vested interest in favor of novel technologies and undervalue of traditional solutions

A regional approach could overcomes this. A region's air mass data, hydrology, soil, topography and species distribution can be used in regional models. Regionally documented ethnography, archeology, and documentary evidence evidences results of human activities and past choices which encompass the entire system. Multiple regional environmental changes can identify sensitive geographical locations. Interregional relationships may then be established and integrated with global data. This approach fosters creativity and the development of local and regional answers to global situations in which sensitive cultural issues play an important part.

HISTORICAL ANALOGS AND LANDSCAPES

Two types of historical analogs can be made:

(1) purely environmental: the global effects of the volcanic eruption of El Chichon in 1982 was similar to Krakatoa in 1883
(2) environmental and human interactions in different time periods

To study the dialectical human-environmental relationships, interactive long term sequences may be traced through the study of changing landscapes. Landscape ecology is the study of structure, function, and change of a heterogeneous land area composed of interacting ecosystems. Historical ecology or landscape history is study of past ecosystems by charting the change in landscapes over time. Thus, evidence for the historical interrelatedness of humans and environments may be read in the landscape. By interference, changing human attitudes may also be identified and their effects studied. For example, the existence of a forest is the result of both location-which determines temperature and rainfall patterns-and previous and current human management practices.

The introduction of historically informed environmental analyses into regional studies offers an important opportunity for anthropologists, archeologists, historians, and geographers. Archeology is multidisciplinary in nature (natural/physical sciences + humanities) and temporal and spatial breath required for long term analyses. Regional archeology has gone beyond the individual site, seeking to understand distribution, population and economies. Ethnohistorians are anthropologists who critically examine documents for evidence of human actions, relations and attitudes. This includes written (diaries, government documents), oral (stories about storms or pest invasions), and visual (dated drawings) documents. Enthographers study customs based on observations and understandings that guide indigenous peoples' adaptive strategies. This cultural information is transferred in complex ritual behavior or casual conversation.

Historical Ecology is the practice of a globally relevant archeology, ethnohistory, ethnography and related disciplines. While geographic information systems can give practical integration of spatial structures (habitations, soils, river drainage), practical understanding of past and current relationships among these environmental and human systems require a culturally specific temporal and spatial perspective applied at a regional scale.

An Historical Ecological Approach to Global Climate Change Expects to Identify

- The duration and frequency of air mass patterns that characterizes earlier warm episodes (bv. middle Holocene, Roman Climatic Optimum, Medieval Climatic Optimum)
- What regions where affected?
- How did biotic and human communities respond to these conditions?
- What spatial patterns are characteristic of biotic communities (species diversity and distribution) and human communities (settlement and land-use, population and agglomeration) in the earlier warm episodes?
- How might patterns be mapped in advance of contemporary global warming?
- What measures could contemporary societies employ to cope with supra-annual cycles?
- What human behaviors, attitudes, beliefs, economic strategies, and forms of governance are associated with periods of stable or unstable climate?
- What measures could contemporary societies employ to cope with a marked increase in climatic instability?
- What values ensure the greatest flexibility in adapting to changed or unstable environment. ?
- Can environmental flexibility be taught?
- How can a global environmental ethic also be culturally sensitive?

- Are some governmental structures better able than others to employ the necessary strategies of adaptation?

Integrative Themes and Considerations

Practices are maintained or modified, decisions are made, and ideas are given shape; a landscape retains the physical evidence of these mental activities.

- *Contradictions:* Contradictions emerge between human groups because people occupying particular localities develop models of their environment. based on their specific needs and experiences: these models may be at variance with other group, leading to competition, religious conflicts, etc. Contradictions constitute the raw materials for change. Landscapes manifest the resolutions of these contradictions.
- *Scale:* Landscapes cannot be studied in their totalities. Investigation are done at different scales. When a particular scale is chosen during one moment of the analyses, it is because at that effective scale one can comprehend patterns.

Factors of duration, intensity, and periodicity at specific temporal and spatial scales must be examined. These parameters must be considered relative to a specific environment. , because a small change in one environment. could be a major change in another.

- *Culture:* Culture determines the thresholds at which a response will be generated and also the particular response itself. It frames a society's resilience in the face of environmental and other disturbances.
- *Region:* Any area may be termed region for the purpose of the study of human-environment. relationships, so long as demonstrable homogeneity can be recognized. Its temporal relations (connections with the past and the future) and its spatial relations (connections with other areas at the same scale and larger and smaller areas) need to be specified. A region can be recognized at a certain scale because of its distinctiveness from an interrelations with other such units. This pattern simply begins the analysis.
- *Boundaries:* Boundaries have inherent duality. Arbitrary boundaries are to be avoided, except in the initial stage of investigation. Instead a research area defined at a number of different scales, from observation of a multiplicity of not necessarily coincident boundaries, offers a fertile ground fir discovering the contradictions those divisions manifest. Boundaries are interesting both for social and natural scientists to explore relationships with living organisms. There is a high correlation between the position of biomes (and their ecotones) and the position of climate driven air-mass activity. Administrative boundaries do not nest with but overlap environmental, social, and economic boundaries.

- *Biodiversity:* Biodiversity is critical to the maintenance of ecosystems. Richness and innovative potential of cultural diversity can also be seen as a potent tool in the mitigation of human/environment. relationships.
- *Heterachy:* Heterarchical complex systems are systems in which the elements have the potential of being unranked (relative to other elements) or ranked in a number of ways, depending on systematic requirements. Hierarchical systems are systems in which some elements on the basis of certain factors, are subordinate to others. A common error of researchers is to uncritically nest levels of analysis, confusing scalar (global-regional-local) with control hierarchies (court system), and leading to the misinterpretation of chains of causation. It is quite possible that effects that occur at the "subordinate level" have major systemic effects: they can change parameters (boundaries) or control levels (center-periphery shifts, scale changes) or the ranking of various elements. Heterarchy reminds us of a natural, multidimensional fluctuation in the importance of elements. This flexibility is essential to a dynamic approach.

HISTORICAL ECOLOGY

Evolutionary biologists define historical ecology as an attempt to understand ecological interactions from a phylogenetic perspective (Brooks 1985; Brooks and McLennan 1991). If two species experience a strong interaction, is the strength of this interaction due to a long shared history, or have they recently come into contact? Although this question has long been a part of ecological debate, phylogenetics has the potential to actually illuminate the "ghost of competition past". For example, consider two interacting species that are suspected of showing niche differentiation, such that one species is large and one is small. If a phylogenetic analysis shows that each species is the same size as its closest relatives from other areas, then it is not necessary to invoke niche differentiation to explain the differences in size.

With respect to community ecology, a phylogenetic framework can help to understand dynamics of community assembly (Cunningham and Collins 1998; Grosberg 2000; Ricklefs and Schluter 1993). Which species have been in residence for a long time (and how long)? Which species have arrived in the recent past (and how long ago)? Are there any generalities about which species have recently arrived?

A Grand Natural Experiment: the Impact of the Trans-Arctic Interchange on the Recent History of the North Atlantic

The temperate North Atlantic is an ideal model system in which to address issues of historical ecology because of a natural experiment in biogeography

(Cunningham and Collins 1998; Vermeij 1991). A large proportion of species-approximately 80% of rocky intertidal benthic mollusks in New England-have arrived in the North Atlantic from the Pacific since the opening of the Bering Strait 3-5 Ma. (Marincovich and Gladenkov 1999) (Vermeij 1991). This trans-Arctic interchange united the cold water biotas of the Pacific and North Atlantic/ Arctic basins, which had evolved independently until that time.

Like most other biotic interchanges, the direction of interchange was highly asymmetric (Pacific to Atlantic, Figure 1(Vermeij 1991)). This natural experiment placed closely related species throughout the northern hemisphere, on coasts which differ dramatically in almost every way.

This experiment allows direct comparison of the ecology of these closely related taxa, so that observed differences between regions cannot be attributed to taxon based differences. For example, the crustacean isopod Idotea balthica is found in a broader range of algal and seagrass habitats, in New England populations than in European populations, and plays a more dominant role in the New England community.

The differences between the northwestern and northeastern Atlantic can be used to investigate community assembly. The last glaciation was much more extreme in the NW Atlantic than in the NE Atlantic, and is thought to have caused local extinction of many benthic species (Vermeij 1989). In some cases, these extinctions may have been followed by post-glacial colonization from the NE Atlantic (Cunningham and Collins 1998). Population genetics, in a geographic context (phylogeography, Avise 2000), has the potential to distinguish between taxa that did or did not survive the last glaciation in the NW Atlantic (Wares and Cunningham in revision). Once the recent colonists have been identified, we can ask which are likely to have been natural or human-mediated introductions, and search for generalities such as what organismal characteristics allow species to survive glaciation in the NW Atlantic. Despite this incredible potential, there have been virtually no comparisons of species found in both coasts of the North Atlantic. Rectifying this situation is one of the central purposes of the North Atlantic Project.

Three Views of Generality in Historical Ecology and Biogeography

A major outstanding question in historical ecology, and biogeography in general, is what role organismal characteristics play in determining composition of communities. Although it may seem obvious that organismal characteristics determine range limits of species, the issue of how those species came to be found in a particular region is open to question.

Interestingly, two completely independent intellectual traditions in Biogeography downplay the importance of organismal characteristics. The first is island biogeography (MacArthur and Wilson 1967), and its intellectual descendants (Hubbell, 1997,2001). This tradition considers raw species numbers, and considers individual species largely interchangeable. Although dispersal and extinction are both central to these theories, the difference in dispersal abilities between individual species are assumed to average out in the end.

The second great intellectual tradition is vicariance biogeography (Humphries and Parenti 1986; Nelson and Platnick 1981). Whereas dispersal is central to island biogeography, in vicariance biogeography the emphasis is on the signal of past fragmentation that can be gleaned from the species that do not disperse from their areas of endemism. If species collected from the same areas show congruent phylogenies, this is considered evidence that they experienced the same series of vicariance events (geographic subdivision). Vicariance biogeography emphasizes huge events that affect entire biotas, regardless of individual organismal characteristics. In this sense, it is similar to island biogeography in that it seeks generality by downplaying organismal characteristics.

In contrast, a third view considers the possibility that organismal characteristics are important. Diamond's controversial assembly rules (1975) argued that the composition of many communities depends on organismal characteristics (see also the forthcoming book "Ecological Assembly Rules" (Weiher and Keddy 2001)). In this vein, Cunningham and Collins (1998) have argued that phylogenetic history has the potential to reveal the influence of organismal characteristics in biogeographic histories. If we are able to identify a set of species that have experienced a common biogeographic history, we can ask whether they share particular organismal characteristics. While this may sound at first like vicariance biogeography, it doesn't assume that there is a single overriding historical pattern (determined by vicariance) that defines an entire biota. Common patterns of dispersal, such as the trans-Arctic interchange itself, can generate patterns as well. In marine systems, with their porous barriers, it is unlikely in most cases that vicariance will affect more than a subset of the biota (with obvious exceptions such as the rise of the Isthmus of Panama). In many cases, we expect that subsequent dispersal between vicariated areas will be extremely common (Cunningham and Collins 1994).

With respect to the North Atlantic, this perspective can be framed in terms of two likely patterns. The first is glacially induced extinction in the NW Atlantic. If a species experiences local extinction without recolonization from elsewhere, the range of this species has been restricted. Vermeij(1989) pointed out that paleontology is the only discipline that can unambiguously identify cases of restriction. Cunningham and Collins (1998) argued that population genetic and phylogenetic data can accomplish the converse, and unambiguously identify sets of species that have long endemic histories in the NW Atlantic, and have therefore resisted glacial extinction (Cunningham and Collins 1998

Wares and Cunningham, in revision). Since repeated extinctions and recolonizations may appear in a low resolution fossil record as a coninuous presence, genetic data are important in this context. In high resolution mcrofossil records, these repetitive local extinctions and recolonizations can be directly observed. These stratigraphic records can then be compared to the conclusions of phylogeographic studies.

The first observed pattern is one of long term residence on both coasts of the North Atlantic. Homarus gammarus in the NE Atlantic and Homarus americanus in the NW Atlantic are sister species, and have had independent evolutionary histories for roughly 1 million years or so (Tam and Kornfield 1998). This "reciprocal monophyly" is strong evidence that Homarus has been in residence in both the NE and NW Atlantic for at least 1 million years (Cunningham and Collins 1998). What is it about Homarus that has allowed it to resist extinction in the NW Atlantic through several glacial maxima? The second is a population genetic pattern shown by many species strongly suggesting post-glacial colonization of the NW Atlantic region from the NE Atlantic (e.g. the seastar Asterias rubens, and the snails Littorina obtusata, and Nucella lapillus (Wares and Cunningham in revision)). What characteristics allowed these species to invade across the Atlantic? Since the latter two species have no pelagic dispersal, dispersal ability is not the only important factor in colonization ability. Other factors inlude the ability to withstand the wide temperature fluctuation in the NW Atlantic, and the tendency to occupy dispersal vectors such as floating algae (Ingólfsson, 1995).

CLIMATE, ECOLOGY, AND HUMAN HEALTH

Environmental conditions, interacting with the biology of disease agents, can exert profound effects. Changes in how land is used affect the distribution of disease carriers, such as rodents or insects, while climate influences their range, and affects the timing and intensity of outbreaks. In this review we examine how our health is influenced by the interplay of social conditions, local environmental factors, and global changes. The discussion focuses primarily on the environment, for—given its scale and pace of change—this sometimes forgotten determinant seems destined to play an ever-increasing role in determining disease patterns in the future.

At any time and in any age, human health tends to follow trends in both social systems and the natural environment. In periods of relative stability—measured in the number and distribution of people, their use of natural resources, and their generation of wastes—natural, biological controls over pests and disease organisms (or *pathogens*) can function efficiently. In times of accelerated change—often associated with economic or political instability, natural disasters, or war—infectious diseases can spread. Today, an increasingly unstable climate, the accelerating loss of species, and growing economic inequities challenge the resilience and resistance of natural systems. Acting together, these elements of change are contributing to the emergence, resurgence, and redistribution of infectious disease on a global scale.

An expected redistribution of infectious disease is but one of the biological consequences of global environmental change. In some regions of the globe, warming may at first appear beneficial. Plants may be fertilized by warmth and moisture, an earlier spring, and more carbon dioxide (CO_2) and nitrogen. But warming and increased CO_2 can also stimulate microbes and their carriers, and added heat can destabilize weather patterns.

The consequences for agricultural pests and crop yields, for the health of livestock and fisheries, and for human illness may be significant; and the costs of epidemics can cascade through economies and ripple through societies. The resurgence of infectious diseases thus poses threats to food and biological security, and to economic development.

Water, food, and health are among our most basic needs. These requirements are also interrelated, and environmental changes now underway threaten all three. Maintaining health demands clean water, safe food, and unpolluted air, and in the modern world the latter depends upon clean energy. In the past, widespread diseases that affect multiple continents, called *pandemics*, have often precipitated social disruption and major shifts in human settlements. In other, more productive instances, the resurgence of infectious disease has inspired social and environmental reforms that addressed the underlying causes. What will be our course this time?

A recent report of the United Nations' World Health Organization records that, since 1976, thirty diseases have emerged that are new to medicine. The reappearance of old diseases—once thought under control—is of equal concern: Drug-resistant tuberculosis, exacerbated by HIV/AIDS, now causes three million deaths annually, while childhood diphtheria, whooping cough, and measles—which are also transmitted person-to-person—are also on the rise, particularly in those places where social systems have recently changed. Malaria, dengue (or "breakbone fever," a severe, sometimes-deadly tropical disease transmitted by mosquitoes and accompanied by headache, rash, and severe joint pain), yellow fever, cholera, and a number of rodent-borne viruses are also appearing with increased frequency. The distribution of the latter diseases, that rely on animals or water as vehicles (or vectors) for transmission, reflect both environmental and social change. In 1995, U.S. mortality from infectious disease attributed to causes other than HIV/AIDS rose 22 percent above the levels of fifteen years before, and 58 percent in all.

Malaria as an Example

Malaria is an ancient, mosquito-borne disease that played a significant role in the history of Africa. For centuries, the presence of sickle cell and other types of red blood cell "anomalies" limited the impact of malaria on native Africans. The disease also served to ward off foreign colonizers, who lacked these evolved defenses, and helped deter deep penetration of the continent until the latter part of the 19th century. In the first phases of the scramble for African territory, Europeans selectively colonized highland regions to escape from swampy regions of malaria, or "bad air": a choice that also contributed to the separation of the races. For further protection, they drank water flavoured with quinine—a natural remedy, derived from the bark of the cinchona tree, discovered in Peru in the 15th century. To make the tonic more palatable, they added gin.

Eventually, control measures in Africa and the Americas, where malaria was also found, included environmental improvements and the application of insecticides, and by the 1950s there were dramatic drops in the incidence of the disease, worldwide. It was not conquered, however, but only held at bay. By the late 1970s, dwindling investments in public health programs, growing insecticide-resistance, and prevalent environmental changes, such as forest clearing, contributed to a widespread resurgence. By the late 1980s large epidemics were once again the rule, often associated with warm, wet periods.

In the past five years, the worldwide incidence of malaria has quadrupled, influenced by changes in both land development and regional climate. In Brazil, satellite images depict a "fish bone" pattern where roads have opened the tropical forest to localized development. In these "edge" areas malaria has resurged. Temperature changes have also encouraged a redistribution of the disease: Malaria is now found in higher-elevations in central Africa and could threaten cities such as Nairobi, Kenya (at about 5000 ft., or the altitude of Denver, Colorado), as freezing levels have shifted higher in the mountains. In the summer of 1997, for example, malaria took the lives of hundreds of people in the Kenyan highlands, where populations had previously been unexposed. The anopheles mosquitoes that can carry malaria are present in the U.S., and, earlier this century, the disease was prevalent. After initially coming under control, small outbreaks of locally-transmitted malaria have occurred in this decade in Texas, Georgia, Florida, Michigan, New Jersey, and New York—and again, as in the 1980s, in California—primarily during hot, wet spells. A persistence of similar climatic conditions, combined with inadequate (or ineffective) control methods, could lead to further localized outbreaks.

Worldwide, up to 500 million people—roughly twice the present population of the U.S.—contract malaria every year, and between 1.5 and 3 million, primarily children, die. Africa is most affected. Mosquito resistance to insecticides and parasite resistance to many drugs are widespread, and there are no operational vaccines, nor any foreseen in the near future. Ecological changes, along with increased weather variability and a warming trend, appear to be playing increasing roles in the spread of this disease.

ENVIRONMENTAL CHANGE AND OPPORTUNISTIC SPECIES

Regulatory mechanisms are a feature of all living systems. Some cells within the body stand guard to repel invading organisms, or to reject cells that develop malignantly. In the environment, predators serve a similar role, keeping populations of pests under control.

Weeds, rodents, insects, and microorganisms are opportunists that reproduce very rapidly. Rodents, for example, have huge broods, plus small body sizes, wide-ranging appetites, and well developed dispersal mechanisms.

In stable environments, large predators fare well and keep smaller, opportunistic species in check. But opportunists can readily colonize overly-stressed environments, much as opportunistic infections take hold in patients with weakened immune systems. Mosquito populations, for example, are naturally controlled by reptiles, birds, spiders, ladybugs, and bats—as well as by pond fish that feed on mosquito larvae. Mosquitoes provide nourishment for these animals, but some carry malaria, yellow fever, dengue fever, and several types of encephalitis. Similarly, owls, coyotes, and snakes eat rodents; and rodents can devour grains and transport Lyme disease ticks, hantaviruses (a debilitating viral infection), arenaviruses (such as South American hemorrhagic fevers and Lassa fever), leptospirosis bacteria, and human plague. In the marine environment, fish, shellfish, and sea mammals consume algae that form the base of the marine food web. A reduction in these plankton feeders as a result of overfishing or disease may thus contribute to blooms of harmful algae. Harmful algal blooms, or "HABs," that despoil beaches and devastate shoreline birds and other animal life, can occur as oxygen-rich "red tides," or as oxygen-poor or hypoxic "brown tides." Plankton blooms can also harbour cholera and other bacteria, and threaten the health of swimmers, or those who consume affected fish and shellfish.

Environmental Change and Biological Controls

Today the activities of one species, humans, are reducing the diversity of all others and transforming the global environment. Ecosystems subjected to the stresses of "global change" (including climate change and altered weather patterns, the depletion of stratospheric ozone, deforestation, coastal pollution, and marked reductions of biological diversity) become more susceptible to the emergence, invasion, and spread of opportunistic species. When subject to multiple stresses, natural environments can exhibit symptoms that indicate reductions in resilience, resistance, and regenerative capabilities. Conversely, ecosystems have inherent flexibilities and survival strategies that can be strengthened by systematic stress, such as the seasonal battering they must endure in temperate latitudes. But their tolerance for abuse has its limits. Several features of global change tend to reduce predators disproportionately, and in the process release prey from their biological controls. Among the most widespread are:

- Fragmentation and loss of habitat
- Dominance of monocultures in agriculture and aquaculture
- Excessive use of toxic chemicals
- Increased ultraviolet radiation, and
- Climate change and weather instability.

The breaking up of large tracts of forest or other natural wilderness into smaller and more diverse patches reduces the available habitat for large predators, and favours many pests.

Land and climate changes may act synergistically, as when constricted habitat frustrates a species' ability to migrate north or south to survive altered climatic conditions. Extensive deforestation and climate anomalies—such as the delayed monsoon rains that resulted from this year's El Nino—can also act synergistically, with costly results.

A ready example is the massive haze from burning that covered much of Southeast Asia in September and October, causing acute and chronic respiratory damage and losses in trade, investment, and tourism—the latter, a $26 billion a year industry.

The dedication of land to *monoculture,* that is, the cultivation of single crops with restricted genetic and species diversity, renders plants more vulnerable to disease. Simplified systems are also more susceptible to climatic extremes and to outbreaks of pests.

Over-use of pesticides kills birds and beneficial insects, as noted in 1962 by Rachel Carson. The title of her book, Silent Spring, made reference to the absence of the chorus of birds in springtime, and the resulting resurgence of plant-eating insects—that had also evolved a resistance to pesticides. The worldwide response to her message transformed agricultural policies and generated more enlightened pest management. But today, the heavy application of pesticides still carries risks to both human health and natural systems. Over-use of pesticides in Texas and Alabama to control the boll weevil has alarmed farmers, for friendly insects such as spiders and lady bugs have died off and other plant pests have rebounded.

Ecosystem Health

As noted earlier, one of "nature's services" is to keep opportunistic species under control. Maintaining this service entails sustaining the health and integrity of ecosystems. One of the essentials is genetic and species biodiversity to provide alternative hosts for disease organisms. Another is sufficient stability among functional groups of species (such as recyclers, scavengers, predators, competitors, and prey) to ensure the suppression of opportunists and preserve essential ecological functions. Habitat is crucial.

Stands of trees interspersed with agricultural fields, for instance, support birds that control insects; clean ponds with healthy populations of fish serve to control mosquito larvae; and adequate wetlands filter excess nutrients, harmful chemicals, and microorganisms.

As a case in point, in tidewater Maryland, buffer zones around farms and the restoration of wetlands and river-bed trees can absorb the flow of sediments, chemicals, and harmful organisms into Chesapeake Bay, and thus reduce the emergence and spread of algae, toxic to fish. Ecosystems are also interrelated: healthy forests and mangroves in Central America, for example, are crucial to coral reefs that spawn fish stocks, formed at the origin of the great Gulf Stream. Maintaining the integrity of natural environmental systems provides generalized defenses against the proliferation of opportunistic pests and disease.

Population explosions of nuisance organisms, be they animals or plants or microbes, often reflect failing ecosystem health: a sign of systems out of equilibrium, in terms of the balance of organisms required to perform essential functions. The damage done, moreover, can be cumulative, for multiply-stressed systems are less able to resist and rebound when other stresses come along.

Rodents, insects, and algae are thus key biological indicators of ecosystem health. Their populations and species compositions respond rapidly to environmental change—particularly to an increase in their food supply, or a drop in the number of their natural predators. These indicator species are also linked to human health.

Impacts of a Loss of Biodiversity

The present rate of species extinctions around the world is a potential threat to human health when one considers the role that predators play in containing infectious disease. From the largest to the smallest scales, an essential element in natural systems for countering stress is a diversity of defenses and responses. Thus, animals that seem redundant may serve as "insurance" species in a natural ecosystem, providing a back-up layer of resilience and resistance when others are lost from disease, a changing environment, or a shortage of food or water. In 1996 the World Conservation Union reported that one-fourth of all species of mammals—and similar proportions of reptiles, amphibians, and fish—are threatened. The current rate of extinctions (estimated at 100 to 1,000 times the rate of loss in the pre-human era) falls heaviest on large predators and "specialists," and thus may initially favour the spread of opportunistic species.

ENVIRONMENTAL DISTRESS SYNDOME: MONITORING GLOBAL CHANGE

Some ecologists describe an evolving "Environmental Distress Syndrome," with several recognizable symptoms that integrate local and global stresses. Such signals include the rapid decline (and widespread malformations) in frogs in 140 countries on six continents, which may be the result of habitat loss, toxic chemicals, and increased ultraviolet-B radiation. Additional and more general symptoms of environmental distress are given in the adjoining box. Monitoring these biological signs—as well as the populations of key biological indicator species such as rodents, insects, and algae—can strengthen observing systems that currently track chiefly chemical and physical parameters, such as nitrogen flow into coastal waters and sea surface temperatures. Interactive geographical mapping that visually integrates the biological, chemical, and physical measurements can help define and analyse the consequences, costs, and the causes of global environmental change.

Climate And Emerging Diseases

Models of how the climate system will respond to enhanced greenhouse warming predict (1) increased air temperatures at altitudes of two to four miles above the surface in the Southern Hemisphere; (2) a disproportionate rise in minimum temperatures (TMINs), in either daily or seasonally-averaged readings; and (3) an increase in extreme weather events, such as droughts and sudden heavy rains. There is growing evidence for all three of these tell-tale "fingerprints" of enhanced greenhouse warming, and each of them is related to infectious diseases.

Persistent hot, humid weather spells can threaten the health of people who live in temperate latitudes. Farm animals are also adversely affected, especially when the air temperature remains uncommonly high throughout the night.

During the summer of 1995, excess deaths in Chicago and other large cities around the world were directly associated with heat waves, compounded by social isolation. In many instances, according to meteorologists, the key factor was the lack of relief at night. In the latter half of this century, TMINs over land areas have risen at a rate of 1.86°C per 100 years, while maximum temperatures have risen at 0.88°C per 100 years. Mild conditions and recurrent winter thawing can also damage forests and can allow harmful insects to survive.

Warmer Temperatures and Vector-borne Disease

Changing social conditions, such as the growth of "mega-cities," and widespread ecological change, are contributing to the spread of infectious diseases. But climate restricts the range in which *vector-borne diseases;*nbsp (VBDs) can occur, and weather affects the timing and intensity of their outbreaks. Rates of insect biting and the maturation of microorganisms within them are temperature-dependent, and both rates increase when the air warms. Warming can also increase the number of insects, provided adequate moisture, although excessive heat can decrease survival of either microorganisms or their hosts. Between the limits of too hot and too cold is an optimum range of temperature in which warmer air enhances metabolism and the chances for disease transmission.

Most insects are highly sensitive to temperature change: ants even run faster in warmer weather. Findings from paleoclimatic (fossil) studies demonstrate that changes in temperature (and especially in TMINs) were closely correlated with geographic shifts of beetles near the end of the last Ice Age, about 10,000 years ago. Indeed, fossil records indicate that when changes in climate occur, insects shift their range far more rapidly than do grasses, shrubs, and forests, and move to more favourable latitudes and elevations hundreds of years before larger animals do. "Beetles," concluded one climatologist, "are better paleo-thermometers than bears."

Computer models of global greenhouse warming project increased temperatures that will, in turn, favour the spread of VBDs to higher elevations and to more temperate latitudes. While 42 percent of the globe presently offers conditions that can sustain the transmission of malaria, the fraction could rise to 60 percent with a global increase of a few degrees C. Mosquitoes are hot weather insects that have fixed thresholds for survival. Anopheline mosquitoes and falciparum malaria transmission are sustained only where the winter temperature is kept above 16°C (61°F), while the variety of mosquito that transmits dengue fever, Aedes aegypti, is limited by the 10°C (50°F) winter isotherm. Shifts in the geographic limits of equal temperature (*isotherms*) that accompany global warming may extend the areas that are capable of sustaining the transmission of these and other diseases. The transmission season may also be extended in regions that now lie on the margins of the temperature and moisture conditions that allow disease carriers to reproduce. Similar considerations apply to cold-blooded agricultural pests, called *stenotherms*, that require specific temperatures for their survival.

Some of these projected changes may already be underway, for, as summarized, there are now reports from several continents of new outbreaks of VBDs in mountainous regions— findings that are consistent with the recorded temperature increase, the general retreat of alpine glaciers, and the reported upward displacement of temperature-sensitive plants.

The consistency among physical and biological indicators agrees with the most recent, 1996 consensus findings of the Intergovernmental Panel on Climate Change (IPCC) that climate appears to be changing, and that some of the anticipated impacts are now observable. The IPCC also concluded that human activities, including fossil fuel combustion and forest clearing and burning, are apparently contributing to these changes. There may be some positive impacts such as fewer winter deaths, or a drop in schistosomiasis in areas where excessive heat kills off the snails that can carry the parasite larvae. But overall, the current evaluation is that the impacts of an unstable and rapidly changing climate on human health are likely to be overwhelmingly negative.

THE EFFECTS OF CLIMATE VARIABILITY ON EPIDEMICS

Another significant climate trend that has been linked to systematic changes in temperature and precipitation is an increase in the variability, or extremes, of climate. This change in extremes can alter not only the intensity of individual events, such as storms and floods, but the timing and spatial patterns of weather as well. Since the mid-1800s the average surface temperature of the globe has risen about 0.4°C-0.6°C, and periods of persistent warming can, in general, be associated with increased variability. The IPCC projects that the warming trend may be accompanied by more intense heat waves and altered drought and rainfall patterns.

As reported in the first issue of Consequences, data from the National Climatic Data Centre—this nation's main repository for meteorological data—indicate that, since the 1970s, extreme weather events have indeed increased in the continental U.S.

On average, periods of drought are systematically longer, and bursts of precipitation (greater than two inches of rain over twenty-four hours) are more frequent. A warmed atmosphere accelerates evaporation, and for every rise of 1°C, the air can hold 6 percent more water.

One consequence is that we are now receiving a greater percentage of precipitation in the form of sudden, intense bursts that are more typical, for example, in the tropics. Longer droughts and more heavy bursts of rain, accompanied by flash floods, were more common in the 1980s than in the 1970s, and more so in the 1990s than in the 1980s.

Extreme events—floods, storms, droughts, and uncontained fires—can be devastating for agriculture, for human settlements, and for health. More, brief cold snaps are also possible, and winter storms, like heat waves, bring an increase in cardiac deaths. Floods spread bacteria, viruses, and chemical contaminants, foster the growth of fungi, and contribute to the breeding of insects. Prolonged droughts, interrupted by heavy rains, favour population explosions of both insects and rodents. Extreme weather events (often associated with the recurring climatic conditions that are initiated by large-scale changes in sea surface temperatures in the Pacific, known as El Nino/La Nina events) have been accompanied by new appearances of harmful algal blooms in Asia and North America, and—in Latin America and Asia—by outbreaks of malaria and various water-borne diseases, such as typhoid, hepatitis A, bacillary dysentery, and cholera.

Disease Clusters

In August 1995 the eastern, tropical region of the Pacific Ocean surface turned cold, initiating a La Nina event that would last until late 1996. Along the Caribbean coast of Colombia a summer 1995 heat wave was followed by the heaviest August rainfall in fifty years, ending a long drought that accompanied the preceding, prolonged El Nino conditions of 1990-1995. The heat and flooding precipitated a cluster of diseases involving mosquitoes (Venezuelan equine encephalitis and dengue fever), rodents (leptospirosis), and toxic algae (that killed 350 tons of fish in their largest coastal lagoon). Prolonged anomalous conditions of the sort that applied in 1990-1995 can also have cumulative biological consequences. In New Orleans, for example, five years without a killing frost was associated with an explosion of mosquitoes, termites, and cockroaches. Termites persisted inside trees into the cold winter of 1995-1996, and now threaten to destroy stands of New Orleans' fabled "mighty oaks." We may have only just begun to understand the true biological impacts of the persistent anomalous climate of the 1990s.

Rodents: Synergies and Surprises

Rodents are today a growing problem in the U.S., Latin America, Africa, Europe, Asia, and Australia. These preeminent opportunists are believed to be the fastest reproducing mammal and they eat everything humans do, thrive on contaminated water and food, and are extremely capable swimmers. Meadow voles, whose numbers are kept in check by predatory marsh hawks, can have up to seventeen broods a year, for example, each of half a dozen offspring. Rodents consume 20 percent of the world's grain, including almost a seventh in our own country, and up to three quarters of what is grown and stored in some African nations. Rodents can also carry diseases. A controlled experiment with Canadian snowshoe hares depicts how multiple factors can act synergistically to greatly increase the number of rodents. Excluding predators by confining the rabbits to cages led to a population doubling, compared to the fate of a number of similar animals in the wild. Augmenting food tripled hare density. Together the interventions in the controlled experiment resulted in more than a ten-fold population explosion.

Rats, Mice, and the Hantavirus

The story of the hantavirus illustrates a similar synergy in the case of microbial agents.

A prolonged drought in the U.S. southwest in the early 1990s reduced the populations of animals such as owls, coyotes, and snakes that prey on rodents. When the drought yielded to intense rains in 1993, the grasshoppers and pinon nuts on which rodents feed became more abundant. The result, when combined with the drop in predators, was a ten-fold increase in rats and mice by June of that year. An outcome was the emergence of a "new" disease called Hantavirus Pulmonary Syndrome: from a virus—perhaps already present, but dormant—transmitted through rodent saliva, urine, and droppings. Predators returned, however, and by summer's end the outbreak had abated.

Rodent-borne hantaviruses have resurged in several European nations, and most notably in the former Soviet Union and in Yugoslavia. In late 1996, hantavirus infection emerged in South America in western Argentina. Within the first few months at least ten deaths resulted, frightening off tourists and threatening the economic livelihood of the region. Hantavirus Pulmonary Syndrome has now appeared in Bolivia, Brazil, Canada, Chile, Ecuador, Paraguay, and Uruguay, with about 50 percent mortality and several cases of person-to-person transmission.

Some other Examples

Evidence of another rodent-borne disease —leptospirosis— is increasingly reported in U.S. urban centres, in areas where the disposal of sewage and other measures to protect public health have declined. In 1995, there were substantial outbreaks of the disease in Central America and Colombia, as heavy (La Nina) rains, following the prolonged El Nino drought, drove rodents scurrying from their burrows. Leptospirosis is treatable with antibiotics; but there were fatalities in 1995 before the diagnosis was established.

A combination of stresses contributed to the sudden appearances of several rodent-borne viral hemorrhagic fevers in rural Latin America in the past several decades: Junin in Argentina (1953), machupo in Bolivia (1962 and 1996), guaranito in Venezuela, and sabia in Brazil. In Bolivia, systematic clearing of trees apparently shifted populations of a variety of disease-carrying mice, known as calomys, from forest to field settings where they became dominant. Heavy applications of DDT —meant to eradicate malaria— helped reduce their natural predators. When cats were reintroduced to the area in 1962, the epidemic of Bolivian hemorrhagic fever was abated, although not until it had killed 10 to 20 percent of the inhabitants of the small villages in which the disease was present. Habitat loss and excessive use of toxic chemicals acted together in this case. In southern Africa, rodent populations exploded as a consequence of climate variability, when heavy and then lighter rains came in 1993 and 1994, on the heels of six years of prolonged drought. When the rains came, rodents found themselves in a world where avian and land predators were virtually absent. Moreover, because so many draft animals had also succumbed, there was little tillage of the land and the underground burrows in which rodents live went largely undisturbed. After an initial successful harvest in 1993, the maize crop in Zimbabwe was decimated by rodents. Soon after, human plague broke out in Zimbabwe and on the borders of neighbouring Malawi and Mozambique, carried—as in the devastating plague of 14th century Europe—by fleas on rats. Subsequently, a rodent-borne virus took the lives of eighty-one elephants in South Africa's Kruger Park, and plague returned in the summer of 1997.

Plague in India resurfaced in 1994, following a blistering summer when temperatures reached 124°F, leaving animals prostrate in the northern part of the country and fueling the breeding of fleas in houses that held stored grain. The unusually heavy monsoons following the 1994 heat wave led to population crowding in Surat on the western coast, north of Bombay, and an apparent outbreak of pneumonic (person-to-person) plague. Cases of malaria and dengue fever also surged in the wake of flooding. Meanwhile, in Australia, rodents emerged as serious crop pests in 1995, accompanying the same prolonged El Nino of the early 1990s and the ensuing years of intense drought.

Current land-use practices and the overuse of chemicals to control pests may increase the chances for such "nasty synergies." Climate variability is also a key element in upsurges of pests—and were climate to become more unstable, it could exert an even greater influence on ecological dynamics and the patterns of infectious diseases in the future. A disturbance in one factor can be destabilizing; but multiple perturbations can reduce the resistance and the resilience of a entire system.

MARINE COASTAL ECOSYSTEMS

Seashores throughout the world are subject to increasing pressures from residential, recreational, and commercial development. These stresses may become more severe, for human population in the vicinity of sea-coasts is growing at twice the inland rate. Some of the pressures that we exert on coastal ecosystems are summarized in the accompanying box. All can increase the growth of algae.

Among the possible consequences of disruption in almost any marine ecosystem is an increase in the opportunistic pathogens that can abet the spread of human disease, sometimes to widespread proportions. One example is cholera.

Cholera

We often think of our modern world as cleansed of the epidemic scourges of ages past. But cholera —an acute and sometimes fatal disease that is accompanied by severe diarrhea— affects more nations today than ever before. The Seventh Pandemic began when the El Tor strain left its traditional home in the Bay of Bengal in the 1960s, travelled to the east and west across Asia, and in the 1970s penetrated the continent of Africa. In 1991, the cholera pandemic reached the Americas, and during the first eighteen months more than half a million cases were reported in Latin America, with 5,000 deaths. Rapid institution of oral rehydration treatment—with clean water, sugar, and salts—limited fatalities in the Americas to about one in a hundred cases. The epidemics also had serious economic consequences. In 1991, Peru lost $770 million in seafood exports and another $250 million in lost tourist revenues because of the disease. The microbe that transmits cholera, Vibrio cholerae, is found in a dormant or "hibernating" state in algae and microscopic animal plankton, where it can be identified using modern microbiological techniques. But once introduced to people—by drinking contaminated water or eating contaminated fish or shellfish— cholera can recycle through a population, when sewage is allowed to mix with the clean water supply.

Five years ago, in late 1992, a new strain of Vibrio cholerae—O139 Bengal—emerged in India along the coast of the Bay of Bengal. With populations unprotected by prior immunities, this hardy strain quickly spread through adjoining nations, threatening to become the agent of the world's Eighth Cholera Pandemic. For a time, in 1994, El Tor regained dominance. But by 1996, O139 Bengal had reasserted itself. The emergence of this new disease, like all others, involved the interplay of microbial, human host, and environmental factors.

The largest and most intense outbreak of cholera ever recorded occurred in Rwanda in 1994, killing over 40,000 people in the space of weeks, in a nation already ravaged by civil war and ethnic strife. The tragedy of cholera in Rwanda is a reminder of the impacts of conflict and political instability on public health and biological security—just as epidemics may, in turn, contribute to political and economic stability.

Is The Ocean Warming?

Surface temperatures of the ocean have warmed this century, and a gradual warming of the deep ocean has been found in recent years in oceanographic surveys carried out in the tropical Pacific, Atlantic, and Indian Oceans, and at both poles of the Earth. These findings could be indicative of a long-term trend. Corresponding temperature measurements of the sub-surface earth, in cores drilled deep into the Arctic tundra, show a similar effect.

The water that evaporates from warmer seas, and from vegetation and soils of a warmer land surface, intensifies the rate at which water cycles from ocean to clouds and back again. In so doing it increases humidity and reinforces the greenhouse effect. Warm seas are the engines that drive tropical storms and fuel the intensity of hurricanes. More high clouds can also contribute to warmer nights by trapping out-going radiation.

Some Biological Impacts

A warmer ocean can also harm marine plankton, and thus affect more advanced forms of life in the sea. A northward shift in marine flora and fauna along the California coast that has been underway since the 1930s has been associated with the long-term warming of the ocean over that span of time.

Warming—when sufficient nutrients are present—may also be contributing to the proliferation of coastal algal blooms. Harmful algal blooms of increasing extent, duration, and intensity—and involving novel, toxic species—have been reported around the world since the 1970s. Indeed, some scientists feel that the worldwide increase in coastal algal blooms may be one of the first biological signs of global environmental change.

Warm years may result in a confluence of adverse events. The 1987 El Nino was associated with the spread and new growth of tropical and temperate species of algae in higher northern and southern latitudes. Many were toxic algal blooms. In 1987, following a shoreward intrusion of Gulf Stream eddies, the dinoflagellate Gymnodimuim breve, previously found only as far north as the Gulf of Mexico, bloomed about 700 miles north, off Cape Hatteras, North Carolina, where it has since persisted, albeit at low levels. Forty-eight cases of neurological shellfish poisoning occurred in 1987, resulting in an estimated $25 million loss to the seafood industry and the local community. In the same year, anomalous rain patterns and warm Gulf Stream eddies swept unusually close to Prince Edward Island in the Gulf of St. Lawrence. The result, combined with the run-off of local pollutants after heavy rains, was a bloom of toxic diatoms. For the first time, domoic acid was produced from these algae, and then ingested by marine life. Consumption of contaminated mussels resulted in 107 instances of amnesic shellfish poisoning, from domoic acid, including three deaths and permanent, short-term memory loss in several victims.

Also in 1987, there were major losses of sea urchin and coral communities in the Caribbean, a massive sea grass die-off near the Florida Keys, and on the beaches of the North Atlantic coast, the death of numerous dolphins and other sea mammals. It has been proposed that the combination of algal toxins, chlorinated hydrocarbons like PCBs, and warming may have lowered the immunity of organisms and altered the food supply for various forms of sea life, allowing *morbilli* (measles-like) viruses to take hold.

The 1990s

For five years and eight months, from 1990 to 1995, the Pacific Ocean persisted in the warm El Nino phase, which was most unusual, for since 1877 none of these distinctive warmings had lasted more than three years. Both anomalous phases—with either warmer (El Nino) or colder (La Nina) surface waters— bring climate extremes to many regions across the globe.

With the ensuing cold (La Nina) phase of 1995-1996, many regions of the world that had lived with drought during the El Nino years were now besieged with intense rains and flooding. Just as in Colombia, flooding in southern Africa was accompanied by an upsurge of vector-borne diseases, including malaria. Other areas experienced a climatic switch of the opposite kind, with drought and wildfires replacing floods. During 1996 world grain stores fell to their lowest level since the 1930s.

Weather always varies; but increased variability and rapid temperature fluctuations may be a chief characteristic of our changing climate system. And increased variability and weather volatility can have significant consequences for health and for society.

Decadal Variability

The cumulative meteorological and ecological impacts of the prolonged El Nino of the early 1990s have yet to be fully evaluated, and another is now upon us.

In 1995, warming in the Caribbean produced coral bleaching for the first time in Belize, as sea surface temperatures surpassed the 29°C (84°F) threshold that may damage the animal and plant tissues that make up a coral reef. In 1997, Caribbean sea surface temperatures reached 34°C (93°F) off southern Belize, and coral bleaching was accompanied by large mortalities in starfish and other sea life. Coral diseases are now sweeping through the Caribbean, and diseases that perturb marine habitat, such as coral or sea grasses, can also affect the fish stocks for which these areas serve as nurseries.

A pattern of greater weather variability has begun and is expected to persist with the El Nino of 1997 and 1998. Since 1976, such anomalies in Pacific Ocean temperatures and in weather extreme events have become more frequent, more intense, and longer lasting than in the preceding 100 years, as indicated in records kept since 1877.

DISCONTINUITIES AND INSTABILIBY

The common perception that the natural world changes only gradually can be misleading, for discontinuities abound. Animals switch abruptly between two states—awake and asleep—that are sharply divided and marked by qualitative differences in levels of activity in the central nervous system. Water can rapidly change from vapour to liquid to solid. Ecosystems have equilibrium states that are also at times abruptly interrupted. An extensive fire in an old growth forest, for example, can radically change the types of plants and animals within it.

Climate regimes can also change surprisingly fast. Recent analyses of Greenland ice cores indicate that significant shifts, called rapid climate change events (RCCEs), have taken place in the past in the span of but several years—not centuries, as was previously believed. While the oceans may serve as a buffer against sudden climate change, this mechanism may be limited, for some of the RCCEs seem to be associated with abrupt changes in ocean circulation.

The climate system exhibits equilibrium states as well, of which three may have been most common: when the poles of the Earth were covered with small, medium, or large ice caps. The present, Holocene period of the last 10,000 years—with medium-size caps and an average global temperature of 15°C (about 60°F)— has been associated with the development of modern agriculture and advancing civilization. But our present climate regime may be becoming less stable. Increased variance—that is, more extreme swings—in natural systems is inversely related to how stable and balanced the systems are, and how sensitive they are to perturbations. Wider and wider variations can occur as a system moves away from its equilibrium state.

Trends in the 20th Century

The gradual warming that characterized the climate during the first four decades of the present century, for example, was accompanied by substantial temperature variability, as borne out in the record of degree-heating-days in the U.S. grain belt. The ensuing cooling trend from 1940 to the mid 1970s showed less variability. From 1976 to the present day, the variability—apparent in hot and cold spells, drought, and floods—has again increased. Greenland ice core records suggest that the last time the Earth warmed abruptly, ending the last Ice Age, there was also a pattern of increased variability.

The connection between human health and environmental stability increases our need for a better understanding of the present state of the global climate system. There are several unanswered questions regarding the system's stability. Was the drift toward earlier springtimes that began in this country in the 1940s indicative of the first minor readjustment in the climate regime? Are the more frequent and intense El Nino events since the mid 1970s another such indicator? Has the baseline of ocean temperatures shifted? Does the present climatic volatility—evident in altered weather and precipitation patterns—increase the potential for an abrupt "jump" in the climate system? And might further stresses lead to abrupt discontinuities of the type found in the Greenland ice cores, when the last Ice Age rapidly came to an end?

THE COSTS OF CLIMATE VARIABILITY AND DISEASE OUTBREAKS

Regardless of what caused it, the recent rise in severe wind and flood-related events worldwide has had extraordinary consequences for property insurers. Prior to 1989, no single-event insured loss in the U.S. had ever exceeded a billion dollars. Since then, annual insured losses have risen dramatically—from almost $1.6 billion annually in the 1980s to $10 billion in the 1990s: a jump that is only partially explained by more intensive exploitation of rivers and land and seashore property. Federal relief bills, chiefly from flooding, totalled $13 billion for the last five years, compared to $3.3 billion for the preceding five.

Because they combine exposure with weather-related events, the costs to the property insurance industry may be the most telling indicator of the non-sustainability of our interference with natural global systems. With continued extreme climate variability, health and environmental restoration costs may grow in a similar manner. It is significant that we are having difficulty insuring our future.

The economic impacts of disease in humans, livestock, and food crops can also be severe and far-reaching. Today the white fly—whose numbers swell when there is drought—is injecting at least eighteen types of geminiviruses into tomato, squash, and bean plants throughout Latin America, depleting the primary source of protein for many who live there. Recently a necrosis virus (vectored by soil-based fungi) that attacks rice has appeared in Colombia. Further spread of a disease of this staple food source could have enormous impacts on world food supplies.

While the 1991 cholera epidemic cost Peru over $1 billion in tourist income locally, international airline and hotel industries lost from $2 to $5 billion from the 1994 Indian plague. Cruise boats, quite understandably, have begun to avoid islands racked by dengue fever. In the Caribbean, this trend could threaten a $12 billion-a-year tourist industry that employs more than half a million people. The 1997 California floods left fungi and root rot that threatens that state's $22 billion citrus industry. Indeed, the global resurgence of malaria, dengue fever, and cholera, and the emergence of relatively new diseases like Ebola, toxic

Escherichia coli and Mad Cow disease —which are related to ecology and animal husbandry practices— affect not only the health of individuals but also of national economies.

An Historical Notes on Pandemics

Pandemics emerge out of social and environmental conditions, and they can induce changes in both of them. At times the resulting changes have been disruptive; in other instances they have stimulated significant social reform.

The Rise and Fall of Infectious Disease

From a long-term historical perspective, pandemics have often been associated with major social transitions and overtaxed infrastructure. Their impacts have been lasting and profound.

A pandemic, of debated cause but remembered as the Plague of Justinian, struck Europe in A. D. 541. It came as the Roman Empire was in decline, and it raged for two centuries, claiming over 40 million lives, in an era when the total population of the Earth was at most 300 million. Urban centres were abandoned and the plague helped drive population resettlement into rural, feudal communities before it disappeared.

After a 600-year hiatus, plague again appeared, in A.D. 1346—at the depths of the Middle Ages—when growing urban populations had again outstripped the capabilities of cities to sustain sanitation and basic public health. Several other factors played compounding roles: Human populations had migrated from East to West; the Medieval Warm Period of the 12th and 13th centuries may have contributed to the proliferation of rats and fleas that carried the so-called bubonic plague; and cats had been killed in the belief that they were witches. In the ensuing five years of the so-called "Black Death," about 25 million lives were taken—about one of every three persons who lived in Europe at the time. Social relations and labour patterns were dramatically altered throughout Europe.

A third outbreak of widespread epidemic disease, almost 300 years later, had a more positive outcome. In the course of the early Industrial Revolution, improvements that accompanied development led to a substantial decline in mortality from infectious disease. Then, in the 1830s, under the burgeoning weight of industrialization and the growth of population—seven-fold in London from 1790 to 1850—the conditions in European cities described in the novels of Charles Dickens became breeding grounds for three major infectious diseases: cholera, smallpox, and tuberculosis. Suddenly growth and development had outgrown infrastructure, and infectious diseases rebounded. But the resurgence of infectious disease this time precipitated protests throughout the European continent, and ultimately led to constructive responses. In England, the Sanitary and Environmental Reform Movements were born; and the field of epidemiology ushered in modern public health principles and eventually, led to a national health program. The epidemics abated in the course of several decades, three-quarters of a century before the advent of anti-microbials.

Recent History

By the 1960s widespread improvements in hygiene, sanitation, and mosquito control led most public health authorities to believe that we would soon conquer infectious diseases. In the 1970s public health schools turned their attention instead to chronic ailments, such as heart disease, stroke, diabetes, and cancer. But the so-called "epidemiological transition" to diseases of modernity never materialized in many developing nations. And, in the 1980s, the global picture shifted dramatically.

According to the U.N. World Health Organization's 1996 report, drug-resistant strains of bacteria and other microbes are having a deadly impact on the fight against several diseases, including tuberculosis, malaria, cholera, and pneumonia —which collectively killed more than 10 million people in 1995. Spread of resistant organisms resulted from antibiotic overuse, microbial mutations, and the geographic movement of humans, insects, rodents, and microbes. Ironically, our very means to control infectious disease—antibiotics and insecticides—are, themselves, rapidly driving the evolution of new and unaffected strains. Notably, two thirds of antibiotic use is in animal husbandry, agriculture, and aquaculture.

In the 1990s, diphtheria rose exponentially in the former USSR as the public health system deteriorated following political and economic changes. The incidence rose from 4000 cases in 1992, to 8000 in 1993, and 48,000 in 1994, claiming the lives of over 4000 residents since 1990. Incidence has risen in fifteen nations of Eastern Europe, although recent immunization campaigns have begun to control this infection.

Dengue fever, for which no vaccine is yet available, had essentially disappeared from the Americas by the 1970s, but has resurged in South America, infecting over 300,000 people in 1995— which was, notably, the warmest year of this century. "Aedes aegypti is now well established in all areas of the Americas except Canada and Chile," ran a recent editorial in the British medical journal Lancet. Settlements that surround typical mega-cities, where discarded non-biodegradable containers serve as ideal mosquito breeding sites, provide especially vulnerable settings; milder "cold" seasons and weather extremes can both help precipitate large outbreaks. Additionally, previous exposure and a change in the type of viral dengue circulating may lead to Dengue hemorrhagic fever, that carries a 5 to 10 percent mortality.

In 1995 the largest epidemic of yellow fever since 1950 — carried by the same mosquito that transmits dengue —hit the Americas. Peru and the Amazon basin were heavily impacted, and there is a growing potential for urban yellow fever. While there is a yellow fever vaccine, the current supply may be inadequate for future needs.

Finally, in 1996 the largest epidemic ever recorded of meningitis struck West Africa, associated with pervasive drought, since dry mucus membranes may aid the invasion of the colonizing organisms. Over 100,000 persons contracted the disease and more than 10,000 people died. A vaccine is available, but must be used early to stop an epidemic.

Who is at Risk?

Conditions conducive to the spread of epidemic infectious diseases now exist worldwide, according to the WHO report, and domestic environmental and social conditions that favour the spread of these diseases are present in the U.S. today. Infectious diseases that have emerged, like Hantavirus Pulmonary Syndrome, Lyme Disease, and toxic E. coli were not imported from other nations. E. coli, for example, spreads in cattle raised in close quarters.

The transmission of tuberculosis, another example, is facilitated in homeless shelters and in prisons. And while poorer populations are at greatest risk, outbreaks of infectious disease are not restricted to disadvantaged regions, for today's population movements facilitate "microbial traffic" between nations and economic groups.

What can be Done?

The concerns that have been elaborated here are not hopeless: there are solutions to all of them. The steps that are needed, moreover, would benefit our own and future generations regardless of the future course of climate or the inevitable environmental surprises that await us in years ahead. Solutions can be divided into three levels, ranging from tactical and immediate, to strategic and long-term, and all are within our present capabilities.

The first-level solution is improved surveillance and response capability for the public health sector, that includes the development of vaccines, better treatments, and more widespread support, around the world, for public health measures. The second is the integration of health surveillance as an element of the kind of environmental monitoring that is called for in the accompanying article in this issue of CONSEQUENCES. We need to make greater use of remote sensing and climate forecasts—as for El Nino/La Nina occurrence—to develop health early warning systems to alert communities of conditions conducive to the outbreak of infectious diseases.

The third level is the evaluation of environmental and energy policies in the context of their impacts on human health and well-being. Maintaining the integrity of ecosystems, such as forest habitat and wetlands, can provide defence against outbreaks of the opportunists that carry disease, and provide a buffer against climatic vagaries and extremes, whether or not there is any change in the overall climate regime. Early interventions can save money and lives.

A Personal Conclusion

There are more and more fingerprints of an impending change in the global climate, and ever more evidence of our own ecological footprint on natural systems. We are living in a period of accelerated social, ecological, and climatic change. But will our global society react to the symptoms of environmental dysfunction in time to take corrective measures?

We are changing the chemistry of the air, and in the process altering the heat budget of the world. It is the multiple changes induced in the Earth's atmosphere—carbon buildup, sulfate accumulation, and ozone depletion—that constitute a destabilizing array of forcing factors. Together they may already have begun to alter natural climatic modes, such as the frequency and strength of the El Nino-Southern Oscillation. These modifications—along with the changes in coastal ocean chemistry—have begun to affect biological systems and human health.

Behind these chemical, physical, and biological changes is our ever-increasing use of the Earth's finite resources, and our generation of wastes at rates beyond which biogeochemical systems can adequately recycle them. These patterns of consumption are simply not sustainable and come at costs that are real, often very high, and not acknowledged by current systems of economic accounting. Practices affecting forestry, fisheries, petrochemicals, and fossil fuels need all be examined in light of their costs across the full range of their ultimate impacts, including their effects on biodiversity, climate, and the global resurgence of infectious diseases. Some of these practices now facilitate the spread of diseases by altering the environment, and others by undermining social infrastructures.

The global environment is most drastically at risk from changes in the climate that are almost certain to follow our escalating combustion of fossil fuels. Air pollution—by particles and smog from fossil fuel combustion—add to the health hazards of warming. Ultimately, according to the first IPCC report, the world must reduce present greenhouse gas emissions from 60 to 70 percent to stabilize the concentrations in the atmosphere and, we can hope, allow natural systems to readjust. The U.N.-sponsored Framework Convention on Climate Change that addresses the burning of fossil fuels is an essential step, for the global carbon budget is key to all living systems.

The instability of many economies also jeopardizes the public health. Population growth and the relocation of people, driven by economic, environmental, and political factors, exert enormous pressures on the environment. Migration levels of the past two decades—within and between nations—surpass the great migrations of the 1800s. World Bank figures, not surprisingly, confirm that the ability of a society to stabilize its population—and as a consequence, bring public health and environmental degradation under control—is directly related to the degree of equity of income within it.

Unfortunately, international burdens of debt, binding austerity programs, unequal terms of trade, and numerous subsidies negate many of the policies, plans, and projects designed to alleviate poverty, preserve the environment, and stimulate economic growth and security. Short-term, microeconomic goals are hampered by stronger macroeconomic forces, creating social instability and ultimately retarding healthy development.

The global resurgence of infectious disease in the last quarter of the twentieth century—a backward step that few would have anticipated twenty years ago—is a clear consequence of combined and compounding changes in physical, chemical, biological, and social systems. Greater disease surveillance and response capability are the first, essential, steps. But viewed as a symptom, the resurgence of infectious disease across a wide taxonomic range may indicate that we may be vastly underestimating the true costs of "business-as-usual."

Fortunately, consciousness and values can change even more rapidly than do the natural systems we all depend upon. We face important decisions in the way we use and re-use the finite resources that are available to us. Perhaps we are also vastly underestimating the economic opportunities and employment benefits to society as a whole as we make the transition to use resources more efficiently, generate energy cleanly, and restore essential functions of the natural environment. Curbing our unhealthy addiction to fossil fuels may be the lever that opens the portal to a healthy and productive future.

THE ECOLOGICAL EFFECTS OF ROADS

Despite heightened recognition (by informed people) of the harmful effects of roads, road density continues to increase in the US and other countries. Federal, state, and local transportation departments devote huge budgets to construction and upgrading of roads. Multinational lending institutions, such as the World Bank, finance roads into pristine rainforest, which usher in a flood of settlers who destroy both the rainforest and the indigenous cultures. Public land-managing agencies build thousands of miles of roads each year to support their resource extraction activities, at a net cost to the taxpayer. The US Forest Service alone plans to build or reconstruct almost 600,000 miles of roads in the next 50 years. Most public agencies disregard the ecological impacts of roads, and attempt to justify timber roads as benefiting recreation and wildlife management. Even when a land manager recognises the desirability of closing roads, he or she usually contends that such closures would be unacceptable to the public.

This chapter will review some ecological effects of roads, with emphasis on impacts to wildlife (broadly defined). My concern is with all roads, from primitive logging roads to four-lane highways. Although the effects of different types of roads vary, virtually all are bad, and the net effect of all roads is nothing short of catastrophic. The technical literature that pertains to this topic is vast, and an entire book would be needed to summarise it adequately. Consider this only an introduction, or an "executive summary" of a massive tragedy.

Direct effects, such as flattened fauna, are easy to see. In contrast, many indirect effects of roads are cumulative and involve changes in community structure and ecological processes that are not well understood. Yet, these long-term effects signal a deterioration in ecosystems that far surpasses in importance the visual and olfactory insult to us of a bloated deer by the roadside.

DIRECT EFFECTS

Roadkills

The above statement notwithstanding, roadkill can have a significant impact on wildlife populations. The Humane Society of the US and the Urban Wildlife Research Centre have arrived at a conservative figure of one million animals killed each day on highways in the United States. When I-75 was completed through a major deer wintering area in northern Michigan, deer road mortality increased by 500%. In Pennsylvania, 26,180 deer and 90 bears were killed by vehicles in 1985. These statistics do not account for animals that crawl off the road to die after being hit. Also, roadkill statistics are invariably biased toward mammals, against reptiles, amphibians, and probably birds, and do not include invertebrates at all (who wants to count the insects smashed on windshields and grills?).

Vehicles on high-speed highways pose the greatest threat to wildlife. Unpaved roads, particularly when "unimproved", are less dangerous. Roadkill usually increases with volume of traffic. In one Texas study, however, mortality was greatest on roads with intermediate volumes, presumably because higher-volume roads had wider rights-of-way that allowed better visibility for animals and drivers alike. Increases in traffic volume do result in more collisions on any given road, and in our profligate society more people means more cars on virtually every road.

Florida is a rapidly developing state with more than 1000 new human residents each day and over 50 million tourists annually. Primary and interstate highway mileage has increased by 4.6 miles per day for the last 50 years. Hence it is no surprise that roadkills are the leading known cause of death for all large mammals except White-tailed Deer.

Roadkills of Florida Black Bear, a subspecies listed as threatened by the state, have been rising sharply in recent years, from 2-3 per year in the 1970s to 44 in 1989. Many of the bears are killed on roads through public lands, in particular the Ocala National Forest. Seventeen Florida Panthers, one of the most endangered subspecies of mammals in the world, are known to have been killed on roads since 1972. Since 1981, 65% of documented Florida Panther deaths have been roadkills, and the population of only about twenty individuals is unlikely to be able to sustain this pressure. An average of 41 Key Deer, a species listed as Endangered by the US Fish and Wildlife Service, were killed on roads yearly from 1980 through 1986, and 57 were killed in 1987. Roadkill is also the leading cause of mortality for the American Crocodile, also an Endangered species, in south Florida. The Florida Scrub Jay, a Threatened species, has been found to suffer considerable mortality from collision with vehicles, and researchers have concluded that these birds cannot maintain stable populations along roads with considerable high-speed traffic.

Snakes are particularly vulnerable to roadkill, as the warm asphalt attracts them; yet their carcasses are seldom tallied. Herpetologists have noted dramatic declines of snakes in Paynes Prairie State Preserve near Gainesville, Florida, which is crossed by two four-lane highways. This preserve was once legendary for its diversity and density of snakes, but no more. Similarly, a study of south Florida herpetofauna by Wilson and Porras attributed declines in many snakes to the increasing road traffic in that region. Roadkill is a classic death-trap phenomenon. Animals are attracted to roads for a variety of reasons, often to their demise. Snakes and other ectotherms go there to bask, some birds use roadside gravel to aid their digestion of seeds, mammals go to eat de-icing salts, deer and other browsing herbivores are attracted to the dense vegetation of roadside edge, rodents proliferate in the artificial grasslands of road verges, and many large mammals find roads to be efficient travelways. Songbirds come to dustbathe on dirt roads, where they are vulnerable to vehicles as well as predators. Vultures, Crows, Coyotes, Raccoons, and other scavengers seek out roadkills, often to become roadkills themselves.

ROAD AVERSION AND OTHER BEHAVIOURAL MODIFICATIONS

Not all animals are attracted to roads. Some have learned that roads bring unpleasant things, such as people with guns. Species that show road aversion exhibit decreasing densities toward roads. Various studies report that Turkey, White-tailed Deer, Mule Deer, Elk, Mountain Lions, Grizzly Bear, and Black Bear avoid roads. When these animals are disturbed by vehicles, they waste valuable energy in flight. Other studies show conflicting results, which usually can be explained by differences in road use. Certain bird species also have been found to avoid roads, or the forest edges associated with roads. In the Netherlands, researchers found some bird species to be displaced up to 2000 meters from busy highways.

The American Elk is one of the best-studied species with respect to road aversion. Elk avoidance of roads is clearly a learned response (they do not avoid natural edges), and is related to traffic volume and hunting pressure. In western Montana, Jack Lyon found that Elk avoid areas within 1/4-1/2 mile of roads, depending on traffic, road quality, and the density of cover near the road. According to work by Jack Thomas in Oregon, a road density of one mile per square mile of land results in a 25% reduction in habitat use by Elk; two miles of road per square mile can cut Elk habitat use by half. As road density increases to six miles of road per square mile, Elk and Mule Deer habitat use falls to zero. Elk in some areas have learned that roads are dangerous only in the hunting season, and do not show road aversion in other seasons. Other studies suggest that Elk avoid open roads, but not closed roads. Where hunting pressure is high however, even closed roads may be avoided because so many hunters walk them.

Grizzly Bears also may be displaced by roads. In British Columbia, Grizzlies were found to avoid areas within 1/2 mile of roads. A study in the Cabinet Mountains of northwestern Montana determined that the mean distance of Grizzly radio-telemetry signals from open roads (2467 m) was significantly greater than the mean distance from closed roads (740 m). Other studies have found that Grizzlies avoid areas near roads, especially by day, even when preferred habitat and forage are located there. This is particularly alarming, because in Yellowstone National Park, which has the second largest Grizzly population in the lower 48, roads and developments are situated in the most productive Grizzly Bear habitat Natural movements of Grizzly Bears may also be deflected by roads, as Chuck Jonkel has documented in Montana. In other cases, however, Grizzlies may use roads as travelways, particularly when they find off-road travel difficult due to dense brush or logging slash. Grizzlies have also learned to exploit the hastened growth of forage plants near roads in spring. Similarly, the abundance of soft mast such as Pokeberry and Blackberry along road edges attracts Appalachian Black Bears in summer. Any advantages associated with roads for either bear species are outweighed by the increase in sometimes fatal (usually for the bear, unfortunately) encounters with humans.

Wild animals can become habituated to roads. Thirty years ago, for example, bears in Yellowstone, the Great Smokies, and other parks often sat along the roadsides and picnic areas waiting for handouts from tourists. When parks disallowed handouts and relocated habituated hears, the attraction subsided. In any area where animals are exposed to frequent human activity, habituation can be expected. This is not necessarily a desirable response, however. Although animals that are attracted to roads and vehicles do not waste energy reserves in flight response, some of them become aggressive toward people. Aggressive behaviour of habituated animals has been noted in bears, Mule Deer, Elk, Bighorn Sheep, Bison, and other species. Conflicts occur most often when humans approach animals closely in order to feed or photograph them. A few years ago in the Smoky Mountains, a bear reportedly chomped on a baby's face when a parent held it close for a kissing photo-the baby's cheek had been smeared with honey. Such encounters usually result in relocation or killing of the "problem" animals, though the real problem is human stupidity. Studies of Grizzly Bears in Montana and British Columbia have found that bears habituated to human activity especially moving vehicles, are more vulnerable to legal and illegal shooting.

FRAGMENTATION AND ISOLATION OF POPULATIONS

Some species of animals simply refuse to cross barriers as wide as a road. For these species, a road effectively cuts the population in half. A network of roads fragments the population further. The remaining small populations are then vulnerable to all the problems associated with rarity: genetic deterioration from inbreeding and random drift in gene frequencies, environmental catastrophes, fluctuations in habitat conditions, and demographic stochasticity (i.e., chance variation in age and sex ratios). Thus, roads conrtribute to what many conservation biologists consider the major threat to biological diversity: habitat fragmentation. Such fragmentation may be especially ominous in the face of rapid climate change. If organisms are prevented from migrating to track shifting climatic conditions, and cannot adapt quickly enough because of limited genetic variation, then extinction is inevitable.

In one of the first studies on habitat isolation by roads, D.J. Oxley and co-workers in southeastern Ontario and Quebec found that small forest mammals such as the Eastern Chipmunk, Grey Squirrel, and White-footed Mouse rarely ventured onto road surfaces when the distance between forest margins (road clearance) exceeded 20 meters. The authors suggested that divided highways with a clearance of 90 meters or more maybe as effective barriers to the dispersal of small mammals as water bodies twice as wide. Earlier work in Africa had shown that tortoises, and young Ostrich, Wart hogs, and African Elephants, had difficulty crossing roads with steep embankments. In Germany, Mader found that several species of woodland carabid beetles and two species of forest-dwelling mice rarely or never crossed two-lane roads. Even a small, unpaved forest road closed to public traffic constituted a barrier. All of these animals were physically capable of crossing roads but appeared to be psychologically constrained from venturing into such openings.

In Ontario, Merriam and co-workers found that narrow gravel roads were "quantitative barriers" to White-footed Mice in forest fragments; many fewer mice crossed roads than moved an equal distance in the forest alongside roads.

Expect that the barrier effect of roads would be less severe in more open habitats, where the contrast between the road and adjoining habitat is less. Yet, a study by Garland and Bradley of the effects of a four-lane highway on rodents in the Mojave Desert found that rodents almost never crossed the road. Of eight species captured, marked, and recaptured, only an adult male Antelope Ground Squirrel crossed the entire highway.

No roadkills were observed, suggesting that few rodents ever ventured onto the highway.

Animals far more mobile than rodents and beetles may hesitate to cross roads. In the Southern Appalachians, Brody and Pelton found that radlo-collared Black Bears almost never crossed an interstate highway. In general, the frequency at which bears crossed roads varied inversely with traffic volume. Bears appeared to react to increasing road densities by shifting their home ranges to areas of lower road density. The power of flight may not override the barrier effect of roads for some bird species. Many tropical forest birds are known to be averse to crossing water gaps no wider than a highway. Further research is needed to determine if these species react to road clearings as they do to water gaps.

Thus, populations of many animal species divided by a heavily travelled road may be just as isolated from one another as if they were separated by many miles of barren urban or agricultural land. Larry Harris and Peter Gallagher, writing in a recent Defenders of Wildlife publication on habitat corridors ("Preserving Communities & Corridors" available from Defenders, 1244 19th St. NW, Washington, DC 20036; $10 each), put the road fragmentation problem into proper perspective:

"Consider this triple jeopardy: At the same time that development reduces the total amount of habitat, squeezing remaining wildlife into smaller and more isolated patches, the high-speed traffic of larger and wider highways eliminates more and more of the remaining populations."

To the extent that various plant species depend on road-averse animals for dispersal, roads fragment plant populations as well.

Pollution

Pollution from roads begins with construction. An immediate impact is noise from construction equipment, and noise remains a problem along highways with heavy traffic. Animals respond to noise pollution by altering activity patterns, and with an increase in heart rate and production of stress hormones. Sometimes animals become habituated to increased noise levels, and apparently resume normal activity. But birds and other wildlife that communicate by auditory signals may be at a disadvantage near roads. Highway noise can also disrupt territory establishment and defence. A study by Andrew Barrass found that toads and tree frogs showed abnormal reproductive behaviour in response to highway noise.

Vehicles emit a variety of pollutants, including heavy metals, carbon dioxide, and carbon monoxide, all of which may have serious cumulative effects. Combustion of gasoline containing tetraethyl lead, and wear of tires containing lead oxide, result in lead contamination of roadsides. Although unleaded gasoline now accounts for more than half of all gasoline used in the US, lead persists in soils and the food web for long periods. In Kansas, lead levels in roadside soils and vegetation in the early 1980s were two to three times greater than from near roads with similar traffic volumes in 1973 and 1974, when the use of unleaded gasoline was 42% lower.

Many studies have documented increasing levels of lead in plants with proximity to roads, and with increases in traffic volume. Plant roots take up lead from the soil, and leaves take it up from contaminated air or from particulate matter on the leaf surface. This lead moves up the food chain, with sometimes severe toxic effects on animals, including reproductive impairment, renal abnormalities, and increased mortality rates. Food chain effects can switch between aquatic and terrestrial pathways. Lead concentrations in tadpoles living near highways can be high enough to cause physiological and reproductive impairment in birds and mammals that prey on tadpoles.

3

Plant Ecology

Plant ecology is a branch of the scientific field of ecology which focuses specifically on plant populations. There are a number of applications for plant ecology, ranging from helping people develop low water gardens to studying endangered ecosystems to learn about how they can be protected. Researchers from this field tend to come from an interdisciplinary background which can feature training in a wide variety of scientific pursuits, including plant anatomy, general ecology, biology, and so forth.

The field of plant ecology includes the study of plants and their environment. Rather than just looking at plants in a vacuum, researchers consider how they interact with each other and their environment to create an interconnected system. Plant ecology can include the study of entire ecosystems, such as the rainforest or plateau, or the study of specific areas of interest, like plant populations which manage to survive next to a polluted stream. Plant ecologists also look at animals, soil conditions, and other influences on a plant's environment.

Ecology is a complex and vast field of study which can encompass everything from understanding how natural environments function to how humans interact with the natural world, and how various behaviors can fundamentally alter the natural environment. In plant ecology, people can focus on topics like climate change and its effect on plants, plant evolution, how plants disseminate themselves in nature, symbiotic relationships between plant species, plant diseases, and so forth.

A great deal of field work is involved in plant ecology, as researchers like to see their subjects in nature so that they can learn in context. A single sample of a plant can provide interesting information and data, but actually seeing that plant growing can provide a researcher with a great deal more data. For example, looking at a plant alone, a researcher might not understand why its leaves are shaped the way they are, but when the researcher sees the plant in nature, he or she might realize that the leaves conferred some sort of benefit on the plant or the surrounding environment, ranging from signaling the presence of the plant to pollinators to providing shelter for seedlings so that they can grow up.

Plants make up a vital part of the natural environment, and plant ecologists are well aware of this. In a healthy ecosystem, plants provide food and shelter for animals, secure the soil to prevent erosion, cast shade to create microclimates, conserve water to keep it in the ecosystem instead of allowing it to be lost, and participate in the breakdown and recycling of organic material to keep the ecosystem thriving. Plants are also of critical interest because they produce oxygen, and plants have been heavily implicated in the creation of the Earth's currently oxygen-rich atmosphere.

The relation of organisms and their processes individually to the physical conditions of their internal and external environments is the especial province of the plant physiologist but that of the plant ecologist is to study the integrated effects of the interaction of these physical conditions and the organisms they support, having due regard to the important part played by what we comprehensively term competition. It is the purpose of this article to present some of the salient trends in the study of the causal factors which influence the character and composition of plant communities.

Often in the past it has been found convenient to consider the habitat factors in separate categories, the historic, the climatic, the edaphic and the biotic, but there is an inevitable danger in such abstraction that we underrate the degree to which these interact to affect their influence on plant life. Those influences which have operated in the past to produce the conditions of the present can be classed as historic factors and these, it is manifest, must often have been secular in character.

The replacement of the prevailingly Pteridophytic and Pteridospermous flora of the Coalmeasure Period by the predominantly Gymnospermous vegetation of the succeeding epochs, must have depended upon prolonged changes in the environment, both physical and biotic, as also, no doubt, the transition to the predominantly Phanerogamic vegetation of the present era. The persistence or survival of any one group that marked the facies of plant communities may well reflect, not so much the inherent capacity of the gene complexes involved, to provide organisms of survival value, as their capacity, relative to those of other organisms, to change with sufficient rapidity.

The distinction is important since the one implies an intrinsic lack of physiological plasticity, the other a genetic complex that is merely resistant to adjustment. The one would lead to complete extinction under changing conditions, as with the Pteridosperms, the other to a rare persistence as exemplified by the Royal Fern *(Osmunda)* and the Quill-wort *(Isoetes)* alike survivals of very ancient lineage. Though very remote in the time of their initiation these secular changes are probably still operative in their effects.

Indeed the vegetation of the Earth's surface today has, we all recognize, been profoundly modified by the age of steam and the internal combustion engine which alike depend for their source of power on our heritage of fossil fuel from the extinct floras and faunas of the past; their exploitation has accelerated the progressive replacement of natural plant communities by the semi-natural and the quasi-artificial, a transition that the geometrically increasing population of the world is continually augmenting.

If the effects of the remote, and even of the immediate, past are often difficult to evaluate that in no degree denigrates their significance. In our own time man's influence in changing the protective cover of vegetation has disastrously accelerated erosion in many areas. By regulating waterways and creating hard road surfaces he has speeded up drainage and lowered water tables in an ever increasing area, whilst through forest destruction on catchment areas the regulatory influence of the organic sponge has been reduced so that floods are liable to alternate with drought and bring changes far beyond the extent of obvious interference. Anti-erosion measures have recognized the important role that vegetation has to play and the time must one day come when foresters, agriculturists, water engineers and others will recognize a common interest and responsibility in initiating changes in the ecology of the plant cover which they severally exploit.

From the nature of evidences of the past and their often fragmentary character it is only in relation to the most recent events that it is possible to do more than note the contemporaneous occurrence of vegetation changes and physical alterations so that historical ecology is more often descriptive than causal and so outside the scope of this present consideration. The more obvious climatic influences of wind, precipitation, humidity, temperature, and illumination were, in the earlier ecological studies, considered far too much in isolation from the point of view of the average conditions and with little regard either to their interaction or their indirect effects. Furthermore, it was not till attempts were made to correlate vegetation with the climatic pattern that it was realized how complicated this pattern might be.

PLANT ADAPTATIONS

A wetland is a harsh environment physiologically. Aquatic plants can't deal with periodic drying and temperatures tend to be more extreme because the water's shallow terrestrial plants can't deal with long floods. Stresses include anoxia and wide salinity and water fluctuations. Adaptations to these conditions have an energy cost, either because the organisms cells are working less efficiently (conformers) or because it expends energy to protect cells from external stress (regulators).

Protists aren't plants, of course, but this is a convenient spot to put them. They are eukaryotic (membrane bound organelles), unicellular, colonial, or simple multicellular organisms, including the protozoa, algae, and slime molds. Bacteria are generally unicellular prokaryotes and not plants either, but they are vital to the detrital energy web of a wetland, so we'll include them here too.

Problems associated with flooding:

- *Anoxia*: When an organic soil is flooded, the oxygen available is quickly depleted through metabolism by organisms that use oxygen. Because oxygen diffuses much more slowly through water than through air, atmospheric oxygen doesn't help. The bacteria that survive in this situation need to be facultative anaerobes meaning they can switch from using aerobic respiration (using oxygen as an electron receptor in the process of producing energy) to anaerobic respiration (using something other than oxygen). Some bacteria will only grow under anaerobic conditions, using sulfate rather than oxygen. These are the ones that produce hydrogen sulfide which accounts for the rotten-egg smell one associates with wetlands.
- *Salt*: In a freshwater aquatic or soil environment, the osmotic concentration of the cytoplasm in bacterial cells is higher than that of the surrounding medium. This allows the cells to absorb water until they develop turgor which means that the pressure of the cytoplasm is balanced by the resistence of the cell walls---the cells are firm, neither collapsing nor exploding. Salt has two dangers, osmotic and toxic. The cell will dehydrate of explode, depending on outside salinity due to osmosis, unless it is adapted. Wetland bacteria generally maintain their salt balance by actively transporting some other ion (often potassium) across their membranes to maintain osmotic balance. Taking in sodium itself would not work. Emergent plants are more complex than protists and bacteria, so they have a wider range of adaptations, but evolution has eliminated their capacity to use something other than oxygen as an energy source, *i.e.* they cannot respire anaerobically. Plants are sessile (stuck in one place), but it's only their roots that are stuck in the anoxic or salty environment of wetland substrate. A flood sensitive plant when inundated rapidly loses its oxygen supply to the roots. This shuts down aerobic metabolism thus reducing nearly all metabolic activities such as cell division and nutrient absorption. Anaerobic glycolysis (same thing your muscles do when you ask them for a "burst" of energy) works for some needs inititally, but it is inefficient and toxic endproducts

accumulate. These two problems will cause death fairly rapidly, as you know if you overwater your houseplants. Hydrophytes (flood tolerant plants) have adaptations to survive these problems.

Structural Adaptations

- *Aerenchyma*: The primary plant strategy in response to flooding is the development of air spaces in the roots and stems which allow diffusion of oxygen from the aerial portions of the plant into the roots. Thus the roots don't have to depend on getting oxygen from the soil. "Regular" plants may have a porosity (% air space in roots and stems) of 2-7% of their volume, while a wetland plant may be up to 60% pore space by volume. Water Lilies offer an example: air moves into the internal gas spaces of young leaves on the water surface and is forced down through the aerenchyma of the stem to the roots by the slight pressure caused by the heating of the leaves. The older leaves lose their capacity to support pressure gradients so gas from the roots returns out through the old leaves.
- *Adventitious roots*: roots above the ground (or the anoxic zone or the level of the water) which are able to function normally in an aerobic environment.
  - *Ex*: prop roots on mangroves have numerous small pores called lenticels above the tide level which end in long, spongy, air-filled submerged roots.
  - *Ex*: pneumatophores-"air roots" on black mangroves. These stick out of the mud from the main roots and are exposed during low tides.
  - *Ex*: "knees"-these were traditionally thought to be important in oxygen exchange, but no one has really shown this to be the case. It's currently thought that while these may be helpful in gas exchange (and probably also support) they are not vital.
- *Rapid early shoot growth*: Under flooded conditions, several herbaceous and woody species exhibit this which gets the shoot above the surface of the water quickly to facilitate gas exchange
- *Stem and lenticel hypertrophy*: Hypertrophy is the enlargement of an organ without an increase in the number of constituent cells. An example of this is butressing or butt swell which is an increase in the diameter at the base of the stem. The role of this seems to be to increase air space which allows for increased movement of gases. Besides that, the wide base provides extra support for shallow rooted structures on a soggy substrate.

Reproductive Adaptations

The ability of seeds to germinate while inundated has both advantages and disadvantages, depending on the conditions of the inundation. Species whose seeds can germinate and grow under flooded conditions experience less competition. Rice, American Elm, cottonwoods, and Black Willows can do this. The ability of seeds to survive long periods of flooded conditions while buried in sediments in a dormant state is also helpful. Infrequent droughts would expose soil surfaces and those surviving seeds would have the opportunity to germinate. Cypress and Tupelo trees do this.

Frequent flooding can result in good seed dispersal if the seeds can float and avoid getting waterlogged. They can float until they get hung up on a dry spot, perhaps appropriate for germination. Some plants can delay flowering or speed production during floods, or accelerate flowering during dry periods. Vascular plants deal with salt water with specialized cells controlling import and export of salt. Mangroves, Almost completely exclude salt. When you squeeze their leaves you get almost pure water. Marsh grass, on the other hand, lets salts in but selectively excretes it--hence the salt crystals you find on their leaves.

Interestingly, wetland plants in saltwater have the same problem plants in arid climates have---difficulty in getting and keeping water. Because of the salt levels, water tends to leave the plant via osmosis, or at least not enter the plant. The same fleshy structures (consider Salicornia or pickleweed), and adaptations such as the capacity to store carbon dioxide and use water more efficiently in photosynthesis which allows the plant to keep its stomata closed (pores on the leaves and stems) more during the day.

The sun is the energy source that keeps most organisms alive. Photosynthesis converts radiant (solar) energy to chemical energy. Almost all organisms depend on photosynthesis directly or indirectly. Exception to this are the hot vent ecosystems found at the bottom of the oceans. Producers are organisms that can make organic molecules from inorganic substance. Most producers are photoautotrophs and use light as energy source for manufacturing organic compounds from CO_2 and H_2O. Organisms that cannot make their own organic compounds and must obtain them from other organisms are called heterotrophs. Consumers and decomposers are heterotrophs.

CHEMICAL CHANGES DURING PLANT GROWTH

The simple compounds which the plant absorbs from the atmosphere and soil are elaborated within its system, and converted into the various complex substances of which its tissues are composed, by a series of changes, the details of which are still in some respects imperfectly known, although their general nature is sufficiently well understood. They may be best rendered intelligible by reference, in the first instance, to the changes occurring during germination, when the young plant is nourished by a supply of food stored up in the seed, in sufficient quantity to maintain its existence until the organs by which it is afterwards to draw its nutriment from the air and soil are sufficiently developed to serve that purpose.

Changes Occurring during Germination

When a seed is placed in the soil under favourable circumstances, it becomes the seat of an important and remarkable series of chemical changes, which result in the production of the young plant. Experiment and observation have shown that heat, moisture, and air, are necessary to the production of these changes, and though probably not absolutely essential, the absence of light is favourable in the early stages. The temperature required for germination varies greatly in different seeds, some germinating readily at a few degrees above the freezing point, and others requiring a tolerably high temperature.

The rapidity with which it takes place appears to increase with the temperature; but this is true only within very narrow limits, for beyond a certain point heat is injurious, and when it exceeds 120° or 130° Fahrenheit, entirely prevents the process. The presence of oxygen is also essential, for it has been shown that if seeds are placed in a soil exposed to an atmosphere deprived of that element, or if they be buried so deep that the air does not reach them, they may lie without change for an unlimited period; but so soon as they are exposed to the air, germination immediately commences.

Illustrations of this fact are frequently observed where earth from a considerable depth has been thrown up to the surface, when it often becomes covered with plants not usually seen in the neighbourhood, which have sprung from buried seeds. When all the necessary conditions for germination are fulfilled, the seed absorbs moisture, swells up, and sends out a shoot which rises to the surface, and a radicle which descends—the one destined to develop the leaves, the other the roots, by which the plant is afterwards to derive its nutriment from the air and the soil. But until these organs are properly developed, the plant is dependent on the matters contained in the seed itself. These substances are mostly insoluble, but are brought into solution by the atmospheric oxygen acting upon the gluten, and converting it into a soluble substance called diastase, which in its turn reacts upon the starch, converting it first into dextrine, and then into cellulose, and the latter is finally deposited in the form of organised cells, and produces the first little shoot of the plant.

At the first moment of germination, the oxygen absorbed appears simply to oxidize the constituents of the seed, but this condition exists only for a very limited period, and is soon followed by the evolution of carbonic acid, water being at the same time formed from the organic constituents of the seed, which gradually diminishes in weight. The amount of this diminution is different with different plants, but always considerable. Boussingault found that the loss of dry substance in the pea amounted in 26 days to 52 per cent, and in wheat to 57 per cent in 51 days. Against this, of course, is to be put the weight of the young plant produced; but this is never sufficient to counterbalance the diminished weight of the seed, for Saussure found that a horse bean and the plant produced from it weighed, after 16 days, less by 29 per cent than the seed before germination.

The same phenomenon is observed in the process of malting, which is in fact the artificial germination of barley, the malt produced always weighing considerably less than the grain from which it was obtained. It was believed by Saussure, and the older investigators, that the carbonic acid evolved was entirely produced from starch and sugar; and as these substances may be viewed as compounds of carbon and water, the change was very simply explained by supposing that the carbon was oxidised and converted into carbonic acid and its water eliminated.

But this hypothesis is incapable of explaining all the phenomena observed; for woody fibre, which is one of the chief constituents of the young plant, contains more carbon than the starch and sugar from which it must have been produced, and we are, therefore, forced to admit that the action must be more complicated.

There is every reason to believe that the nitrogenous constituents of the seed are most abundantly oxidized, for they are remarkably prone to change; but the action of the air is not confined to them, and it appears most probable that all the substances take part in the decomposition, and the process of germination may, in some respects, be compared to decay or putrefaction, which, like it, is attended by the absorption of oxygen and evolution of carbonic acid; but while in the latter case the residual substances remain in a useless state, in the former they at once become part of a new organism.

Changes Occurring During the After-growth of the Plant

When the plant has developed its roots and leaves, and exhausted the store of materials laid up for it in the seed, it begins to derive its subsistence from the surrounding air, and to absorb carbonic acid, water, ammonia, and nitric acid, and to decompose and convert them into the different constituents of its tissues.

These changes take place slowly at first, and more rapidly as the organs fitted for the elaboration of its food are developed. The roots and the leaves are equally active in performing this duty, the former absorbing the mineral matters along with the carbonic acid, ammonia, nitric acid, and moisture in the soil, or the manure added to it; the latter gathering the gaseous substances existing in the air. Each of these undergoes a series of changes claiming our consideration.

Decomposition of Carbonic Acid

Carbonic acid, which appears to be absorbed with equal readiness by the roots, leaves, and stems, undergoes immediate decomposition, its carbon being retained, and its oxygen, in whole or in part, evolved into the air. This decomposition occurs only under the action of the sun's rays, and has been found to be proportionate to the amount of light to which the plant is exposed.

It takes place only in the green parts of plants, for though the roots absorb carbonic acid, they cannot decompose it, or evolve oxygen; and the coloured parts, the flowers, fruits, etc., have an entirely opposite effect, absorbing oxygen and giving off carbonic acid.

The absorption of carbonic acid and escape of oxygen has been proved by numerous direct experiments by Saussure and others, in which both atmospheric air and artificial mixtures containing an increased quantity of carbonic acid have been employed.

Saussure allowed seven plants of periwinkle (Vinca minor) to vegetate in an atmosphere containing 7·5 per cent of carbonic acid for six days, during each of which the apparatus was exposed for six hours to the sun's rays.

In this experiment the whole of the carbonic acid, amounting to 431 volumes, was absorbed, but only 292 volumes of oxygen were given off. Had the carbonic acid been entirely decomposed, and all its oxygen eliminated, its volume would have been equal to that of the acid, or 431, so that in this instance 139 volumes of the oxygen of the carbonic acid have been retained to form part of the tissues of the plant.

On the other hand, the nitrogen is found to be increased after the experiment. It might be supposed that the nitrogen evolved had been derived from the decomposition of the nitrogenous constituents of the plant, but this cannot be the true explanation, because in this particular case it greatly exceeded the whole nitrogen contained in the plants experimented on. Its source is not well understood, but Boussingault supposes it to have existed in the interstices of the plant, and to have escaped during the course of the experiment. Saussure found that the oak, the horse-chesnut, and other plants, absorb oxygen and give off carbonic acid in less volumes than the oxygen, while the house-leek and the cactus absorb oxygen without evolving carbonic acid.

The absorption and decomposition of carbonic acid takes place only during the day, and matters are entirely reversed during the night, when oxygen is absorbed and carbonic acid eliminated from all parts of the plants. Although the action occurring during the night is the reverse of that which takes place during the day, it is in no degree to be attributed to a re-oxidation of the carbon which had been deposited in the tissues of the plant.

It appears, on the contrary, to be a purely mechanical, and not a chemical process. During the night the sap continues to circulate through the vessels of the plant, and moisture, carrying with it carbonic acid in solution, is absorbed by the roots; but when it reaches the leaves, where the sun's light would have caused its decomposition during the day, it is again exhaled unchanged.

The oxygen absorbed during the night must, however, take part in some chemical processes, for if it were merely mechanical, the absorption would not be confined to that gas alone, but would be participated in by the other constituents of the air. Moreover, the amount of absorption varies greatly in different plants—being scarcely appreciable in some, and very abundant in others.

Plants containing volatile oils, which are readily converted into resins by the action of oxygen, or those containing tannin or other readily oxidizable substances, take up the largest quantity. This is remarkably illustrated by an experiment in which the leaves of the Agave americana, after twenty-four hours' exposure in the dark, were found to have absorbed only 0·3 of their volume of oxygen, while those of the fir, in which volatile oil is abundant, had taken up twice, and those of the oak, containing tannin, eighteen times as much oxygen.

In the flowers, both by day and night, there is a constant absorption of oxygen, and evolution of carbonic acid. In fact, an active oxidation is going on, attended by the evolution of heat, which, in the Arum maculatum and some other plants, is so great as to raise the temperature of the flower 10° or 12° above that of the surrounding air.

SYSTEMS OF SOIL CLASSIFICATION

The systems of soil classification developed particularly in relation to highly differentiated climatic conditions, as for example by K. Glinka, soon led to the recognition of climatic soil types but also the appreciation that under less extreme conditions, such as may obtain in western Europe and especially in Britain, the climatic conditions can cease to be the main factor in soil genesis and the nature of the substrate from which the soil is derived becomes of great significance. In Britain the criss-cross, of changing climatic characteristics from East to West and North to South, superimposed upon the rapidly changing geological strata from the more recent towards the South and East to the older in the West and North, has produced in the British Isles a peculiarly intricate mosaic of soil conditions that has been still further complicated by the glaciations and the post-glacial loess that now appears to have been even more widespread than had hitherto been envisaged as shown by the investigations of Perrin, Coombe and others.

These various soils may enhance or ameliorate the effect of present-day local climate and this has enabled a greater diversity of immigrant species to persist in British plant communities than might otherwise be able to survive. For a long time the significance of soil aeration was ignored and Clements in 1921 did a service to this aspect of ecology by bringing together much of the relevant literature. See also. Recent work would seem to emphasize its importance not merely by reason of its influence on the extent of the root development but also because the actual intake of the nutrients appears to be directly related to efficient aeration of the adsorbing cells that can provide the energy for intake against an adverse gradient. From the data furnished by Hopkins and his associates it would appear that the intake, of plant nutrients generally, decreases with the reduction of the oxygen content of the atmosphere that surrounds the root-system. The effect upon the intake of the trace elements appears to be less than for the major nutrients whilst sodium intake would seem actually to augment with diminished oxygen supply, a feature that may be of considerable import for vegetation growing on soils liable to flooding by sea-water.

Both the oxygen content of the soil-atmosphere and its carbon-dioxide content are important and depend upon the activity of soil organisms and the freedom of diffusion with the air above, which latter is facilitated by volumetric changes due to temperature fluctuations. So it is that under turf or woodland litter high carbon-dioxide concentrations may obtain, in illustration of which we may note that Russell and Appleyard recorded over 3 per cent under grassland and Harley and Brierley under beech-leaf litter from three to eleven times the amount in the atmosphere above.

A high organic content is often associated with a large microbial population so that the production of carbon dioxide is copious and the surface litter tends to retard diffusion as well as insulating the surface soil from rapid temperature fluctuations. In assessing the climatic and edaphic factors as they affect plant life we have in the past been perhaps too apt to regard climate and soil conditions as separate abstractions so that a true soil ecology has been distorted by the partialities that are only valid in isolation.

The investigations of plant physiologists during recent decades have contributed to our appreciation of the direct influence of environment upon vegetation, notably in relation to two types of factors, the climatic and the edaphic. It is now over thirty years since Garner and Allard published the results of their classical experiments demonstrating the influence of the relative duration of daylight and darkness upon growth and reproduction.

Since that time the vast volume of literature on the photoperiodic response has revealed that, for a large number of species of flowering plants, flower formation is dependent either on the stimulus of a short period of darkness and a long day or the stimulus of a longer period of darkness and a shorter day. Variations in the relative duration of day and night could moreover retard or inhibit reproduction by seed and also influence the degree and character of vegetative growth.

For annual species whose growth rhythm is adjusted to such stimuli the latitudinal changes in photoperiodism may clearly operate as a limiting factor to their distribution, but for spreading perennials the substitution of vegetative multiplication for the production of fruit may well extend their geographical range.

Mercurialis perennis, for example, so abundant in our basic woodlands, achieves success by means of its rhizomatous aggression although the reproductive capacity from seed towards its northern limits is negligible. The specialization, which response to such stimuli implies, may therefore be advantageous, or the reverse, when the species concerned extends beyond the climatic conditions of its original home. It is significant therefore to note that some species have not developed any response relation to photoperiodic stimulation, as a time keeper of their growth rhythms, and that these include some of our commonest weeds such as the Chickweed *(Stellaria media),* the Shepherd's Purse *(Capsella spp.),* and Poa annua which flower and fruit at all seasons when temperature conditions permit and are well-nigh cosmopolitan in their distribution.

For these and other such species the lack of photoperiodic response is manifestly a factor in their success and determines in part the role they play in vegetation. It is also to be noted that photoperiodic response can be markedly influenced by temperature and humidity whilst within one and the same species long-day and short-day strains can be evolved. Probably the chief contribution of physiology to an understanding of the habitat's direct influence in recent years was the discovery of what have been termed the micronutrients or trace elements. That extremely small quantities of certain elements, mostly only requisite in parts per million, were nevertheless essential for plant life is due to their role in forming catalytic agents of various metabolic activities. Such micronutrients now regarded as generally necessary for the higher plants are boron, copper, zinc, manganese, and molybdenum.

But in addition to these, various other elements would appear to be at least beneficial, if not actually essential, to certain plants, as for example sodium and iodine, whilst though there is some experimental evidence for stimulation of growth by minute traces of, for example, titanium and arsenic, it seems unlikely that these play any significant part in determining the composition of plant communities or the degree of dominance of species. It should, however, always be borne in mind that owing to the "compound interest law" minute initial advantages may lead to significant final effects.

Quantitative Estimation of Amounts

The quantitative estimation of amounts of such diminitude as that in which the trace elements occur, with an accuracy of within 10 per cent or less, is one of the triumphs of modern spectroscopic technology and these determinations have shown that deficiencies may often occur either through their inadequacy in the soil, through their absence, or through being rendered non-available. The last condition is exemplified in respect to manganese, zinc, and boron in markedly alkaline soils whilst copper deficiencies or manganese deficiencies can be brought about by microbiological activity. The observation that certain characteristic appearances are associated with deficiencies of each of the various nutrients, both macro- and micro- alike, made practicable the survey of such occurrences over a far wider area than would have been possible if analyses alone could have sufficed. The outcome has been the recognition that the availability of most of the essential elements for the nutrition of the higher plants is very variable. In natural soils rainwater charged with CO_2 readily brings the calcium bicarbonate into solution and by base exchange with potassium and magnesium these also are readily leached from the soil so that deficiencies of all three are by no means uncommon.

Calcium is never wholly absent from soils that can support higher plants since it is an essential constituent of their cell walls but the great range of concentration, from the so-called non-calcareous soils, devoid of free carbonates, to the highly calcareous soils of downs and dunes, is accompanied by a corresponding change in the character of the vegetation which may involve the replacement of a calcifuge by a calcicole species occupying a similar niche or the change from acid moorland to calcareous grassland. A recent review of the role of magnesium as a plant nutrient shows that many natural soils in Europe may contain very small amounts, sometimes less than 0.01 per cent and magnesium deficiency is, in fact, frequent. The large areas in South Australia that have been rendered fertile, by amending deficiencies of molybdenum, zinc, and copper, is sufficient evidence for the ecological significance of the distribution and availability of trace elements. Though this is admittedly an extreme example the areas where deficiencies of one type or another have been recognized are continually being added to.

It is of considerable import that evidence has been furnished that some species are much more susceptible to such deficiencies than others whilst some plants can accumulate trace elements in a marked degree so that, when these are essential nutrients, such capacity must be an important asset in competition. On seleniferous soils grass herbage may be quite innocuous to stock whilst species of *Astragalus* if present can accumulate selenium to such an extent as to render the herbage lethal. So, too, clovers will accumulate molybdenum and the Sun Spurge, *Euphorbia helioscopia,* is known to be able to accumulate boron, facts which suggest that competition for the micronutrients may, because they are frequently marginal in concentration, be more severe than for the macronutrients which are more commonly considered from this standpoint. Of these latter, deficiency of nitrogen is common in acid soils and those containing little organic material, whilst phosphate deficiency also characterizes acid soils in areas of high rainfall but especially when these are rich in organic matter since phosphorous in organic combination is even less readily available to the plant than from inorganic compounds such as iron-phosphate. Potassium deficiency is common on chalk, sandy soils, and peat.

Although much is known as to the respective demands that crop plants make upon the various nutrients and of their susceptibility to toxic concentrations of manganese or aluminium, our knowledge of wild species in these respects and of their powers of accumulation of nutrient ions is as yet fragmentary although these might well furnish the clue to many apparent idiosyncrasies of presence and absence in communities. That the precise form in which an element is present may be far more significant than its amount is manifest from the efficiency of chelated compounds of iron and manganese for relieving deficiencies of these elements where other compounds are wholly ineffectual.

For the ecologist, as for the agricultural chemist, the problem is not the accurate determination of the total amounts of the various nutrients present but the estimation of the proportion of each which is in a form that the plant can assimilate. A recent investigation of New Zealand soils by D. E. Hogg, with respect to potassium, is illuminating in this connection. Utilizing a number of standard methods of assessment he found that determinations of the exchangeable potassium corresponded closely to the response made by plants when potassium was supplied but only in the regions of high rainfall. In the areas of low rainfall assessment based upon nitric acid extraction showed a closer relationship with crop response. It is manifest that the varying availability of the macro- and micro-nutrients may have a direct effect upon the distribution of species and communities but the possibilities of indirect effects must not be ignored. We have already referred to the differential absorption of such potentially lethal elements as selenium and molybdenum which can be economically serious in relation to agriculture, but under natural conditions such differences might materially influence the biotic pressure exerted by the grazing animal.

So obvious is it that a plant community is a social aggregate of its constituent species that one is apt to forget its implication, that all these must have similar environmental preferences or tolerances, except in so far as the presence of one or more species ameliorate, or exacerbate, the conditions for others. The obvious manifestation of this is the creation of shelter by taller species but there may be many other influences more subtle, as for instance the capacity of some species to tolerate and accumulate ions of alumina and manganese which may conceivably render conditions acceptable to other plants more susceptible to their toxic action.

It may be urged with some justice that many of the features we have mentioned as affecting distribution are mostly as yet only known to operate locally and determine the success of individual species rather than communities. That individual species can bring about vegetation changes of a widespread character is, however, witnessed by the disastrous extension of *Opuntia inermis* in Queensland or the spectacular spread of RosebayWillow-herb in Britain. It would appear to be the initial establishment and the build up of the population of a species to the requisite "infection pressure" that presents the major obstacles to marked extension and it is not least in this context that one should perhaps take particular cognizance of such discriminating causes.

So far we have made no reference to one class of biotic influences, namely the effects of animal life upon the nature of the plant community. No doubt in some degree it is true that the vigour of growth of vegetation and its rate of reproduction is adjusted to the hazards of the predators upon it, but it has been shown that Herbert Spencer's facile generalization is invalid and even were it true the imposed burden for survival is a serious handicap in competition.

Recently C. B. Huffaker has expressed the view that "changes in plant populations and insect populations are often reciprocally related phenomena". The profound effect of a high rabbit population in Australia and in Britain and its drastic diminution by myxomatosis has recently brought into prominence the differential influence that an animal population can impose. Only in recent years have population studies shown what high numbers vegetable feeders such as field-voles can attain and whilst the importance of animal life, both large and small, is doubtless profound, yet the assessment of its differential effects on plant communities still remains largely the subject-matter for future research.

Competition between species and its severity in a plant community is dependent upon the requirements of the constituents both as to what demands each makes upon the habitat and the degree of intensity of these demands with respect to time. All flowering plants require water and mineral nutrients and most require light but the claims made upon these may vary greatly with the species concerned. Competition ensues only when the supply is inadequate to meet the full requirements of all, a condition which may be attained with respect to light in open communities and with respect to water in aquatic ones. Competition for light we have already briefly referred to. It is largely dependent upon potential height and leaf area on the one hand and on the other upon the specific compensation point. Competition for water and nutrients is clearly dependent upon the differing capacity of a species to obtain these and to develop a root system, in the presence of others, adequate to its demands with sufficient rapidity and this can only be accomplished if, *inter alia,* the requisite photosynthetic products are available to effect this growth. In assessing the adequacy of supplies of essentials it is necessary to distinguish, as in the human counterpart, between mere subsistence and what is requisite for vigorous growth.

It has been asserted that there is no competition between the herbaceous layer of a forest and the dominant trees but, as we have pointed out, the former may deprive the deeper-rooted trees of their water supply although in general it is between the species of the same stratum that competition is most severe.

Competition is perhaps most acute in the early stages of growth when mortality is highest. Between individuals of the same species an equilibrium may be established so that over a wide range of population density the total productivity is very similar as has been shown in numerous crop spacing experiments. Between different species the reactions vary greatly.

Some, which are closely allied and make similar demands upon the habitat (e.g. *Cerastium semidecandrum and C. tetrandrum*) may attain a measure of equilibrium but with open communities priority of establishment is significant and hence the mode and times of germination and the processes of dispersal play their part. In perennials the mode of growth and rate of potential spread can play significant roles.

Plant succession can be thought of as in large part a competitive drift in which at each phase until the climax the constituent species render the habitat more favourable to their successors than to themselves. From this aspect the few species that appear to be able to establish an almost static condition, gain a special significance. The maritime communities dominated by *Halimione portulacoides and Spartina townsendii* may be cited as possible examples though their seeming stability may be but an illusion due to the slowness of their change.

The importance of the competition aspect of succession is that it emphasizes the slow rate at which competitive influences may operate, masking the almost imperceptible decline or augmentation of individual species despite the vagaries of seasonal fluctuations.

One of the desiderata is for more actual data as to the time scale involved. We know, for instance, that weeds of arable land that reverts may survive for perhaps half a century, that some pioneer dune species may persist nearly a century, but the rate of a decline under various degrees of competitive pressure for the characteristic perennial species of communities could materially assist in estimating the relative importance of reproduction, vegetative spread, and life span as factors in aggressive capacity.

From this brief survey it is apparent that future progress demands a far more detailed analysis of the habitat factors alike in space and time and parallel with this a more meticulous assessment of the constituent organisms amongst which the importance of sub-specific taxa may far transcend the specific aggregates in ecological significance, alike with respect to their biological behaviour and their physiological attributes.

KNOWLEDGE OF CLIMATIC CONDITIONS

Calcium would appear to be present in amounts ranging from one to six parts per million and though such amounts be small their repeated addition to the soil whenever there is a fall of rain does not permit their being ignored. It would, however, seem that variations in the amounts of micronutrients present in rainfall is likely to have but a negligible influence upon plant distribution. The advances in our knowledge of climatic conditions have emphasized the importance of detailed studies, both spatial and temporal, that take cognizance of all types of humidity and precipitation both above and within the soil. The clue to the presence of vegetation in so-called rainless desert! has been found to rest in the dew formation that even in temperate communities may play an important role.

Quite recently the probable importance of high humidity under exceptional environmental conditions has been further emphasized through the experimental proof by Breazeale*et al.* that plants can absorb water through their leaves from a saturated atmosphere and that this together with contained solutes can exude through the roots into the soil which may thereby attain field capacity. To descriptive ecology we owe the recognition of a number of major vegetation types that are associated with particular climatic conditions, as for example the occurrence of the deciduous forests in areas where a favourable climate alternates with an unfavourable, due to low temperature or inadequate humidity. Another example is the association of evergreen coniferous forests with areas where the length of the growing season is restricted.

Relations of Plant Communities

But now that the broader features of the relations of plant communities with climatic types have come to be recognized the unexplored areas of the world's surface, though likely to provide further examples and interesting variants, are unlikely to contribute materially to our real understanding of the causal factors of distribution unless investigated in considerable detail. Further progress demands a detailed analysis of climatic and other habitat conditions throughout the seasonal cycle and experimental studies of individual species to determine their tolerances and the critical phases in their development which climatic conditions may promote or inhibit and the temperature and humidity limits these demand.

Other features of the climatic complex that call for more detailed analysis are the responses of individual species to direct and indirect effects of wind action and the influence of radiation of different intensities and wave lengths. The comprehensive work edited by Professor Duggar constitutes a valuable summary of the position attained at that period, since when the amount of research, especially upon photoperiodism, to which we shall revert, has been both extensive and significant. In the competition for radiant energy potential heights and spread are morphological features that determine the degree to which one kind of plant or individual can become a sunshade to another but clearly the time factor is here significant and in a population of seedlings, for example, those individuals that germinate first will have an advantage over those germinating later which emphasizes the survival value of what has been termed germination energy.

The more continuous the light screen provided by the foliage of a species the more effective will be its suppression of the plants in its shade though the mechanical vulnerability to wind imposes on leaf area the compromise presented by the compound character of most large leaves, although the rosette-leaves of many biennials which have the support of the soil or other vegetation beneath are immune from this type of injury and are often large and quite entire. We can, indeed, in many morphological features discern indications of this struggle for light. The dominance of the tree habit in the climax phase where habitat conditions can support forest is but an expression of the fact that in the struggle for light the tallest members tend to survive. The wane of the arboreal vegetation is probably an accompaniment of man's increasing interference with nature making ever-augmented inroads upon woody vegetation so that today, almost throughout the world, herbaceous communities are becoming more conspicuous.

It is, perhaps, due to the importance of the time factor that the more successful species are in general those that have the potentiality of large seed-output and the marked association of average seed size with the shadiness of the plant community that a species normally colonizes is a further emphasis on the importance of the light factor in competition at the juvenile phases of developments. In the competition for nutrients the extent and rate of development of the root system to which we have already referred, is manifestly correlated with the success of the assimilating organs and the mode of spread of a species whether by seed or vegetatively will mainly determine the habitat conditions that it can invade.

From experiments with Barley growing in competition with *Holcus mollis* H. H. Mann and T. W. Barnes concluded that though the root space and supply of plant food was apparently ample for both they reduced the growth of each other and the dominant appeared to be determined by the *time of development* as well as by the density. One could multiply examples but it is clear that temporal factors play an appreciable part in the competition both for light and nutrients and emphasize the need for a much more detailed knowledge than we at present possess concerning the life histories of the chief species contributing to plant communities and the conditions that modify them. An interesting example of the differential effect of species upon one another was exhibited by some experiments carried out with *Juncus effusus.* A. Lazenby found that the number of seeds of this Rush which germinated and the subsequent growth differed strikingly according to the other species of seeds sown with them. Thus when sown with Bent *(Agrostis tenuis)* and White Clover *(Trifolium repens)* only about one-tenth of the population of Rush plants was obtained as when the accompanying species were Ryegrass *(Lolium perenne)* and White Clover.

It is only natural that the visible, overground, parts of the plant should have received major attention from both morphologists and ecologists though it is perhaps remarkable, having regard to the early recognition of the importance of the root-system, from the nutritional as well as the mechanical aspect, that its nature, extent and mode of development should have so long been neglected. Such neglect is perhaps partially to be explained by the difficulty of exhuming the entire root system, in most soils, as a consequence of which their extent has often been underestimated.

The valuable researches of Weaver and his associates in America have served to call attention to this neglected field of study. From these the considerable labour involved in such studies can be appreciated but also the great diversity and significant distinctions that obtain. Sandy soils afford an especially favourable medium for such investigations since by blowing away the sand from a working face as it dries entire root systems can be excavated without risk of losing the finer ramifications and by appropriate means these can be supported in their original positions as they emerge from the matrix. The present writer's own studies on the root systems of plants characteristic of various phases of dune development have shown how varied these can be not merely between different species but also between different individuals of the same species when growing in conditions of diverse water supply and aeration. Root studies have emphasized the distinction between those that exhibit a restricted but richly branched system, which exploit a relatively small volume of soil intensively, and those in which the root system is extensive but the large soil volume is much less completely interpenetrated.

Modern studies of economic plants have shown what marked differences in this respect may obtain between cultivars of the same species as, for example, the root systems of the "Wealthy" and "Doucin" apples or the various East Malling Apple stocks, and there is no reason to suppose that similar differences both interspecific and intraspecific, do not occur with respect to the root systems of wild plants and that they play an important role in their competitive equipment. The recognition of the fundamental importance of a number of trace elements and their frequent presence in inadequate amounts, or in more or less non-available condition, has brought into prominence the great significance that may well attach to the type and degree of root exploitation.

Furthermore it has been shown that the availability of some trace elements, such as zinc, in the early stage of development of a species, can be decisive for the subsequent healthy growth and its early supply will differentiate between failure and success. The importance therefore of the *rate* of development of the root systems of different kinds of plants in what we may perhaps be permitted to describe as their race for the necessary nutrients which are in short supply, scarcely requires emphasis. The great success of the grasses may be in no small degree due to the extent and rapidity of their root development. Weaver showed that the latter is frequently more than 12 mm in a day whilst the root of a maize plant may extend more than 50-60 mm in the same period.

With uniform genetic material the extent of the root system is very susceptible to the influence of water soluble substances, for example the calcium ion is known markedly to affect root growth. The extent of the root surface in the presence of calcium was several times that in its absence and the volume of soil that can be exploited is probably proportionately increased. The extent of the root system is also affected by the soil texture and indeed one aspect of cultivation is that it reduces the resistance that the growing root has to overcome in its penetration of the soil. Again, optimum moisture content and above all good aeration promote not merely the extent of the root system but in particular the development of root hairs.

One may note that root hairs can augment the absorbtive surface sevenfold, so that factors affecting their production and growth may be of great significance. All these conditions affecting the size and efficiency of the absorbing structures stress the importance of the morphological-physiological relations and one may expect that future ecological studies will tend to integrate still further the two angles of approach, but if this is to be achieved it is essential that the physiologist should be apprehensive of the extent to which field competition is likely to modify the laboratory indications and the ecologist must be alert to appreciate the field significance of the controlled experiments which, however oversimplified they may be from the point of view of their translation to the plant community, can rarely fail to make their contribution to our understanding of the more complex conditions.

In 1929 I called attention to the striking reduction in the extent of the root system of a species when subjected to the competitive influence of the root systems of other plants. Eight years later Pavlychenko furnished remarkable quantitative data respecting the magnitude of this effect as exhibited by cereals in competition with weeds and with one another. The importance of the competition factors in natural communities cannot be over-emphasized and such may well be operative from the earliest phases of plant development since seedling mortality, which is very high, appears to be influenced not only by the physical conditions but by the proportions in which the seedlings of different species are present.

Statistical studies have confirmed what general observation had suggested that individual plants are not normally dispersed in a random manner. This was for instance clearly brought out in regard to grassland communities by G. E. Blackman, in 1935, but it yet remains to be ascertained to what extent such lack of uniformity in dispersion reflects the lack of uniformity in the habitat conditions. For example, the marked tendency towards aggregation of the individuals of the herbaceous species of *Salicornia* is clearly to be expected from the crozier-like hairs upon the testa which anchor the seeds to suitable surfaces, such as the wefts of salt-marsh algae, and to one another, when they are dispersed by the rising and falling tides.

So, too, the classical examples of the hygroscopic arms of the dissected spore-coats of *Equisetum* which ensure some measure of aggregation of the unisexual gametophytes. These and other similar morphological determinants may clearly be important for survival but unrelated to any permanent feature of the habitats concerned.

We still do not know why it is that the annual vegetation of a desert, superficially uniform, may present a Joseph's coat with large areas each dominated by a different species of *Helipterum.* Are such phenomena visual expressions of vagaries of dispersal, or evidences of survival from selection accompanying real though obscure habitat conditions? Attention has more than once been drawn to the phenomenon of certain species that occur with great abundance in an area and produce copious seed only to disappear for a long period subsequently or, if not completely absent, they are rare. A striking example that has been observed both in this country and on the Continent is afforded by the Yellow-wort *(Blackstonia perfoliata),* which is very pertinent to our present context because its root system is of comparatively small extent.

The output of its small, almost dust-like, seeds which exhibit a high percentage germination is large. So it is not unreasonable to assume that these are in fact broadcast over the entire area. Hence, one may ask, is it that such species require some nutrient condition, perhaps a trace element in short supply and that this becomes depleted? The discontinuity of the densest population of *Blackstonia* would not warrant suggesting that its roots completely exploit the entire surface soil but it may well be that, from a vast population of seedlings, the mature plants we see are in fact survivors where the requisite nutritional conditions obtain and that the discontinuity of occurrence does indeed reflect the heterogeneity in this respect of a habitat otherwise apparently uniform.

MANAGEMENT OF ECOSYSTEM

Practical ecosystem management usually involves maintaining a natural or artificial homeostasis in which the end product is of benefit to man, and in which violent or pathologic imbalances can be controlled. An example of a natural ecosystem which man might wish to maintain for esthetic or recreational value would be a wilderness area or National Park. Here the most important consideration is to insure that natural processes are permitted to continue. In a forest this would mean, for example, that fire, if already a natural part of the ecosystem, be permitted to occur at natural frequency and intensity.

Several recent studies have shown that certain forests depend upon intermittent burning to recycle nutrients and minerals. In the lowland conifer forests of Alaska, if fire is excluded a thick carpet of moss may accumulate and raise the permafrost level. This encourages the growth of black spruce, a species with little food or timber value. Browsing animals such as deer, moose and bear cannot survive on black spruce. They depend on the Tarai fires to maintain a suitable cycle of vegetation. Many foresters now feel that the underbrush and leaf litter in the Ponderosa pine forests of western United States should be removed by light ground fires every few years to maintain soil fertility, to prevent excessive accumulation of organic matter in the form of cellulose and also to prevent more devastating fires that destroy the entire forest.

In the pine forests of the South, very efficient fire suppression techniques allowed dangerous accumulation of combustible materials, and a pine fungus disease was favoured in the accumulated litter. In all of these forests, proper management should not exclude all fires, but should prevent totally devastating fires. These examples illustrate the need for understanding natural processes in ecosystems in order to maintain them properly.

The Everglades of Florida provide another example of the importance of understanding natural ecosystem processes before the system can be properly managed or maintained. The unique flora and fauna of the Everglades depends upon the proper balance of fresh and saline water flowing through its channels. If a significant decline in fresh water input occurs, as has been taking place due to the diversion of fresh water to the growing megalopolis of Miami, numerous important species of plants and animals may die and the characteristic features of the system may be destroyed. In times of drought, many animals depend upon alligator wallows as a source of water. These are pools hollowed out by alligators, and they tend to retain water longer than other parts of the swamp. If alligators decline through shooting or any other.

It is increasingly important to understand the dynamics of ecosystem, their patterns of succession and evolution, and their patterns of succession and evolution, and their patterns of diversity and stability. E.P. Odum has written a major review of these topics and has shown that ecosystem may be characterized as pioneer, developmental and mature. Various stages within this continuum possess certain properties of production, respiration, community structure, nutrient cycling, homeostasis, etc. For example, young developmental stages of an ecosystem tend to have greater gross production in relation to respiration, but lower species diversity and less stability than mature stages.

Thus, developmental stage to be favoured in agricultural practice, but they are also more vulnerable to ecologic damage or catastrophe. We will explore these relationships in more detail throughout subsequent chapters after various components of the ecosystem are considered seperately, diversity and stability. E.P. Odum has written a major review of these topics and has shown that ecosystem may be characterized as pioneer, developmental and mature.

Various stages within this continuum possess certain properties of production, respiration, community structure, nutrient cycling, homeostasis, etc. For example, young developmental stages of an ecosystem tend to have greater gross production in relation to respiration, but lower species diversity and less stability than mature stages. Thus, developmental stage to be favoured in agricultural practice, but they are also more vulnerable to ecologic damage or catastrophe. We will explore these relationships in more detail throughout subsequent chapters after various components of the ecosystem are considered seperately.

THE PRINCIPLES OF ECOSYSTEM MANAGEMENT

Even if some synergies between the different international arrangements and processes relating to the biodiversity of freshwater resources still deserve more attention and none of the international treaties and institutions already deals fully with freshwater ecosystems, there is an increasing consensus on the highest political levels to manage water, water-related processes, and ecosystems in a sustainable manner.

However, at the level of implementation the value of ecosystems is rarely taken fully into account. In order to close this implementation gap the contracting parties of the CBD and other advocates have proposed a so-called "ecosystem-based approach" as an appropriate way of managing natural resources.

The Ecosystem Approach

The ecosystem approach is a strategy for the integrated management of land, water and living resources that promotes conservation and sustainable use in an equitable way. The term ecosystem is used more as a mental construct suggesting complexity and systems interaction rather than a geographic entity. An emphasis on the complexity of system-wide interactions highlights scientific uncertainty and results in the need to deal with this uncertainty explicitly by acting conservatively and managing adaptively: setting a course of action based on a set of hypotheses, monitoring what happens, and re-evaluating the direction on what one learns. At its most fundamental level, an ecosystem approach maintains diversity as a means of building resilience against catastrophic events in biological, economic, organisational, and political systems. At its second meeting in 1995, the Conference of the Parties of the CBD adopted the ecosystem approach as the primary framework for action, and subsequently has referred to the ecosystem approach in the elaboration and implementation of the various thematic and cross-cutting issues work programmes under the Convention. The issues concerned include:

- Biological diversity of inland water ecosystems.
- Marine and coastal biological diversity.
- Agricultural biological diversity.
- Forest biological diversity.
- Indicators of biological diversity.
- Incentive measures and environmental impact assessment.

By recommending the ecosystem approach as the guiding concept, in May 2000 the fifth COP took a next step towards its practical verification in the frame of the CBD.

Concerning inland water ecosystems a work programme was adopted by the COP which highlights the importance of designing integrated watershed, catchment and river basin management strategies. Particularly the interrelation between water management and agriculture was stressed, as well as the need to use the ecosystem approach in all sectors which have an impact on inland water biodiversity.

The ecosystem approach was initially developed as a research paradigm and not intended to serve as the basis for resource management. With the political application of the notion "ecosystem-based approach" advocates intended to find an adequate language in response to the shortcomings of classical nature conservation approaches.

Although classical nature conservation (*e.g.* designation of protected areas) can be considered successful in many regions and also is an important module in ecosystem management, its recognition of human needs and other legitimate sectoral interests was rather insufficient. It did not put enough emphasis on the biological diversity outside protected areas. Furthermore, the primary method of protecting freshwater biodiversity has been to designate particular species as threatened or endangered making them subject to national recovery programmes or international protection. Unfortunately, this approach is failing and it demonstrates the need for a more holistic approach in order to overcome the shortcomings of traditional efforts in nature protection policy. In the United States, for example, no aquatic species has ever graduated from the government's endangered species list, but 10 species of fish have been removed due to extinction. Equally, ecosystem management responds to the obvious shortcomings of classical single-resource approaches focused on exploitation.

The 12 Malawi Principles

- Management objectives are a matter of societal choice.
- Management should be decentralised to the lowest appropriate level.
- Ecosystem managers should consider the effects (actual or potential) of their activities on adjacent and other ecosystems.
- Recognising potential gains from management there is a need to understand the ecosystem in an economic context. Any ecosystem management programme should:
  - Reduce those market distortions that adversely affect biological diversity.
  - Align incentives to promote sustainable use.
  - Internalise costs and benefits in the given ecosystem to the extent feasible.
- A key feature of the ecosystem approach includes conservation of ecosystem structure and functioning.
- Ecosystems must be managed within the limits to their functioning.
- The ecosystem approach should be undertaken at the appropriate scale.
- Recognising the varying temporal scales and lag effects which characterise ecosystem processes, objectives for ecosystem management should be set for the long term.

- Management must recognise that change is inevitable.
- The ecosystem approach should seek the appropriate balance between conservation and use of biological diversity.
- The ecosystem approach should consider all forms of relevant information, including scientific and indigenous and local knowledge, innovations and practices.
- The ecosystem approach should involve all relevant sectors of society and scientific disciplines. These principles were agreed at CBD's COP-5 under decision V/6 with minor modifications.

Therefore, ecosystem management is proposed as a modern way of managing natural systems and generally intends to use natural resources within their natural limits. However, although there are still some controversies on how to translate ecosystem management into concrete management terms, parties of the CBD have already agreed on basic principles to guide the *modus operandi*.

A key point is that the ecosystem approach is a holistic process for integrating and delivering in a balanced way the three objectives of the CBD: conservation and sustainable use of biological diversity combined with equitable sharing of biodiversity's benefits. In particular, the agreed principles of the ecosystem approach stress the importance of:

- Societal choice concerning management objectives.
- The "economics" of biodiversity (internalisation of costs and benefits, balance between conservation and use).
- Adequate institutional structures (decentralisation, management at the appropriate scale).
- Adaptive management which enables policy makers to anticipate and cater for the natural dynamics of ecosystems.
- Consideration not only of scientific knowledge but also of indigenous and local knowledge.

In order to translate this rather abstract principles into guidelines for water management it is first necessary to define the appropriate management level to meet the general objectives. While the cited principles stress the importance of decentralised approaches in general terms, the idea of river basin management is considered an adequate starting point for the implementation of the ecosystem approach in water management.

The reasoning is that river basins offer many advantages for strategic planning and that they represent the most appropriate geomorphologic units on which to base ecosystem management practices.

However, concerning ecosystem protection there are some limits: groundwater catchments only rarely match with surface water catchments;

water quality and quantity inside the river basin interacts with other influences outside the catchments boundaries; estuarine ecosystems, for example, can only be sufficiently protected by taking into account the interaction of freshwater and tidal currents.

Therefore, river basin management should not be perceived as a panacea but it does provide a sound geographical basis for implementation. Briefly, ecosystem management should be an integral component of comprehensive river basin management strategies. Hence, the explicit switch to ecosystem management leads to an accentuation of the main focus in water management because ecosystem management demands:

- A broader perspective: whole ecosystems and the full range of services, no sectoral view.
- Efforts to balance natural ecosystem robustness and human-induced alterations.
- Collation of information on the status of, and threats to, the biodiversity of the freshwater ecosystem concerned (including impacts of the introduction of alien species).
- Explicit consideration of land-use, in-stream flow and water temperature for maintaining ecological functions.
- A long-term perspective.
- Consideration of the full economic value of freshwater ecosystems (include its biodiversity).
- Recognition of ecosystem's change as a matter of fact (*i.e.* restoration of damaged or destroyed ecosystems will never lead to the "pristine" state; adaptive management to deal with uncertainties).
- Integration of scientific knowledge and modern management tools (Decision Support Systems, Geographical Information Systems etc.) into decision-making.
- Identification of win-win options between protection and use of freshwater ecosystems: "use them, but don't lose them".
- Consideration of the full range of policy instruments applicable in water management (economic and legal instrument, co-operation etc.)

As most of these elements are widely agreed upon the rhetoric of international water policy, the next steps must include attempts to tackle the implications of the ecosystem approach in practice. For example, only little is known about the value of ecosystem management in political terms for at least two reasons:

- The concept appears highly demanding because much information – sometimes on "invisible" relationships between human-induced pressures and natural reactions – is needed, and effective vertical and

horizontal co-ordination of sector policies and planning instruments has to take place. Today, even in wealthy nations a lack of integration across sectors in managing water resources can be identified.
- It is necessary to decide which services of water receive priority, and how the costs and benefits are to be distributed. The developed world, for example, can "afford" to stop or to remove development projects in favour of ecosystem integrity (*e.g.* Great Whale Hydropower Project in Canada, Edwards Dam in the US) and to use sometimes generous subsidies to compensate land owners for restricting their use of the lands. The restoration of river ecosystems in the developed world also is an example for costs emerging in the short terms. Although long-term economic benefits are regularly provided, political decision are often dominated by short-term considerations.

WATER AND FORESTED ECOSYSTEMS

Ecologists consider water to be the defining part in an ecosystem, including the forest ecosystem. Water shapes the physical landscape through erosion Undulating forest surrounds meadows, lakes, and rivers of the Charlevoix Conservation Area, a coastal watershed in Quebec, Canada. This region, which illustrates a high-quality forested watershed, has been designated a biosphere by the United Nations Educational, Scientific and Cultural Organization (UNESCO). and deposition. It also shapes the biological parts of the ecosystem by its presence or absence; its quantity and quality; and its occurrence and distribution. The water cycle plays a key role in ecosystem functions and processes. Forests, in turn, are vital to the water cycle and to water quality. In essence, the forest acts like a giant sponge, filtering and recycling water. Approximately 80 per cent of U.S. fresh-water resources are estimated to originate in forests, which cover one-third of the U.S. land area.

Tree leaves intercept water from rain, snow, and fog; the leaves also release water back to the atmosphere by evapotranspiration. Tree roots extract water from the soil while helping hold the soil in place. Forested land reduces the surface impact of falling rain through interception and delay of water reaching the surface. Forestland also decreases the amount and velocity of storm runoff over the land surface. This in turn increases the amount of water that soaks into the ground, a portion of which can ultimately recharge underlying aquifers. Conversely, water from hydraulically connected surficial aquifers may enter streams and wetlands, helping to maintain their water levels during dry periods.

Forests and the Hydrologic Cycle

The surface water in a stream, lake, or wetland is most commonly precipitation that has run off the land or flowed through topsoils to subsequently enter the waterbody. If a surficial aquifer is present and hydraulically connected to a surface-water body, the aquifer can sustain surface flow by releasing water to it. In general, a heavy rainfall causes a temporary and relatively rapid increase in streamflow due to surface runoff. This increased flow is followed by a relatively slow decline back to baseflow, which is the amount of streamflow derived largely or entirely from groundwater.

During long dry spells, streams with a baseflow component will keep flowing, whereas streams relying totally on precipitation will cease flowing. Generally speaking, a natural, expansive forest environment can enhance and sustain relationships in the water cycle because there are less human modifications to interfere with its components. A forested watershed helps moderate storm flows by increasing infiltration and reducing overland runoff. Further, a forest helps sustain streamflow by reducing evaporation (*e.g.*, owing to slightly lower temperatures in shaded areas). Forests can help increase recharge to aquifers by allowing more precipitation to infiltrate the soil, as opposed to rapidly running off the land to a downslope area.

Riparian Areas

The riparian zone is broadly defined as the area between a body of water and the upland parts of the landscape that are rarely flooded except under the most extreme conditions. But the term also can refer more specifically to the immediate streamside area. Riparian areas represent less than 10 per cent of most forest ecosystems, yet these areas often are the most productive portions. Compared to upland regions, riparian areas have more water available; the vegetation is more robust; the soils are deeper; the timber often is of higher quality; and the waterbodies have more shade. The riparian zone also may include wetlands bordering streams and lakes. This combination of factors makes riparian areas among the most heavily used portions of a forest. Riparian and wetland areas provide abundant and reliable forage for wildlife, as well as transportation corridors. They also may receive heavy human use for recreation.

Riparian zones also are attractive destinations for logging and for livestock grazing; as a result, riparian areas in forests are sometimes heavily damaged, especially in the forests of the arid American Southwest. Fortunately, riparian areas respond well to good management practices.

Aquatic Biodiversity

Forest lands and waters are vitally important in maintaining biodiversity and providing habitat for fish and wildlife, including threatened or endangered aquatic species. In the United States, over one-third of national forest lands are critical for maintaining aquatic biodiversity and protection of listed species.

For aquatic species, watersheds provide the basic unit of any conservation strategy. Many watersheds also contain isolated habitats with unique characteristics producing a high potential for rare species. Some species occur only near a single spring or in a single stream within a given watershed. Lands set aside to protect these unique habitats also benefit the entire watershed and its ecosystem.

DEVELOPMENT OF COMMUNITY WASTELANDS AND DENUDED FORESTS

Conservation of biodiverstity and protection of forests are the other important components of community forestry. However there has been a lukewarm response to these activities in the past, mainly because of lack of awareness, inadequate benefits and lack of trust between the local communities and government agencies who own these lands. Hence the new strategy should find a suitable solution for these problems.

Development of forest lands: Rehabilitation of denuded forest lands and protection of natural forests are essential to conserve biodiversity. The forests influence the climate and soil moisture conditions and improve agricultural production.

This aspect needs wider publicity in rural areas and the local people should be motivated to take active part in Joint Forest Management. The Village Forest Committees willing to protect the natural forests, should be encouraged to share the benefits in the form of fodder, fuel, timber and NWFP. These committees can also take up reforestation of degraded forest lands, aiming to conserve biodiversity and generate income. While facilitating natural regeneration, the local communities can also introduce fuel, timber and NWFP species of their choice to enhance the productivity on denuded forest lands.

Development of community lands: Lack of people's initiative was a serious problem in developing community wastelands, mainly due to lack of direct benefits. Earlier efforts to establish woodlots could not generate substantial income. Establishment of NWFP species such as tamarind (*Tamarindus indica*), Indian gooseberry (*Emblica officinalis*), neem (*Azadirachta indica*), Pongamia (*Derris indica*), *Madhuca spp*. and a wide range of medicinal species can generate substantial income, regularly for over 50-100 years. With the world's herbal medicine business likely to cross US $ 3 trillion during the next decade, it will be an excellent opportunity for the Asian farmers to enhance their income through cultivation of these species on community lands as well as on private wastelands.

Development of Mined Areas: Rehabilitation of mined areas is another cause of serious concern. Although the industries are obliged to establish a green cover after mining the area, the outcome has been very poor. Such sites are major causes of soil erosion and flooding of rivers. Lack of commitment, inadequate expertise in selection of plant species and their management have been the main reasons for failure. These activities can be entrusted to voluntary organisations and local communities, with research support to raise healthy plantations. Preference should be given to NWFP and timber species which have long gestation period, sufficient to enrich the mined lands.

CO_2 Sinks: There are opportunities for environmental protection by establishing industrial greenbelts, recycling treated effluent and developing carbon dioxide sinks, particularly around urban areas. The polluting industries can be compelled to establish greenery through the involvement of voluntary organisations and local people.

Environmental Awareness and Eco-tourism: Lack of awareness among the common public is a cause for environmental pollution in the developing countries. Hence, continuous efforts are needed to motivate the common public to plant more trees and protect the environment. School children and literate urban population are fairly receptive to participate in environmental protection. This can be undertaken through school based plant nurseries, development of arboretum, botanical gardens and greenbelts around the schools and industries.

While developing industrial greenbelts and afforestation on river banks, special efforts can be made to promote eco-tourism. Creating waterbodies through plugging of gullies, developing, nature trails, shady grounds for resting, selecting suitable plant species to attract wildlife and providing adequate eco-tourism. Environmental exhibitions at these sites can help in motivating the public to take active part in community forestry and environmental protection.

Organisational Development

Development of local organisations is the key to ensure people's participation and to sustain the benefits of investments and efforts made in community forestry.

Tree Growers Organisations

The initial need is to provide leadership to organise local people in afforestation. This can be carried out through formation of local Selp-Help Groups, village level farmers' associations and forest groups. This activity should receive priority during the next decade.

Capacity Building

Training of local farmers, supply of critical inputs, credit and technical advisory services to improve the profitability and developing market networks are the critical inputs which have to be introduced in the field to support tree growers.

Networking of Tree Growers and User Groups

There is an urgent need to set up networks of tree growers, forestry users and concerned scientists in these fields. Such networks should identify the opportunities for tree growers. They can also promote processing and marketing of forestry products and protect the interests of tree growers.

Forestry Information Service

Setting up of information centres to identify the priority of the industries and farmers and provide necessary information to enhance the economic viability of community forestry would help to sustain the interest of tree growers. Forestry Extension Units should closely associate with Information Service Centres to identify appropriate technologies for transferring to the field.

Forestry Research

The networks should identify the problems affecting the production and marketing of the produce and encourage the Forestry Research Institutions to take up relevant scientific studies to solve the problems. The researchers should closely associate with the network and Information Centres to disseminate new technologies to solve field problems and enhance the production.

Forestry research should focus on the following topics:

- Conservation of biodiversity;
- Improving the productivity of wastelands, tree plantations and natural forests;
- Exploring the utility of multipurpose tree species and NWFP;
- Developing of alternatives for conserving wood;
- Selecting various organisational systems to manage community forestry.

The outcome of these research topics can further strengthen the community forestry programme in the country.

EFFECT OF OROGRAPHIC FACTORS IN MODIFYING THE LOCAL CLIMATE

The effect of orographic factors in modifying the local climate was soon appreciated and the numerous studies in montane areas, such as Switzerland, showed clearly the importance of aspect and of the general level of the mountain massif on altitudinal limits of communities and species. This rapidly led to the recognition of what has been termed cold-air drainage and the existence of frost pockets which could result in temperature inversions and accompanying inversions of altitudinal limits, features that have been closely studied by fruit growers for obvious economic reasons.

Our knowledge of the more detailed pattern of climatic features as they affect plant life is, in many areas, inadequate despite the broad correlation between vegetation types and saturation deficits that may obtain in some regions or with length of frost-free periods in others. Moreover our knowledge of the microclimate of the various strata of plant communities and its seasonal variations is generally meagre whilst any concept of the microclimate within the soil is commonly wanting.

So, even though we may know the climatic environment of the shoots with some degree of accuracy, we are often quite ignorant as to the significant environment of the root systems. During prolonged cold spells the depth to which the soil is frozen solid, for example, can vary widely in different plant communities growing on the same type of sub-soil. In one instance bare soil was frozen to a depth 2 to 3½ in., under rough grass to between 1 and 1½ in. and in a hazel copse to only W! in., or not at all, according to the depth of the leaf litter.

Operation of Climatic Factors

The long term operation of climatic factors may clearly limit the capacity of a species to flourish and compete with others or it may even impair or inhibit its power of reproduction. The detailed studies on frost resistance of Apple varieties have, for instance, revealed the diverse times at which temperature-sensitive crises may supervene in the life-history so that if this obtains also in wild populations climatic differentiation in the occurrence of strains as well as species may obtain. But the elucidation of such relations demands a knowledge, for each species, of these critical periods, such as flower initiation, pollen-tube development, fertilization, etc., and the temperature tolerances of each. The success of any type of plant in the wild state will depend upon its capacity to flourish and reproduce under the local climate which the plant itself in part creates. The determining conditions are not, however, the average but the extremes to which it is subjected and hence the need for continuous records of the climatic factors within the community itself not forgetting the steep vertical gradients that may obtain between different levels, of the same vegetation unit, and the interference effects of the different species with respect to the penetration of light and rainfall.

The climatic pattern is often conditioned by the structure of the community and the physiognomic character of its constituent members no less than these are themselves determined by the climatic pattern which they can modify and endure.

We have referred to the fundamental principle that it is the most severe conditions of habitat, rather than the average, that mainly determine the characteristics of communities. But this, which we may term "the *Principle of Extremes,*" must not be over-simplified and regarded as being in the nature of so many sieves of lethal conditions.

Species that will survive a low temperature during a single winter may succumb to two successive winters of no greater severity. Again, it is commonly the extreme conditions, that are not lethal, but sub-lethal, operating from season to season that undermine the vigour of a species and give advantage to the more tolerant vegetation over the less tolerant.

The crude early concepts as to the relationship of plants to low temperature gave place when subjected to experimental tests to the recognition that resistance of a plant or its parts was largely conditioned by its water content and that the capacity of seeds to survive storage in liquid air was only true so long as their water content was negligible. The degree of toleration of low temperature is well known as a specific character that limits the range of many plants but the complexity of the phenomenon of frost resistance has only been appreciated in the light of recent observations and experiments which have shown that the low temperature toleration of a species varies seasonally and that capacity to endure a certain amount of frost is no guarantee that the same species will not succumb to far less severe conditions if the temperatures be fluctuating. Similarly with respect to drought tolerance the capacity to endure desiccation is one that is partly inherent, partly dependent upon the time of the year and partly on the manner in which the desiccation comes about.

Both with respect to desiccation by drought and by low temperature, the mode and rate of recovery are operative factors in determining survival since rapid expansion of a contracted protoplast, unsupported by the cell wall from which it has shrunk, may involve lethal rupture.

A detailed consideration of the general topic of plant hardiness has been furnished by J. Levitt which emphasizes the diverse qualities that render the protoplasm resistant to disorganization but the particular aspect we would here stress is that the precise pattern of climatic change in a particular habitat or partial habitat, often referred to as the microclimate, can alone provide a clue to the climatic factors as they affect the constituents of a natural community.

Thus the seasonal incidence of precipitation if confined to a few thunderstorms in the hottest months may scarcely support a desert type of vegetation whilst the same average rainfall spread evenly over the cooler period may suffice for a plant community which evades the waterless period by shedding its leaves.

We must not lose sight of the fact that the precipitation itself may vary to a significant degree in kind as well as in amount. For example, rain contains chloride corresponding in amount to the proximity of an area to the sea. Dr. Miller of Rothamsted, half a century ago recorded the chloride content as ranging from 218 p.p.m., near the coast, to between 2 and 3.4 p.p.m. fifty miles inland, whilst for sulphur a range of from 0.6 to over ten times that amount has been determined in open country and much higher values in the polluted atmosphere near industrial areas.

ROLE OF VEGETATION IN THE PROCESSES OF PEDOGENESIS

The role of vegetation in the processes of pedogenesis has been studied under conditions where the distribution of the phases of plant development in space corresponds to their sequence in time and thus provides an unequivocal chronological succession over a prolonged period with respect alike to soils and organisms. For sand dunes it has been shown that the soil development is dependent upon a succession of species that incorporate organic material beneath the surface as well as providing deposition upon it and augment water retention and stability so that less and less specialized types can effect colonization ultimately ousting the pioneer specialists. The original inhospitable soil conditions with an open community of perennial and annual species, characterized by features that enable them to endure the rigorous conditions, is succeeded by conditions favourable to an increasing number of species, far more diverse in their biological equipment, that ultimately constitute a closed community and this in turn may finally give place to scrub and woodland occupying soil that is now favourable to a great diversity of plants but where in fact the number of species has again diminished owing to the dominance of trees and shrubs. The initial edaphic specialization has thus, in the course of perhaps a century, given place to a biotic specialization that in its own way may be almost equally severe. The studies of R. L. Crocker and his associates on the recessional moraines deal with a comparable sequence from an open community of pioneers that in the course of some 120 years has developed to spruce forest and, as in the dune succession, there is an increasing organic content and transition from an initially alkaline soil to one of appreciable acidity with an augmenting gradient in the soil profile.

The recognition of the major role in water retention by the soil played by the organic material gives added significance to its vertical distribution and it thus came to be realized that, in the naturally stratified soil the surface layer might be of sufficient thickness and its organic content so high that it constituted a sponge which could starve the lower layers of water except perhaps in the heaviest rainfall. Thus is indicated one of the ways in which during the course of years a tall deeply rooted layer of dominant species continually adding its quota to the superficial organic accumulations can gradually contribute to its own destruction and an acidophile shallow-rooted community replaces the erstwhile dominants. Each species has its own complex of conditions in which it can best develop. If we grow any one in conditions that vary with respect to one factor, such for instance as soil reaction, we find there is a range over which the plants exhibit maximum growth on either side of which increasing acidity or increasing alkalinity is accompanied by diminishing vigour. In the absence of competition the range of toleration is often wide but in the presence of other species this may become very restricted. This fact emphasizes the fundamental principle of the interaction of habitat factors.

For whether it be soil reaction or any other there is usually no absolute optimum but a relativity that is the more complex because any single one may operate in so many different ways. Soil acidity, for example, may be beneficial as enabling certain nutrient ions to be readily available but it may also be directly harmful by reason of toxicity of the hydrogen ions themselves, or indirectly through excess of ions of alumina or manganese in the soil solution, or again it may adversely affect beneficial soil organisms such as the nitrogen fixing bacteria and encourage harmful ones such as *Plasmodiophora brassicae.* Above all, adverse or beneficial factors cannot be considered in isolation since plants grow where they must and not where they will so that what, in the laboratory experiment, may seem harmful appears in the field as a benefit because the species concerned is more tolerant of this condition than its normal associates. For instance *Viscaria alpina* can apparently tolerate a copper content in the soil toxic to most species. Again what favours vegetative growth is often detrimental to seed production and which of these is the more important may vary from time to time in one and the same plant community. Experiments have repeatedly shown that the optimum conditions with respect to various factors alter with the stage of development of the individual and also its susceptibility.

"The field for the problem and the laboratory for the solution" is only very partially true for ecological studies, for laboratory findings must be transmuted into the far more complex context of so many other variables that experience alone can guide as to what may be applicable and to what degree. But field studies, both observational and experimental, should serve as the means for testing hypotheses based upon what the plant physiologist has ascertained. Ecology is essentially applied plant physiology with the competition factor as an important modifying influence in a physical environment that represents the interaction of climatic, edaphic, and biotic factors that are themselves abstractions from a sequence of continual change.

The emphasis on physiognomy that has formed the basis for some systems of classification of plant communities can be regarded as an attempt to utilize the plants themselves as integrators of the physical conditions and the concept of the so-called indicator species is but another aspect of the same theme. When extreme conditions are under consideration the correlation of physiognomy with habitat conditions is sometimes surprisingly high as is well exhibited, for example, on some of the sandy and areas in South-West Australia, where communities are encountered consisting of species of the most diverse genera and families yet resembling one another so closely in their general physiognomy as to be difficult to distinguish except when in flower or fruit. In less differentiated conditions, however, as for instance in the temperate woodland, the same stratum, where there is relative uniformity of environment, often presents a great range of morphological diversity that suggests either that physiognomy is an unsatisfactory guide or that our knowledge must be greatly increased by experiments, in the field of environmental morphogenesis, before we are in a position to assess what morphological characteristics are significant and what are irrelevant.

Stratification and Seasonal Development of Aerial Shoots

The stratification and seasonal development of aerial shoots, to which attention was drawn by Kerner Von Marilau nearly a century ago, and of the subterranean organs, which the late Dr. Woodhead was one of the first to investigate, both affect the competitive efficiency of the species whilst the periodicity of the important phases of the life history and their modifications by the environment are no less significant though too little investigated. These latter, for economic reasons, are better known with respect to horticultural plants. The gardener is familiar with the fact that most plants are best moved in the dormant state, yet most species of *Helleborus* thrive best if transplanted when in full flower, a difference probably related to the phases of root development. Or again, careful investigations of bulbous species have shown how temperature fluctuations can affect differently diverse cultivars of the same species apparently by reason of their individual rhythms in the production of flower initials. What is true of cultivated plants is probably equally true of wild species and emphasizes for us that the understanding of the communal life of plants is dependent upon a knowledge of the idiosyncrasies of its chief constituents.

The structure and chemical characteristics of the soil as they affected plant life gained no small impetus from the work of Lawes and Gilbert, initiated in the early forties of last century, but the classical work of E. J. Russell on *Soil Conditions and Plant Growth,* which first appeared in 1912 and which passed through eight editions and has been translated into various languages, probably did more than any other single publication to bring before the minds of botanists the complexity as well as the importance of edaphic conditions upon vegetation. The soils that the agriculturist had studied were, however, to a very considerable degree physically homogenized by the processes of cultivation and chemically altered by their manurial treatment. It was not until ecologists began to pay attention to the organization that is exhibited by natural soils that the degree of applicability of the findings of the agriculturists could begin to be assessed. One of the earliest recognitions of the structure of natural soils and its relation to the vegetation which they bear was the study by Gesser and Siegrist of the profiles in the soils of the Aare communities in Switzerland. In this country the present writer called attention to the striking vertical gradients with respect to organic content, water content, soil reaction, and other features exhibited by woodland and sand-dune soils which provide a gradient of conditions for the root system.

These vertical changes not only contribute to the establishment and maintenance of the complementary communities of species but, as soils derived from a calcareous substratum strikingly show, can provide one and the same root system with a diversity of conditions favourable for the easy acquisition of the whole range of nutrient requirement from an acid surface layer from which the ions of iron and manganese may be readily obtained to an alkaline subsoil from which molybdenum is readily available.

4

Plant Phytogeography and Geography

We have briefly outlined the history, scope, and aims of plant geography and have given some selected details of the work on or linked to phytogeography in major phytochoria of the earth. The various realms and regions have been treated somewhat unequally and differently. This was partly done deliberately to illustrate different "vistas," different methods of approach, and different kinds of emphasis.

The subject is so vast, has so many "side-lines," and is once again, with new outlooks, so dynamic that arbitrary limits had to be set. This is the excuse for having to leave out much of interest and importance. There are many subjects within phytogeography that have special problems and some of these have been selected for condensed consideration under a number of headings.

Kinds of Ranges

Ranges of species are of various kinds, though there are intermediates between any classes one makes. Ranges may be exceedingly wide even almost cosmopolitan, as for *Pteridium aquilinum,* or very small as for *Ramonda (Jankaea) heldreichii;* they may be relatively continuous, as for *Pinus halepensis,* or markedly discontinuous, as for *Convolvulus nitidus;* they may show clinal structure, as in *Ajuga chamaepitys,* or they may not, as in *Arbutus unedo;* they may be divisible into subspecific ranges, as in Silene vulgaris, or there may be no marked geographical correlations with intraspecific variation, as in *Fritillaria meleagris;* they may be restricted to a given geographical area when the species is said to be endemic to the area, as *Petromarula pinnata* is endemic to Crete, or they may extend beyond a geographical area, as do the vast majority of the species of the British flora.

Two general statements must be made: the different kinds of ranges just enumerated for species occur, with slight modifications of wording, in connection with taxa of higher rank than species and our data for past ranges as based on reliable fossil evidence is, for the angiosperms in particular, relatively meagre. We must also note that "continuity of range" means only that the species (or other taxon) occurs without wide geographical breaks but ignoring ecological breaks.

If there be no major problem as to dispersal of disseminules from population to population the range is considered continuous in a wide sense. There is, however, every intermediate between isolation of populations within a species, that is, separation of groups of individuals within a phytochorion so that one cannot interbreed with another because of external barriers, and wide geographical isolation.

Some of the problems of discontinuous ranges are well dealt with by Cain, and the statistical study of wide and restricted ranges is the basis of much of Willis's work on "age and area". The importance of clines is discussed by Huxley, though mainly from the zoological standpoint. Corresponding to clines in taxonomy and population studies are ecotones in ecology. Clines are defined as character gradients within groups while ecotones are the transitions between adjoining plant communities.

It is very doubtful if polytopism (the origin of a taxon independently at more than one locality) occurs except at a low taxonomic level, assuming, of course, that the taxonomy be sound. We have to accept that most taxonomic entities have had one place of origin. It is sometimes claimed that the centre of a range, or the place of greatest frequency or of maximum variability or of lushness of development indicates the area of origin more or less precisely. Certainly all of these facts have to be taken into account but none of them is conclusive.

They must all be considered together and with the independent conclusions of taxonomic affinities as based on modern synthetic taxonomy. There are, however, many facts concerned with range that have evolutionary significance. Variation at the margins of ranges is frequently different from that near the centre. Often this can be correlated with different environmental factors and the action of natural selection is plain, as with *Silene martitima* subsp. *islandica.*

The division between species and subspecies is not sharp and there seems circumstantial evidence from the study of ranges (combined with taxonomic data) that subspecies can give rise to fully isolated species. Endemics are defined as species (or other taxa) limited in present range to a given geographical area. Some endemics are such because they are of relatively recent origin, presumably within their present range, and have not yet had time to extend over all their area of tolerance. These are neo-endemics and are often microspecies (or microtaxa).

At the other extreme there are the palaeo-endemics which originated long ago but have either never been able to extend their ranges or have gradually "lost ground" from competition with other species, often correlated with environmental changes for which their sum total of biotype diversification is unsuited except in their now restricted endemic range. This is the explanation of what is sometimes referred to as species senescence. Taxa do die out, as the fossil record proves, but they do not become "old" in the sense of old age of individuals.

Rare and Relict Species

The term "rare" is relative. It may indicate a species that has a very small range but is common within that range, or a species with a more or less wide general range within which it is represented by few individuals, or, in the extreme, it may be a species with a small range with few individuals within that range. For the broader problems of phytogeography we usually mean a species with a small range or at least with a small approximately continuous range.

Rare species may be restricted in their ranges either because they are young and have not had time to spread or because their characters (expressed in one or in more than one biotype) are not suited for any environment outside the narrow range to which access has been obtained or they may be relicts, that is, they have ranges that are smaller than formerly.

There seems no valid reason for supposing that new species are being formed in smaller numbers than at any time, say, since the beginning of Tertiary times. Indeed, with the making of new environments by man, with the greatly increased plant dispersal by man, and by the consequently increased chances of hybridization it is probable that new kinds of plants are appearing at an increasing rate, though how many of these may be acceptable taxonomic species is another matter. On the other hand, palaeobotanical research proves that taxa become extinct.

Unfortunately, we know little about the causes of extinction of taxa; indeed, we know far too little, in any systematic manner, regarding the death of individuals in nature. Two general facts have to be used by the plant geographer: that organic evolution has continued throughout plant history and that environments are are continually changing. Comparisons between phylogeny and ontogeny may be misleading.

Thus it is probably incorrect to talk about the wear-out or old age of a species as similar to senescence in an individual. The most successful species are those that meet with the fewest limiting factors for completing their life cycles over the widest ranges and are able to disperse over these ranges.

The environment, however, may change — as by the on-coming of a glacial epoch or increased aridity, or the appearance of better equipped biotic competitors — and the species may be so specialized, may have so few biotypes, or may have too little potentiality for producing suitable mutations that it cannot survive or at least maintain its existing range.

It may be able to "migrate" or it may be exterminated, or it may indefinitely continue to exist very locally as a rare relict. Space will not allow the enumeration of actual examples. Such are given by Griggs, Stebbins, Cain, Wildeman, and Matvejev.

Vicarious Species

The comparison of taxa that have been thoroughly studied often shows that taxonomically related varieties, species, or genera have distinct nonoverlapping ranges and these can sometimes be clearly correlated with different environments. The ranges may be more or less contiguous or discontinuous. Vierhapper attempted to distinguish between vicarism and pseudovicarism, the former when the nearly related "Sippen" (or as we should now say "taxa") have originated in the areas or formations from a common ancestor, the latter when one of these conditions does not hold or both do not hold.

He introduced the word "vicariads" for the members of a pair of vicarious taxa and notes that they may be separated horizontally (or geographically), altitudinally, ecologically, or seasonally (or temporarily). The pseudovicariads are probably a mixture: either they are not very closely related or it is uncertain that they should be considered derived from a very near common ancestor or it is more or less certain that they represent convergent evolution, and often they belong to different sections of a genus.

It is rather doubtful if one can reasonably speak of vicarious families and tribes in a very strict sense and even some of the supposedly vicarious genera may be questioned. It is at, or below, the species level that vicarism can best be studied from the phytogeographical and evolutionary points of view. There are fairly numerous pairs of closely related species of which one is found in eastern North America and the other in Europe.

Examples are: *Vallisneria americana* and *V. spiralis, Anemone quinquefolia* and *A. nemorosa, Maianthemum canadense* and *M. bifolium,* and Scrophularia marilandica and S. nodosa. Examples of altitudinal vicariads are Myosotis silvatica and M. alpestris, Centaurea pseudophrygia and C. plumosa, Trifolium pratense and T. nivale, Soldanella major and S. hungarica, etc., and quite a marked proportion of high mountain plants in Crete and Greece could be quoted as examples by comparison with lowland congeners.

Ecological vicariads may be correlated with different substratum conditions (degree of acidity, water content, chemical or physical nature), as *Stachys palustris* and *S. silvatica, Lotus major* and *L. corniculatus, Geum rivale* and *G. urbanum, Gentiana clusii* and *G. kochiana, Rhododendron hirsutum* and *R. ferrugineum*. Other limiting factors are temperature and light and there is undoubtedly interaction of factors often involved in determining ranges of vicariads.

Vicariads have usually been paired off as a result of taxonomic and phytogeographical or ecological studies. It is being realized that they can throw much light on evolution when more detailed researches are made on them. Love says that the fundamental difference between true and false vicariads is that the former penetrated into their areas prior to their successive morphological and genetical differentiation while the latter differentiated before their dispersal to the new territory.

He rightly stresses the need for cyto-genetical researches on supposedly vicarious pairs of taxa and shows, mainly on chromosome number and morphology, that some that have been accepted as vicariads are pseudo-vicariads, as *Zostera marina* and *Z. stenophylla, Gentianella procera* and *G. detonsa,* and *Glyceria grandis* and *G. maxima,* while *Populus tremula* and *P. tremuloides* and *Scirpus (Schoenoplectus) lacustris* and *S. acutus* are to be retained as true vicarious pairs.

The comprehensive study of the bladder campions (*Silene maritima* and *S. vulgaris)* by Marsden-Jones and Turrill has shown something of the complexity of the taxonomic, ecological, and evolutionary relationship of pairs of species. The two species, at least in their typical subspecies as found in the British Isles, are ecological vicariads. They have the same chromosome numbers and can cross reciprocally to produce fertile offspring but their ranges are different, though they overlap, and their ecological distribution is, with few exceptions, quite different.

As populations, again with few exceptions, they keep distinct. Yet within each, and especially within *S. vulgaris,* considering the whole of their ranges there are vicariads within the subspecies, for example, *S. vulgaris* subsp. *vulgaris,* subsp. *glareosa,* and subsp. *alpina*. Moreover, *S. vulgaris* subsp. *alpina* might well, on definition, be considered pseudovicarious with *S. maritima* subsp. *maritima* and as showing quite marked evolutionary convergence.

Area Hypothesis

An important view was put forward by J. C. Willis in 1915 and dealt with fully in his book *Age and Area*, Cambridge, and in other publications. Without qualifications, this states that the range of a species is determined by the age of the species, in the sense that a large range indicates an old age and conversely a small range a recent origin. Willis, partly to meet criticisms, hedged round his expression of "the rule" so that it became unworkable.

Thus he says: "The area occupied at any given time, in any given country, by any group of allied species at least ten in number, depends chiefly, so long as conditions remain reasonably constant, upon the ages of the species of that group in that country, but may be enormously modified by the presence of barriers such as seas, rivers, mountains, changes of climate from one region to the next, or other ecological boundaries, and the like, also by the action of man, and by other causes."

It has been found by the present writer and others that it is only by breaking away from the limitations imposed by this "expression" that one can test for any value in the general hypothesis that on the whole a larger range is a criterion of greater age in a given country. The main criticisms of the hypothesis have been that it fails to distinguish new species from "old," that limiting factors do not cancel out in groups compared, and that species formation has a number of "causes" of which sudden large mutation is not so important as Willis believes.

On the other hand, there is no doubt that the hypothesis is useful in that it directs attention to the time factor in range formation and that its application does sometimes explain existing ranges. Further, attention will have to be paid by phytogeographers to many of the questions Willis asks, particularly in a later book.

Hemispherical Ranges

The tropical belt separates a North Temperate from a South Temperate zone. While the floras of these two zones are very largely different, especially in species, genera, and predominance of tribes or families, they have some taxa in common, those round about the generic level being of particular phytogeographical importance. Both floristic resemblances and differences raise problems connected with what has been called "bipolar distribution" but had better be known as "bihemispherical ranges." It is true that there are mountain ranges, particularly in America and Tropical Africa, with a main north to south direction and which might serve as a highway for migration of a number of temperate taxa across the tropics. One has, however, to remember that while attitude affects temperature and precipitation the factors of photoperiodism remain and their influence on north to south (or the reverse) extension of ranges has been largely ignored and, indeed, we have little knowledge on this subject which is one that requires experimental investigation.

A second, and major, difficulty at arriving at any valid conclusion as to the history of present-day bihemispherical ranges is the meagre palaeobotanical evidence available. If the occurrence in Tertiary deposits of the Northern

Hemisphere of what are now taxa limited to the Southern Hemisphere be accepted, and the evidence for this is stronger than it was, then the postulated place of origin of such families as the *Proteaceae* need not be restricted to southern latitudes.

That evolutionary convergence occurs is frequently demonstrated in detailed taxonomic studies but most often it concerns one or a few characters and not the gamut of organs. Polytopy, the origin of taxa in more than one place independently, is possible, indeed sometimes probable, at lower taxonomic levels but the chances of its occurring are proportionally less the greater the number of differential common characters involved.

It is usually unwise to fall back on polytopism to explain discontinuity of generic ranges unless the taxonomy has been thoroughly revised by modern synthetic methods. Moreover, polytopy may only push the problem back a stage, so to speak, and not solve it. Thus, if one said *Empetrum* arose independently in the northern and southern hemispheres, the question of how the ancestor or ancestors attained discontinuous ranges takes the place of the original problem.

Leaving aside the possibility of occasional polytopy, there have been two main theories regarding bihemispherical ranges: that the taxa concerned arose in the northern hemisphere and extended southwards or that they arose in the southern hemisphere and extended their ranges northwards. At present, the main land masses are in the northern hemisphere and the older view, ably supported by Thiselton-Dyer, is that "all the great assemblages of plants which we call floras seem to admit of being traced back at some time in their history to the northern hemisphere."

It is, he notes, "easy on this supposition to account for their possession of common characters which, in their widely scattered southern distribution is not readily explained on other grounds." Similar views have been supported by various botanists and also, on the zoological side, by some zoologists.

In marked contrast are the views of Camp and Croizat, amongst others. Camp, for example, considers the ranges of 103 plant families with restricted territories and shows their concentration in the southern hemisphere. He concludes that most of these families originated in the southern hemisphere and spread northwards, and that this is particularly true of primitive families.

Further, he postulates a more continuous land mass in the south contemporaneous with the Palaeozoic of the northern (Holarctic) land mass and that the divergences of the basic, generalized familial groups had been accomplished on this southern land mass certainly by the Mid-Mesozoic. Du Rietz discussed at length the problems here being considered. It is somewhat difficult to determine his standpoint on the major problem.

He more or less rejects long distance dispersal of disseminules and the hypothesis of continental drift but accepts the need for "epeirogenetic transtropical highland bridges older than the mountain-chains of the Alpine Orogen. Such highland bridges may have existed not only in Africa, but also bordering the transtropical Alpine geosynclines (i.e. the Andean and the Malaysian geosynclines), partly passing over present deep sea bottom."

Since we do not know when, where, or from what the angiosperms were evolved, their early differentiation into families must largely remain a matter for speculation. Even more than phylogeny must the centre or centres of origin be hypothetical. Hypotheses are essential but they must not become dogmas. Two matters are worth bearing in mind. If there has been considerable drifting of continents and large wanderings of the poles the question of northern or southern origin of the families of angiosperms becomes largely meaningless as at present stated.

Secondly, assuming that the continental masses and the positions of the poles have not greatly changed since the origin of the angiosperms, apart from the accepted regressions and transgressions of the sea proved by geological researches there would appear to be good reasons for migrations to have occurred in both north and south directions. Certainly one has to postulate the diversified evolution of some taxa in the temperate regions of the Northern Hemisphere and of others in the Southern Hemisphere independently.

Continental Drift

The Pacific, Indian, and Atlantic Oceans are great expanses of water, separating continental land masses, with floras and faunas having some families, genera, and, more rarely, species in common. To account for common biological features it has frequently been postulated that there were land connections across which disseminules were more or less gradually and continuously dispersed. On the geomorphological side there was the possibility of former connecting land having sunk beneath the oceans or of formerly joined land masses having drifted apart.

It is first essential to be clear concerning the problem involved. Geological evidence is conclusive that there has been throughout the geological periods regressions and transgressions of the sea relative to dry land. All marine sedimentary rocks now forming part of land masses were laid down beneath seas and, whatever the depth of these, they formed barriers to dispersal of land plants as effective as deep oceans relative only to their extent. Conversely, none can dispute that former land linked many islands to continents, as Great Britain to Europe, or peninsula to peninsula, as Asia Minor to Greece.

Even if the Mediterranean Sea be accepted as the relict of a very ancient and more extensive Tethys Sea its outlines have changed enormously through the ages. The problems we have to consider here are both much greater and more controversial. Have the ocean basins, beyond the continental shelf always been very much as they are now or have they previously been land? If the latter, has their formation been due to submergence of land or to drifting of continents? If either submergence or drifting has occurred when did it happen?

Biologists who have demanded continuous land surfaces to account for existing ranges of plants and animals have between them, in imagination, pretty well filled up all the oceans with land. On the contrary, many geologists and geomorphologists have accepted the view of the permanence of the great ocean basins so strongly put forward by J. D. Dana and summarized in his own words as "The continents have always been the more elevated land of the crust, and the basins always basins."

This view has often been stated in geological text-books and was widely accepted though challenged by scientists from time to time, and especially, as far as Gondwanaland was concerned, by Suess and others. Gondwanaland is the name given to a supposed great southern continent, wide enough to include much of South America, South Africa, India, part of Australia, Antarctica, and the intermediate areas now oceanic. It was thought to have persisted through the Palaeozoic era to Upper Cretaceous times.

The geological, palaeontological, and biogeographical evidence for some kind of former linkage of existing and now separated lands in the Southern Hemisphere is considerable but objections to the foundering of huge areas of land to provide the oceans or parts of the oceans now separating the Gondwanaland fragments have been raised by geophysicists and others.

More recently there has come to the fore the idea of drifting continents. This is now largely associated with the name of Alfred Wegener, though it appears it was, in one form or another, put forward by other geomorphologists before Wegener. Briefly, it is postulated that in Palaeozoic times there existed one great original continent, Pangaea, surrounded by a primeval Pacific Ocean. Then, during the Mesozoic and Cainozoic eras this one original continent broke up, and by the drifting of its fragments oceans gradually opened up between them.

Wegener adopted the old idea that the continents are composed mainly of the lighter silicates, having a mean density near that of granite, and float on a layer of heavier, viscous silicates. He postulated a general drift of the continental blocks away from the poles and towards the west. The details of Wegener's scheme have been modified in various ways by more recent workers but the general principle of continental drift is widely accepted and yet, one must add, often opposed.

Many biogeographers are inclined to accept continental drift as solving all their problems, which it certainly does not do, and the main criticisms have come from palaeobotanists and geophysicists, the latter being concerned with the source of the energy needed to shift continents. The whole subject has been complicated by linking continental drift on to hypotheses concerning "wanderings of the poles" and variations in the inclination of the earth's axis. Koppen and Wegener traced polar displacements, with tabulated records of latitude and longitude, from the Devonian to the present positions of the poles.

The majority of palaeobotanists, from a study of the records of fossil plants, especially those around the present North Pole, have been emphatically against polar migrations. Most recently there have been important researches on the permanent magnetization of the rocks and deductions therefrom. Evidence has been produced that the direction of magnetization of rocks (particularly of iron oxide minerals) perpetuates that of the earth's field at the time of their formation.

Hence, by examining rocks of known age it is possible to discover any variations that have taken place in the direction of the earth's field and the conclusion has been reached that the geomagnetic field has undergone repeated reversals in geological time. It has been assumed from these accepted displacements of the magnetic pole that there has been both translation in a meridional direction and rotation of land masses. Thus, Britain is said to have moved a long way northwards in the last 150 million years from a position about 10° north of the equator (roughly the latitude of Southern India) and North America has done the same.

England has also rotated through about 35° relative to the direction of present magnetic north and this could probably be interpreted as an increase of the distance between North America and Britain. Other, and sometimes decidedly different, estimates have also been made. There is apparently a postulate that the magnetic and geographical poles have always been associated much as they are now.

Another line of recent research which may be expected to throw light on the history of the oceans is the study by modern methods of the ocean floors. These are covered with oozes and the depth of these is determined by echoes from high explosives detonated at various depths. Echoes, it is accepted, are reflected both from the surface of the ooze and from that of the solid rock on which it rests. From the records it is possible to estimate the thickness of the ooze.

A further calculation based on the rate of sedimentation then allows an estimate to be made of the minimum age of a given portion of the ocean. On the whole, the recent results obtained by the Swedish *Albatross* expedition are against the theory of continental drift as applied to the Atlantic and as put forward by Wegener, since the estimates are for a time span of 300 to 400 million years, possibly still more.

Very recently actual borings into the sea floor, in fairly deep water, have been made off the Californian coast and it has been suggested that there is no known theoretical reason why borings to considerable depths should not be made into the crust at very considerable oceanic depths. Such might settle many questions at present controversial.

The literature on the subjects outlined above is extensive. The following books and papers may be consulted: Wegener, Koppen*und* Wegener, Du Toit, Brooks, symposium on *"The Theory of Continental Drift"*, Runcorn, Chaney, Petterson, Mayr, Edwards. The theory of continental drift, if accepted, obviously solves some phytogeographical problems, even if it leaves many untouched and raises some new ones. It is, perhaps, right to take the floras of South America and Tropical Africa as the simplest test.

Wegener fitted the Brazilian bulge into the Gulf of Guinea and postulated the separation of Africa and America as commencing in the Cretaceous. We do not know when or where or from what the Angiosperms arose but there were certainly many existing families of flowering plants in existence and widely ranging by Cretaceous, even Lower Cretaceous, times while gymnosperms had evolved long before.

Palaeobotanically the angiosperms and gymnosperms are crucial for the question of dispersal since their seeds are, with few exceptions, large and heavy compared with the spores of cryptogams. What then are the resemblances and differences found on comparing the spermatophytic floras of Africa and South America? There are about 300 species at most known in the natural or subspontaneous state to be common to the two areas.

Many of these are halophytes (some 30 spp.) easily transported by tides and currents, or aquatic and marsh plants (about 100 spp.) often of wide range and frequently dispersed by birds, or pantropical species spread by man. More critical data for our purpose are to be found at the levels of families and genera.

Good lists generic connections across the South Atlantic, excluding pantropical genera, as follows:

America, Africa and/or Madagascar, etc.: 27 genera.

America and continental Africa only: 64 genera.

America and Madagascar only: 4 genera.

Some of these genera are wrongly included, though, on the other hand, some can be added. The total is a fairly large one but needs very much more detailed analysis than it has received. At the family level, connections between America and Africa excluding Madagascar are shown by *Bromeliaceae, Caricaceae, Humiriaceae, Loasaceae, Mayaceae, Rapataceae,* and *Vochysiaceae,* and those between America and Africa including the Madagascan region are shown by *Canellaceae, Hydnoraceae, Strelitziaceae, Turneraceae,* and *Velloziaceae.*

While it appears that the lists of genera and families of angiosperms common to South America and Africa can be given as evidence of a former land connection, and, indeed, of continental drift, some of the ranges can be otherwise explained.

Thus, the *Bromeliaceae* are American except for *Pitcairnia feliciana* from French Guinea and Chevalier accepts the view that "violent aerial currents" carried the light seeds of a species of *Pitcairnia* from the Caribbean islands, or from more eastern islands that have now disappeared, to West Africa and that isolation then led to differentiation from all American known species. *Rhipsalis (Cactaceae)* may have been dispersed by birds or by man, at least, there has been much controversy regarding the history of the present range of this genus.

The possibility that some of the South American-African discontinuities are due to independent migration southwards from some common northern source where the genus or family is now extinct must be kept in mind. It is also important to remember that many genera (and even some tribes and families) are not common to Africa and America. Whether these evolved after separation of Africa and America, if the continents were formerly joined, or if they have died out in one or the other we do not know.

Oceanic Islands

Islands have a fascination for the biogeographer. Their boundaries are definite, the land area is often not too great for a relatively detailed survey, the problems involved are often clear-cut and peculiar. There are, of course, many different kinds of islands: off-shore islands, continental, oceanic, solitary, archipelagos, volcanic, coral, and so on, and they range in size from mere rocks to continents.

As showing isolation from continental land masses, oceanic islands allow the investigation of certain phytogeographical problems under almost experimental conditions of abstraction. In particular, those of volcanic origin, with no indication of any former attachment to continental land have unique conditions for the study of the origin and development of the flora.

They usually have a natural flora poor in species, relatively rich in endemics, and showing taxonomic affinities in one or more directions. Unfortunately, the flora of many of the islands has been greatly modified by man and sometimes largely destroyed, an extreme example being the indigenous flora of St. Helena. The famous lecture by J. D. Hooker on "Insular Floras" summarized the floristic characters of a number of islands. He pointed out that they are rich in cryptogams, have many evergreen but few herbaceous plants and fewer or no indigenous annuals. Species are few in proportion to genera and genera in proportion to families, and the total number of species is small compared with continental areas of equal size and similar conditions.

Many more oceanic islands have been investigated, or much more fully investigated, botanically since Hooker's time and new developments both within the realm of biology and outside it have to be taken into consideration. Nevertheless, several of the major problems remain much as they were in 1866. These oceanic volcanic islands have, or naturally had, a rich vegetation of a limited number of species.

It is extremely unlikely that the ancestors of these species originated by any form of special creation in these islands and they must, therefore, have arrived from other areas, probably continental, either across land that has now disappeared or transoceanically. The efficiency of long distance dispersal has been a matter of controversy. No one disputes that disseminules (spores, seeds, etc.) can be scattered some distance from the parent plant, the distance being commonly a matter of yards to a few miles.

The evidence for long distance transport over oceans, extensive deserts, etc., is indirect or meagre, with one exception. It is generally agreed that ocean currents can transport some disseminules for long distances but these are those either of strand plants or of relatively few species that withstand immersion in sea water for a considerable time. Man, of course, is recognized as the most efficient of all transporting agents but we are here concerned with the floras that originated before the advent of man. The two natural agencies whose efficacy over very long distances is in dispute are wind and birds. There is a little direct evidence of wide dispersal by both but more is difficult to obtain. Modern research is badly needed. Spores and bacteria are certainly carried widely in the upper atmosphere and it is to be hoped that those engaged in aerobiological work will extend their methods and observations to seeds and other disseminules.

Cyclones may be important. Birds are said generally to travel on long distance migrations with empty alimentary systems and with clean feet and feathers. There is, however, an open field for combined botanicalornithological research here. Migrating birds are now ringed in large numbers. If they could always be carefully examined for attached fruits and seeds and if some such could be attached to them experimentally immediately previous to migration, and if the bodies of dead immigrants (at lighthouses, etc.) could be analysed externally and internally for plant parts, much might be learnt.

The question of land connections has been dealt with above and it need only be said now that problems of wide dispersal are also found over many continental areas where they are sometimes at least as puzzling as for oceanic islands.

There is much indirect evidence in favour of some transoceanic dispersal. The richness of many oceanic islands in cryptogams with their light spores, especially of bryophytes and pteridophytes, suggests wind dispersal has occurred for these plants. For seed plants, the poverty in taxa and the mixture of taxa suggest chance dispersal, as does also the absentees which might be expected had there been direct land connections. Sometimes the taxonomic affinities of the flora of an oceanic island, or island group, are correlated with general direction of the wind or with bird migration routes. Finally, we may note that the two hypotheses of dispersal over long distances and of land connections are not mutually antagonistic for both may have happened, one for this island, one for that, or both for the same island.

Given the establishment of a flora on an oceanic island there are the problems concerned with its further development *in situ.* Cytogeneticists and others engaged in population studies now, rightly, stress the pros and cons of isolation. In the evolution and maintenance of taxa (especially of species) isolation means reduced biotic competition, reduced swamping or extermination of mutations since there will be no flow of new immigrants, and absence of hybridization outside a very restricted population.

Compared with a large continental area the agents of natural selection will be different and, on the whole, less intensive. The climate, for example, is usually more equable than in a continental area, while predators, diseases, and pests are often less numerous. Thus evolution may be slower and old kinds or old characters are likely to survive. On the other hand, mutational characters suited to the conditions of an oceanic island, but less suited to those of a continent, will be selected.

PLANT PHYLOGENY

The various adaptations to the terrestrial environment (*e.g.*, waxy cuticles, stomata, vasculature, gametangia, seeds, and fruit) have evolved slowly during the 475 million-year history of plants. With these adaptations in mind, we will move on to a discussion of plant phylogeny and begin our review of the major characteristics of each of the plant lineages. column}

The relationships indicated by the branching pattern of the phylogenetic tree shown on the right reflect the current character states and the evolutionary history of these groups of plants. The base of each of the plant lineages is defined by a significant adaptation to life on land (*e.g.*, the development of vascular tissue, production of seeds, and flowering).

As mentioned earlier, there are many more specialized adaptations to the terrestrial environment found among modern plants; however, these adaptations are found in only a small group of plants. The major adaptations that define each lineage are characteristic of hundreds and thousands of species of plants. The ancestral forms of these plants and those in which the adaptive features first evolved are no longer living, but their remains are present in the fossil record and provide a basis for dating the origin of each lineage. Continuous adaptations to an ever-changing environment over the history of plant life has led to the diversity of species currently in existence.

Before we begin to discuss each of the plant lineages, it is important to understand the phylogenetic relationships among them. According to this figure, are nonvascular plants "older" than nonflowering seed plants? The correct way to interpret a phylogenetic tree is to read which groups are more closely related to one another, and which groups are more primitive or more highly diverged.

Nonvascular plants are not "older" than nonflowering seed plants, but they possess a greater number of primitive character states than do nonflowering seed plants. Also, the origin of the nonflowering seed plant lineage occurred later in time than the origin of nonvascular plants, but this does not mean that currently living nonvascular plants are any older than currently living nonflowering seed plants. Flowering seed plants are the most derived lineage of plants.

MAJOR TAXONOMIC GROUPS OF PLANTS

Now that you have a working knowledge of the major adaptations present throughout the plant kingdom and understand the evolutionary relationships among them, you will be introduced to the four lineages:

1. Nonvascular plants,
2. Seedless vascular plants
3. Nonflowering seed plants, and
4. Flowering seed plants.

Nonvascular plant characteristics will be examined in this tutorial in some detail. Upcoming tutorials will focus on the other groups. Always keep in mind how the adaptations found in each lineage of plants reflect the environmental conditions in which each lineage developed.

Nonvascular Plants

As the name of this group indicates, plants in this lineage do not have vascular tissue (or if present, it is very reduced). Because they lack substantial vasculature, plants in this lineage are generally small in size, lack significant structural support, grow close to the ground in moist areas, and lack significant water-conducting cells. Plants first evolved in environments that were transitional between the land and the sea, and although modern nonvascular plants are dependent on water to complete their life cycles, they are able to withstand long periods of desiccation. Nonvascular plants include mosses, liverworts, and hornworts.

Seedless Vascular Plants

Seedless vascular plants have a waxy cuticle, stomata, and well-developed vascular tissue. Their vasculature allows them to grow to larger sizes than the nonvascular plants, but they still generally occupy moist habitats. This lineage is more highly derived from the common ancestor of all plants than are the nonvascular plants, however, they do not produce seeds. Although the developing diploid embryo is dependent on the haploid gametophyte for survival (like mosses), the diploid sporophyte is more conspicuous and is the prominent generation of seedless vascular plants. Phylogenetically, seedless vascular plants are basal to the seed plants

Vascular Plants With Seeds

Vascular plants with seeds belong to one of two groups: those with flowers, and those without flowers. Those without flowers are also known as gymnosperms, which means "naked seed" and refers to the lack of flowers and fruits in all members of this lineage (as compared to the more highly derived lineage with flowers). The ancestor of modern nonflowering seed plants evolved once plants were already well established on land. Adaptations of a well-developed vasculature and seeds indicate a strictly land-based existence. With the production of seeds, the gametophyte generation is highly reduced in this lineage and the sporophyte generation is most prominent. Nonflowering seed plants include conifers (*e.g.*, pine, hemlock, spruce, and fir trees) and cycads.

Flowering Vascular Plants With Seeds

Flowering vascular plants are also known as angiosperms. Although this group of plants evolved more recently than nonvascular plants, seedless vascular plants and nonflowering seed plants, it includes the greatest number of species currently in existence. The great success of this group is due to their highly evolved and specialized methods for gamete dispersal (many species have insect or other animal pollinators) and seed dispersal (various types of fruits aid in the dispersal and successful germination of their seeds). The adaptations found in this taxonomic group are linked to the great diversity of animal life existing in the terrestrial environment. All of the agricultural crops we depend on for food, the fibreous plants we depend on for clothing, and the plants we grow to beautify our surroundings are from this lineage.

Nonvascular Seedless Plants

We will discuss the various features of nonvascular plants, using mosses as an example. As we review the general characteristics of this group, remember, the liverworts and hornworts also belong to this group

Morphology

Of all the plant lineages, nonvascular plants are the most basal group. This means that throughout the millions of years of plant evolution, this group has retained more primitive characteristics than any of the other plant lineages. They are less derived than seedless vascular plants and seed plants, but this group of plants is highly successful in the environments they inhabit.

As one walks through a wooded area, they are highly likely to find mosses growing on rocks, rotting wood, trees, or on the ground. Nonvascular plants are generally small and do not extend much more than a few inches above the surface they are growing on. Their appearance can best be described as a "carpet of green." The plant body that is most obvious is actually the gametophyte generation, which is haploid.

Nonvascular plants typically grow in moist environments. Their lack of vascular tissue requires them to maintain close contact with water to prevent desiccation. They do not have true roots, true stems, or true leaves (which are distinguished by the organization of vascular tissue). Rhizoids are the root-like structures that function to anchor them to the surface they are growing on, however, they are not capable of water uptake. Water is absorbed throughout the "leafy" plant body of the gametophyte. They also require a moist environment for successful fertilization. They do not produce pollen grains, hence this group of plants has retained the primitive condition of a flagellated sperm. The male gametes are motile in water and must be released into a moist environment so that the sperm can swim to the female gametangium (where the egg cells are located).

MOSS LIFE CYCLE

Alternation of generations is an important concept in the study of plant evolution. During the life cycle of plants, generations alternate between the gametophyte (which produces gametes) and the sporophyte (which produces spores). As mentioned above, the most conspicuous (or prominent) form of all nonvascular plants is the haploid gametophyte generation. To better understand alternation of generations in nonvascular plants, study this figure on the right. It depicts the life cycle of a moss and helps to distinguish the haploid and diploid stages.

Note the prominent form of the moss, the gametophyte, which is haploid (1n). This is the plant body that is most often observed. In the figure there are separate male and female gametophytes; however, the gametophyte can also be bisexual (male and female gametangia are located on the same plant body). In step 1, the gametophyte is the generation that produces gametes; sperm are produced in the male gametangium, the antheridium (plural, antheridia), and eggs are produced in the female gametangium, the archegonium (plural, archegonia). In step 2, the motile sperm has reached the egg, which is retained in the archegonium and fertilization takes place. (Remember, water is required for fertilization because the flagellated sperm must swim to the egg.) In step 3, the diploid (2n) zygote undergoes mitosis and begins to develop into the embryo (also 2n). In step 4, the embryo matures into the sporophyte, the diploid (2n) plant body. The sporophyte is the small, brown, stalked structure that one sometimes sees held above the main body of the moss. In step 5, meiosis takes place in the sporangium of the mature sporophyte and haploid spores are produced. In steps 6 and 7, the haploid spores are dispersed and each spore undergoes mitotic cell division to create a haploid multicellular gametophyte. The prominent haploid gametophyte is then ready to produce gametes (back to step 1).

An important feature of the moss life cycle is that the developing embryo is retained on the gametophyte plant body. This is an adaptation to the terrestrial environment because the embryo is protected from desiccation throughout its development into the sporophyte. (Remember the description of plants as embryophytes?) If one thinks about haploid and diploid stages in terms of the animal life cycle, it will be difficult to make sense of the plant life cycle. As noted above, the plant life cycle includes alternation of generations, with a multicellular haploid stage. Review again, step 5 of the life cycle (where meiosis takes place). Note that meiosis does not occur again when gametes are produced. Once you recognize these differences, you should begin to feel more comfortable thinking about the plant life cycle.

The diversity of plants existing today is the result of 450-700 million years of evolution and adaptation to the terrestrial environment. The common ancestor of all plants is thought to be very similar to species in the group of green algae known as the charophytes. Charophytes are similar to modern plants. Both have cellulosic cell walls, cell plates during cytokinesis, carbon storage in the form of starch, possession of chlorophyll b as an accessory pigment, and similar RNA and DNA sequences for particular genes. Charophytes are aquatic organisms, and it is highly likely that the earliest plants occupied transitional environments between the sea and the land. The transition to the terrestrial environment was advantageous for plants because there was direct access to sunlight and little to no herbivore activity. Early plants were ill-equipped for life out of the water, and desiccation was a major challenge to a land-based existence.

Adaptations to the terrestrial environment enabled generation after generation of plants to successfully exist out of the water. The waxy cuticle and stomata were effective in reducing water loss and preventing desiccation. Vascular tissue further reduced the problem of desiccation because it allowed transport of water and nutrients throughout the plant. Upright growth for improved access to sunlight was also an advantage conferred by vascular tissue because it also functions in internal support of the plant body. Protection of gametes and developing embryos was accomplished by evolution of the jacketed gametangia, and later, the evolution of seeds. More recently in plant history, adaptive features have been influenced by other organisms in the terrestrial environment; some plants produce specialized flower structures and fruits that attract insects and other animals that aid in pollination and seed dispersal.

All of the plants that are currently in existence are highly evolved, however, different taxonomic groups are defined based on the adaptive features that have or have not evolved. The most basal group is the nonvascular plants. They have retained many of the primitive characteristics that are also found in charophytes. Seedless vascular plants are more derived than nonvascular plants and are defined by their lack of seed production and presence of vascular tissue. The more derived lineages, nonflowering seed plants and flowering seed plants, both produce seeds, but only the flowering seed plants produce flowers and fruits.

The nonvascular plants (including mosses, liverworts and hornworts) are highly successful and can be found the world over. They are resistant to desiccation, but prefer a moist environment due to their lack of vascular tissue and motile gametes. Nonvascular plants, like other plants, are embryophytes, and their life cycles are based on alternation of generations. The prominent generation of nonvascular plants is the multicellular haploid gametophyte. The diploid sporophyte generation is completely dependent on the gametophyte for its survival. In the more derived plant lineages, the gametophyte is greatly reduced. Life cycles and the major characteristics of the seedless vascular plants, nonflowering seed plants, and flowering seed plants will be discussed in future tutorials for comparison with the more primitive nonvascular plants.

PLANT STRESS SYMPTOMATOLOGY

Biological research is a practice of conducting experiments wherein a single component is altered. Any changes in growth, for example, are, ipso facto, due to the one factor that was altered. Unfortunately, sometimes multiple uncontrolled factors are changed without recognition by the researcher. This can lead to confusion, which leads to much research, discussion, and dissension. The attached reports are an attempt to explain a presumed pesticide problem. Without access to the plant species originally exposed to deleterious conditions, we chose a sorghum cultivar [Sorghum bicolor (L.) Moench. cv GP-10] that experience has shown to be responsive to every stress we have utilized previously. By varying the culture medium (± organic matter), temperature, and fertilizer, it has been shown that the fungicide is relatively nontoxic even when applied at 5× registered application rates.

But the type of mineral nutrient fertilizer was determinative. The plant responses were identical to the symptomatology of plant growth in acid soils. These symptoms were totally reversed by the addition of magnesium (Mg^{2+}) to the culture medium. This reversal is a major diagnostic symptom for acid soils. Which factor was determinative? H^+ or pesticide? Excess H^+ in the rooting media (pH d"4.3) induces an acid-soil stress, with decreased magnesium and increased manganese and aluminum availability. The aluminum is toxic at virtually any soil pH. But, the quantity of aluminum ($Al3^+$) in the soil is extremely low at pH e"5.0.

Additionally, when fertilizers containing ammonium (NH^+) are utilized, the NH^+ is exchanged through the root plasma membrane for H^+. This exchange results in an acid soil. Thus, the cataloging of plant symptoms to a supposed pesticide influence [stubby (3-in.) black roots, chlorotic leaves with necrotic spots] must include the responses to changed cultural conditions. Response to other stress-produced symptoms are often indistinguishable. And in this case, acid soil–induced symptomatology was determinative.

TEMPERATURE AND FERTILIZATION INFLUENCE ON SORGHUM BICOLOR RESPONSE TO BENLATE DF AND WP

Benomyl[(methyl-1-butylcarbamoyl)-2-benzimidazolecarbamate]—or Benlate— is a systemic, soil-applied fungicide that has been used extensively in the greenhouse, container-grown, ornamental horticulture industry. Recently, extensive losses to that greenhouse, container-grown, ornamental horticulture industry have occurred, which have been putatively explained as being due to contamination of Benlate DF (dry flowable) with a herbicide, plant-growth regulator, or other foreign substance(s), or the Benlate DF itself. After extensive experimentation, the producers of Benlate DF stipulated that (a) they did not know what had caused the problem and (b) the problem was not due to contaminants in Benlate DF. Additionally, the symptoms of the damaged plants (i.e., chlorotic to necrotic foliage and shortened, black roots) could not be reproduced by Benlate applications in the same cultivars and in greenhouses in which the original problem developed.

These symptoms were present in isolated greenhouses and were not generally prevalent throughout the industry. Two methods of benomyl application were registered. One was a foliage spray of approximately 1 to 1 2 lb Benlate DF, which is a 50% benomyl a.i. material, in 200 to 500 gal water per acre. The second technique for use in ornamental container-grown crops in greenhouses was a soil drench at 1 lb Benlate DF per 100 gal water applied as 1 to 2 pints/ft^2. The latter application technique utilizes a 600-mg L"1 benomyl a.i. solution at <"2 pt/ft2 which approximates 54.5 lb of benomyl a.i. per acre (A). Since the water solubility of benomyl is 3.8 mg/L and 1 mg/L applied to the soil at 40 gal/A is approximately equivalent to 1 lb/A in the top 3 in. of soil, a considerable surplus of benomyl would be applied in the 60 mg/L.

The benomyl T1/2 in water approximates 7 hr, so that a single drench application would result in undissolved benomyl in the container for over 56 hr. The undissolved benomyl would be absorbed to the potting mix or any other adsorbent material in the rooting container. The major benomyl degradation products are methyl-1H-benzimidazolecarbamate (MBC) + n-butyl isocyanate (BIC). The latter degrades to n-butylamine + CO_2 with a T1/2 of 7 min. Presumably, the growers would use a commercially available fertilizer (CF). Two major fertilizers were extant and labeled analyses indicated that they were virtually identical in chemical composition. Benlate DF is not registered for use on sorghum [Sorghum bicolor (L.) Moench.]. Sorghum [Sorghum bicolor (L.) Moench. cv GP-10] was chosen as an assay plant because it has been shown to respond readily to chemical or environmental stress. Additionally, sand culture was chosen to permit the deletion of any confounding factors due to benomyl adsorption to soil and/or other potting medium characteristics. Therefore, we evaluated a CF and Hoagland-and-Arnon complete mineral nutrient solution on GP-10 sorghum grown at 38 and 32æ% C as well as ± Benlate DF and Benlate WP (wettable powder).

Discussion

Sorghum responds readily to nutrient deficiencies. Plant growth under acid soil stress (pH d"4.5) has been studied extensively with sorghum.

Because CF (500 mg/L) supplies approximately one-half as much total N to the plants as is present in the H&A, a direct comparison of H&A (pH 5.3) and CF (1000 mg/L) (pH 3.5) shows that the CF is incomplete and does not permit plant growth at the same rate as does the H&A (pH 5.3). The differences due to pH in the CF (500 or 1000 mg/L) (pH 4.0 and 3.5, respectively) and H&A (pH 3.5) show that even under acid-soil–stress conditions the mineral ion incomplete CF does not permit optimum growth. The influence of acid soil stress is shown by the decreased shoot FW (mg/plant), root FW (mg/plant), and total plant FW (g/plant) in plants grown in H&A (pH 3.5) compared to plants grown in H&A (pH 5.3). The differences between plants grown with CF 500 and 1000 mg/L are, primarily, a total N supply response. Inadequate supply of Ca^{2+} and Mg^{2+} exacerbates the problem. CF (1000 mg/L) and H&A (pH 3.5) had equivalent N fertilization, yet growth in the H&A (pH 3.5) was significantly greater than with CF (1000 mg/L) in all growth parameters except root FW (mg/plant) and total plant FW (g/plant). Thus, two basic interacting parameters are demonstrated. These are (a) the supply of a complete mineral nutrient fertilization regime to the plants and (b) the pH of the solution applied. Both of these parameters have a long history of deleterious influences on plant growth. And these parameters are inextricably interactive. The differences in growth of sorghum exposed to H&A or CF is totally explicable on the basis of a combination of several factors: (a) low pH in CF, (b) low concentration of required mineral nutrients in the CF in comparison to H&A, (c) low Mg in the CF, (d) absence of Ca in the CF, and (e) the form of nitrogen applied in the CF.

In sorghum as in other plants, given equal water status, low mineral nutrition equals low growth. Calcium is not supplied by the CF and calcium has been shown to be requisite and to act as a cytosolic second messenger, so that deficiency or excess of Ca in the cytosol results in leaky plasma membranes that are visualized by black roots caused by the induction of polyphenol oxidase activity. Additionally, NH^{+} and 4 Mg^{2+} concentrations are highly correlated in sorghum grown under acid soil stress. Low Mg^{2+} fertility results in severe stress. Thus, these data demonstrate the influence of a multiple stress syndrome. If sufficient water is available, high temperature induces a high evapotranspiration. When the stoma were induced to open by one herbicide, increased water utilization resulted.

This increased water uptake resulted in the absorption of residues of a second herbicide to the extent that the residues of the second herbicide became deleterious or lethal in the presence of the first herbicide, but those residues of the second herbicide were not deleterious when the plants were not exposed to the first herbicide. Or, under high waterutilization conditions (i.e., high temperature) more of whatever was present in the rooting medium was absorbed by roots and translocated to the shoots in the evapotranspiration stream. Thus, at 38æ% C, Benlate DF influenced shoot length (cm), shoot FW (g/plant), and root FW (g/plant). But at 32æ% C, Benlate DF did not influence plant growth in any of the three plant growth measurements. Growth at 32æ% C was less than at 38æ% C. This is explicable as a response to total mineral nutrient supply differences at 38æ% and 32æ% C as influenced by total water evapotranspiration. This concept is corroborated by the greater growth of the untreated plants fertilized by H&A in comparison to those growth with CF.

Additionally, greater growth with H&A resulted in more root uptake of materials in the rooting medium and massively excess application rates of Benlate DF and WP induced decreased growth in all three growth parameters. Benomyl water solubility (3.8 mg/L) is low. The individual Benlate DF and WP applications utilized herein equaled 60 mg/pot. Benomyl degradation T1/2 is reported to be about 7 hr. Or, undegraded benomyl was present for at least 7

T1/2 , and those plants with a high evapotranspiration were constantly exposed to benomyl concentrations greater than the benomyl water solubility for >49 hr. Plants absorb benomyl. And those plants were subjected to nutrient imbalance when exposed to the CF. Therefore, root plasma membranes (PM) were exposed to conditions that resulted in leaky PM, which resulted in black roots that do not function selectively. Therefore, high temperature and fertility imbalances have been demonstrated to be a multistress syndrome where massively excessive applications of Benlate DF and WP can marginally influence plant growth.

INFLUENCE OF ADSORPTIVE SURFACE ON THE RESPONSE OF SORGHUM TO BENLATE DF AND BENLATE WP

The systemic, soil-applied fungicide benomyl (methyl-1-butylcarbamol)-2-benzimidazolecarbamate) has been utilized extensively in the greenhouse-lathhouse, container-grown, ornamental horticulture industry where losses have occurred which were postulated by the growers as being due to contamination in Benlate DF (dry flowable).

The producer of Benlate DF has been unable to document contamination of the Benlate DF by any herbicide, plant-growth regulator, or other substance. The response of plants to massively excessive rates of Benlate DF has been shown, in sand culture, to be influenced by the temperature at which the plants were grown and the fertilizer utilized. A Benlate DF drench application presents benomyl at concentrations which would require >56 hr to degrade. The previously presented data were from plants grown in sand culture without any source of adsorptive surface other than the plant roots. Therefore, the question of presence or absence of an adsorptive surface in the treated pots arose. Could an adsorptive surface prevent the development of deleterious conditions in the root zone? And how would changes in ambient temperature or fertilization influence the response of plants to excessive Benlate DF or WP?

Methods and Materials

Ten sorghum [Sorghum bicolor (L.) Moench. cv GP-10] seeds were planted 1 cm deep in "white quartz flintshot" sand. Plants were grown at 32æ% C. Five replications were utilized. Fertilization was by 100 mL per pot per week of Hoagland-and-Arnon (H&A) complete mineral nutrient solution or 100 mL per pot per week of 500 mg/L commercial fertilizer (CF). Daily water applications utilized deionized water. Benlate DF or WP was applied at 100 mL per pot per week of 600 mg benomyl a.i. (0, 1, 2, and 3 applications). In addition, a duplicate set of pots were utilized in which 3 cm of granular charcoal was added to the top of the plant containers. Plants were grown for 4 weeks and harvested for number of plants per pot, shoot length (cm), shoot fresh weight (FW) (g/plant), and root FW (g/plant).

Elemental contents were analyzed by is explicable on the basis of a removal by the charcoal (or other adsorptive surface) of immediate root exposure to some substance and the maintenance of conditions without acid soil stress in the root zone (pH e" 5.0). The influences of soil type on benomyl uptake have been known for at least two decades. Presence of MBC (the major benomyl degradation product) in leaves of elm seedlings, as amended by planting substrates, was sand > silt loam soil > silt loam + perlite, and peat. Peat moss added to sand reduced benomyl uptake and benomyl was adsorbed to soil but not sand. In soils fertilized with ammonium-nitrogen (NH+ "N), roots induce an 4 increased hydrogen (H^+) ion efflux with a resultant decrease in soil pH.

The interaction of Mg deficiency in the presence of low soil pH induced Al stress has been shown to be highly cultivar-dependent. At soil pH 4.8, Al decreased Mg absorption without major root damage, but the Al induced highly toxic to the roots and shoots. A second problem associated with acid soil stress is the excess Mn^{2+} availability. Manganese is a requisite ion used as a cofactor in gibberellic acid (GA) biosynthesis. Yet different sorghum cultivars respond totally differently to Mn^{2+} concentrations, and while one cultivar is highly susceptible at low Mn^{2+} concentration and does not grow or dies, another cultivar is almost totally resistant to a high Mn^{2+} concentration. Additionally, high Mn^{2+} concentrations at the root surface have been shown to induce high indoleacetic acid (IAA) oxidase activity, which induces massively decreased root growth and is reversed by the addition of exogenous IAA supply. Therefore, the induction of an acid soil stress by repeated applications of fertilizer (pH 4.0) must be considered as a seriously detrimental influence on plant growth.

The overall damage to container-grown plants in the presence of massively excessive rates of Benlate DF has been shown to be a multistress syndrome in which synergistic responses to high temperature, fertilizer imbalance, low pH, and composition of the potting root medium are present. Reduction of any stress: growth of plants at decreased temperatures (40æ% C), balanced fertilizer at neutral pH, type of fertilizers, or presence of a highly adsorptive potting medium results in a greatly diminished plant response to this multistress syndrome. Comparison of Benlate-untreated plants ± charcoal indicates the degree of response of plants to this highly deleterious multistress syndrome.

REVERSAL BY MAGNESIUM OF SUPPOSED BENLATE DF-INDUCED GROWTH RESPONSES

Benlate DF [dry flowable formulation of (methyl-1-butylcarbamoyl)-2-benzimidazole carbamate] has been putatively implicated in growth inhibitions in the container-grown, ornamental horticultural industry. Researchers have been unable to document this to be a response to any contaminant in the Benlate DF. Using a sorghum cultivar [Sorghum bicolor (L) Moench. cv GP-10] that is highly responsive to stress, plant growth was responsive to the type of fertilizer applied in sand culture, temperature, and presence of an adsorptive surface in the rooting medium (see Secs. I and II of this chapter). A commercial fertilizer (CF) commonly utilized in this industry has a pH 4.0 at 500 mg/L and pH 3.5 at 1000 mg/L; applications of fertilizer solution at this pH induces acid soil stress (3–15). Additionally, application of ammonium-nitrogen (NH^{+} "N) fertilizers 4 induced an excess hydrogen (H^{+}) ion efflux by the roots, resulting in a low soil pH.

Growth parameters and mineral element analyses showed inhibitions of shoot length (cm), root fresh weight (FW) (g/plant), and shoot FW (g/plant) when plants were fertilized with NH^{+} -based fertilizers that were highly correlated 4 with the quantity of aluminum (Al) (μg/g DW) in the foliage. Recently, Al toxicity was shown to be highly correlated to the type of N supplied in the fertilizer. In the presence of nitrate-nitrogen (NO″ "N), 3 Al slightly decreased root elongation; but, when NH^{+} "N was present, the highly 4 deleterious responses were correlated with magnesium (Mg^{2+}) deficiency and resulted in root impairment.

Sorghum cultivars varied in their responses to Al. Since the CF supplies a low concentration of Mg^{2+} and utilizes, partially, a NH+ form of N, it is possible that the addition of extra Mg^{2+} might reverse 4 these problems. B. Methods and Materials Ten sorghum (cv GP-10) seeds were planted 1 cm deep in "white quartz flintshot" sand contained in 10-oz nestable plastic cups (9-cm-diam top, 13 cm deep). The pots were treated with 100 mL/pot Benlate DF (600 mg/L) weekly.

Weekly commercial fertilizer applications (500 mg/L) of 100 mL/pot were made. Water status was maintained at field capacity daily using deionized water. Magnesium sulfate (100 mL of 0, 10, 20, 40, 80, 160, or 320 mg/L) was added weekly. After 4 weeks of growth at 32æ% C, plants were harvested for root fresh weight (FW) (g/plant), shoot length (cm), and shoot FW (g/plant). Mineral contents were analyzed by published procedures utilizing perchloric acid digestion and atomic absorption spectrometry. Five replications were utilized and data were subjected to analysis of variance on a randomized complete block design. Means were separated by standard errors. C. Results Addition of MgSO4 (20 mg/L) induced significantly increased growth of plants exposed to excessive Benlate DF to growth levels equivalent to the untreated control pots. Addition of MgSO4 >20 mg/L induced progressively decreased growth. Root mineral ion content increased (i.e., S, P, Mn, Mg, and Cu) as the concentration of Mg mg/L increased when Benlate DF was absent. In the presence of excessive rates of Benlate DF, S, Fe, and Mg mineral ion contents increased as Mg fertilization increased. In shoots, Mg induced significantly increased mineral ion contents (± Benlate DF in S, P, Zn, Mn, Fe, Mg, Al, and Cu). Calcium (Ca) content decreased (± DF). D. Discussion Growth at 32æ% C without $MgSO_4$ and in the presence of Benlate DF was equivalent to similar treatments published previously. Influence of excessive application rates of Benlate DF in the presence of an acid soil stress–inducing incomplete mineral ion fertilization regime is shown by the decreased root FW (g/plant), shoot length (cm), and shoot FW (g/plant). Reversal of the postulated Benlate DF influence by the addition of 20 mL/L indicates an influence of the fungicide on either (a) ion uptake by roots, (b) modification of the low CF Mg^{2+} content to a more balanced fertilizer ratio, or (c) deactivation of the NH^{+} influence on acid soil stress. Addition of $MgSO_4$ to the soil solution altered the root ion content. This is in accordance with previously published data showing that roots absorb whatever is available in the soil solution. But variations occur. Calcium contents (± DF) decreased. Therefore, the addition of $MgSO_4$ (± Benlate DF) decreased Ca uptake. Since (a) Ca concentration in the CF was very low initially, (b) Ca concentration plays an important metabolic role as a cytosolic secondary messenger with normal concentrations near 10"6 μM on a DW basis, and (c) the Ca concentrations are a bit high so that internal metabolism would be disrupted, a decrease in Ca content would be expected to be beneficial.

Similar responses were observed in shoots except that Al contents were significantly increased as Mg concentration increased and ± Benlate DF did not alter this response. These data, then, demonstrate a growth-inhibitory response of plants to a CF that was reversed by the addition of 20 mg/L $MgSO_4$. This is indicative of mineral fertilizer imbalance as well as the imposition of acid soil stress onto the plants. Aluminum hexahydrate ($Al[OH]^{3+}$ hereafter called Al^{3+}) solubility is very 6 low at cytosolic pH (i.e., <"pH 6.0). But Al^{3+} attaches to enzymes that normally utilize Mg^{2+} as a cofactor and the Al^{3+} dissociates from those enzymes so slowly that 1 μM Al^{3+} effectively competes for action sites with value is the average of five replications at 4 weeks after planting and growth at 32æ% C. b +, Benlate DF treatment weekly; ", 0 Benlate DF. c Values within an element followed by the same letter are not significantly different as determined by the mean standard errors.

10 mM $Mg2^{+}$. These include the energy producing systems (i.e., MgATPase) as well as sterol synthesis and other enzyme systems utilize Mg^{2+} as a cofactor. Sterols are requisite for membrane function and membranes become leaky when the sterol quantity is deficient. Thus, Al^{3+} produces deleterious results with Mg^{2+} -containing enzymes and/or any oxygen rich (i.e., PO_4) containing component. Al^{3+} solubility is increased very markedly in soil solutions pH d"5.0.

Therefore, application of fertilizers at pH d"5.0 is equivalent to the application of an extremely toxic Al3+ solution. Recently, acid soils (i.e., pH <4.5) have been shown to develop when NH^{+4} is used as a N-fertilizer. This results in Al^{3+} toxicity, which induces Mg^{2+} deficiency. The CF utilized herein contains 3.96% NH^{+} "N, 5.61% NO" "N, and 10.43% urea-N. The NH^{+} "N, per se, influences soil pH and 3 4 induces $Al3^{+}$ toxicity and Mg^{2+} deficiency. The urea degrades (1 urea '! 2 NH^{+} + CO_2) and further exacerbates the acid soil problem. Additionally, urea, per se, is tolerated by plant leaves at <5 to 15 lb urea/100 gal water. Application of the CF to foliage at 1000 mg/L water was equivalent to <"0.83 lb urea/100 gal water.

But growers often utilize much higher fertilizer rates, and this may induce deleterious results on the foliage due to the urea before it decomposes to NH+ "N and induces acid soil stress problems. Thus, the deleterious responses of plants postulated to implicate Benlate DF have been shown to be a multistress syndrome which includes (a) high temperature, (b) low adsorptive surface within the treated root region, (c) imbalanced mineral nutrition (herein), and (d) acid soil stress. Since (a) cytosolic Ca^{2+} concentration is tightly controlled, (b) Mg^{2+} is requisite for chlorophyll and sterol synthesis, (c) Mn^{2+} is requisite for carotenoid and gibberellin (GA) synthesis, and (d) Zn^{+} is requisite to indoleacetic acid (IAA) synthesis, the data contained herein explain the postulated Benlate DF influence as a multistress syndrome that can be alleviated by removal of any of the individual stresses, most notably Mg^{2+} deficiency. It is still possible that Benlate DF may influence mineral ion uptake. If so, this factor might further confound the condition. But the chloroticnecrotic leaves, stunting, curled leaves, and blackened roots are all symptomatic of plant growth under acid soil stress plus imbalanced fertilizer application. And addition of $MgSO_4$ (20 mg/L) reversed the syndrome.

INFLUENCE OF METHYL-BENZIMIDAZOL-CARBAMATE (MBC), BENOMYL, AND BENLATE DF FORMULATE ON PLANT GROWTH

Benomyl ([methyl-1-butylcarbamoyl]-2-benzimidazole-carbamate) is a systemic fungicide that degrades, T1/2 = 7 hr, to methyl-1H-benzimidazolecarbamate (MBC). However, benomyl water solubility is only 3.8 μg/L, so that excessive applications of benomyl could result in exposure to benomyl per se for extended periods of time. Benlate DF (dry flowable) is a 50% a.i. formulation of benomyl and was shown to be an insignificant factor in deleterious plant responses to a multistress syndrome that included the influence to high temperature, imbalanced fertilizers including absence of calcium and deficient levels of magnesium, and lack of adsorbent material in the rooting medium. The Benlate DF factor was reversed by the addition of 20 mg Mg+ /L into the fertilizer. Since Benlate DF is composed of equal portions of benomyl and a complex formulate, either portion might be the cause of the minor growth responses documented to occur when massively excess applications of Benlate DF were applied. Thus, a question remaining was the response of plants to the long-lived degradation product (MBC) of benomyl, benomyl per se, and the Benlate DF Formulate.

Methods and Materials

1. MBC Concentrations

Ten Sorghum bicolor (L.) Moench. cv GP-10 seeds were planted 1 cm deep in "white quartz flintshot" sand contained in 10 oz nestable plastic cups (9-cm diam top, 13 cm deep), and the plants were grown for 4 weeks at 32æ% C. Weekly fertilization was 100 mL of Hoagland-and-Arnon complete mineral nutrient solution (H&A). Initial chemical treatments were MBC (0, 4.75, 9.5, 19.0, and 38.0 mg/L). At 4 weeks after planting (WAP), the plants were harvested for root fresh weight (FW) (g/plant), shoot length (cm), and shoot FW (g/plant). Five replications were utilized. Data were subjected to analysis of variance on a randomized complete block design. Means were separated by standard errors.

2. Benomyl Concentrations

In sand culture at 32æ% C (see above) sorghum (GP-10) was grown for 4 weeks with weekly applications of H&A (100 mL/pot/week) + initial applications of benomyl (0, 4.5, 9, 18, 36, or 72 mg/L). Five replications were utilized and data were subjected to statistical analysis as described above.

3. Formulate Concentration

As in benomyl concentration study.

C. Results

1. MBC Concentrations: Root FW (g/plant) was not significantly decreased at any level of MBC concentration. Root FW was significantly increased at 38 mg/L MBC. Shoot length (cm) was not significantly influenced by MBC. Shoot FW (g/plant) was significantly increased by all MBC treatments.
2. Benomyl Concentrations: Massively excessive benomyl concentrations (72 mg/L) decreased shoot length (cm) by 15%, shoot fresh weight (g/plant) by 22%, and root fresh weight (g/plant) by 20%.
3. Formulate Concentrations: Massively excessive applications (72 mg/L) of the formulate in Benlate DF did not induce statistically significant changes in shoot length (cm) or root evaluation of the active ingredient, benomyl, and the Benlate DF Formulate and plant growth did not reveal

any consistent deleterious responses except for a 15% decrease in shoot length in the presence of 72 mg/L benomyl and a 19% decrease in shoot FW (g/plant) at 72 mg/L Formulate. These decreases in plant growth are relatively minor in comparison to the major differences in growth that occurred between complete and incomplete mineral fertilizers or when organic adsorptive material was present in the rooting medium. Thus, in the multistress syndrome symptoms associated with the putative "Benlate DF problem," the causative factors have been shown to be (a) application of nutritionally imbalanced fertilizers, (b) low pH, (c) pots without sufficient potting mix adsorptive surfaces, and (d) high temperature. Excessive applications of Benlate DF can be marginally deleterious in the absence of any potting mix adsorptive surface. But, this limited problem is more a response to temperature, adsorptive surface, and pH than to the fungicide. The major benomyl degradation product, MBC, did not induce consistent plant growth reductions.

Decreased growth induced by Benlate DF was observed at >35.84 kg/ha (32 lb/A) or the equivalent of 20× the legally registered Benlate DF application rate. Influence of Benlate DF on plant growth. In plants fertilized with CF, shoot length (cm), shoot FW (g/plant), and root FW (g/plant) were increased by Benlate DF (2.24 kg/ha) (2 lb/A). Addition of Mg^{2+} to CF did not further increase growth (Figs. 10 to 12) over that shown in the presence of Benlate DF (2.24 kg/ha) (2 lb/A). The influence of Mg^{2+} availability in the fertilizer. There was a significant linear increase of shoot length with Mg^{2+} application. The CF pH was <3.5 and is composed of NH^+ "N (3.96%) and urea 4 (10.43%). Urea decomposes to 2 NH^+ + CO_2.

Therefore, the CF created a 4 severe acid-soil-stress syndrome around the roots. This was alleviated by the addition of Mg^{2+} or the addition of Benlate DF (<17.92 kg/ha) (16 lb/A). These Benlate DF–induced growth increases were in sterile sand (initially) or in sufficient Benlate DF to prevent the establishment of pathogens. Therefore, there is some totally unexplained response of the plants to Benlate DF that strongly resembles an influence on mineral nutrient uptake. Most likely candidates to explain this response are either Ca^{2+}, Mg^{2+}, or an interaction between the two mineral elements. Magnesium (1 mM) induced a decreased 45 Ca^{2+} absorption by sorghum root tips (1 cm) while NH^+ induced 4 an increased 45 Ca^{2+} absorption.

Similarly, Benlate DF (2 ppmw) induced a decreased Ca^{2+} absorption by sorghum root tips (1 cm) (unpublished data). Since Ca2+ acts as a second messenger in controlling cytoplasmic metabolism, any modification of Ca^{2+} influx through the root plasma membrane (PM) would create problems to the root. Roots normally absorb far more Ca^{2+} than is requisite, and Ca^{2+} efflux through the PM is effected by the PM Ca^{2+} ATPases. Alteration of that system would result in excess Ca^{2+} in the roots and induce major metabolic problems.

Roots of plants grown in CF (0 Benlate DF) were approximately 4 cm long (severely stunted) and dark brown. Shoots from those plants were stunted, chlorotic, and necrotic. Addition of Mg^{2+} resulted in white healthy roots and nonchlorotic shoots. But these CF + Mg^{2+} (0 Benlate DF) plants were intermediate to the plants treated with H&A (0 Benlate) whose roots were white and had grown to the bottom of the pot and then formed a mat. Since (a) low pH and Al^{3+} inhibit root elongation and Ca^{2+} absorption, (b) the putative Benlate DF damage morphological symptoms have been duplicated in cultures without Benlate DF, (c) the CF produces acid soil stress problems, (d) these problems are reversed by Mg^{2+} which fits the acid-soil-stress syndrome, and (e) Benlate DF (1.12–17.92 kg/ha) (lb/A) has been shown to partially reverse the symptoms of the acid soil stress syndrome, the putative damage by Benlate DF has been completely explained by an acid soil stress imposed on the plants by the utilization of a mineral ion incomplete fertilizer which imposes a deleterious pH (<4.0) onto the plants.

This situation is further exacerbated by the presence of NH^+ and urea in the CF 4 which induces even lower pH in the soil with associated increased acid soil stress problems. Finally, what is the influence of quantity of CF applied to plants? Using H&A as a standard, CF at 1000, 2000, 3000, and 4000 mg/L were planted (10 seeds/pot) (five replications). After 3 weeks, numbers of emerged plants were greatest in the H&A and decreased in CF at any level. Numbers of emerged plants remaining alive after 3 weeks was substantially decreased by CF and was essentially zero (0) at CF >2000 mg/L. Shoot length was essentially a pattern of growth. In H&A complete mineral nutrient solution, the plants thrived. In CF 1000 mg/L, the plants were chlorotic and necrotic and did not thrive. At CF >2000 mg/L, the plants were chlorotic and necrotic and did not thrive. At CF >2000 mg/L, the plants (when alive) were at the size that could be supported by the nutrients in the seed. Then they died.

This is a typical pattern of acid soil stress. GP-10 is a sorghum selection that has high tolerance to acid soil stress and grows fairly well at soil pH >4.2. Below that soil pH, the GP-10 fails to thrive. In other studies with the sorghum cultivar TAM428, at pH <4.8 this cultivar germinates and grows to about 7 cm, then becomes static, and subsequently dies. This pattern has been shown to be a response to another characteristic of acid soil stress [i.e., excess manganese (Mn^{2+})], in that isoprenoid biosynthesis is inhibited by excess Mn^{2+} in TAM but not in cultivars tolerant to acid soil stress. Since acid soils present excess H^+, Mn^{2+} , and Al^{3+} to plants, complete isolation of causes of deleterious plant responses to the syndrome of acid soil stress cannot be absolutely certain. But in the responses of GP-10 sorghum to CF and/or Benlate DF, two major factors are evident. First, the responses of these plants were very typical of responses to $Al3^+$ toxicity–induced Mg^{2+} deficiencies and were reversed by the addition of Mg^{2+}. Second, with Benlate DF <10×, the legal registered application rate was not deleterious to plant growth and the responses to CF without added Mg^{2+} were reversed.

INFLUENCE OF BENOMYL, BENLATE DF, AND BENLATE WP ON THE CALCIUM (45 CA^{2+}) UPTAKE BY ROOTS OF SORGHUM AND MAIZE SEEDLINGS

Benomyl [(methyl-1 butylcarbamoyl)-2-benzimidazolecarbamate] is a systemic fungicide that has been reported to induce various plant-growth regulatory responses. The water solubility of benomyl is approximately 3.8 mg/L at 20æ% C. Yet, a drench application utilizes 2 pt/ft2 of a 1 lb/100 gal solution. Since 1 lb = 453.6 g, 1 gal = 3.785 L; 1 qt = 946.25 mL: 1 gal 453.6 g 1 lb Benlate DF 0.5 a.i. benomyl × × × 100 gal H2 O 1 Benlate 3.7851 L lb = 599.2 mg benomyl L H2O

If 2 pt are applied per square foot, 0.94625 L lb 0.5992 g 1 qt 43560 ft 2 × 2× × × L acre qt 453.6 g ft 54.46 lb benomyl acre The original 1 lb/100 gal water is 600 mg/L benomyl. Obviously, this concentration of benomyl far exceeds the water solubility of benomyl. Thus, an undissolved reservoir of benomyl is present in the system. Since benomyl T1/2 in water exceeds 7 hr, a drench application results in the adsorption of benomyl to any surface available. As the benomyl in the soil solution is absorbed into the plant or degraded, the benomyl concentration will be maintained at saturation by benomyl desorption from the potting media and/or root surface into the soil solution and become available to the plant. Thus, a single benomyl drench application of 600 mg/L would be sufficient to maintain a constant benomyl-saturated soil solution for >6 days.

Benomyl degrades to NBC + BIC (methyl-2-benzimidazolecarbamate + n-butyl isocyanate). The latter degradation product further degrades to nbutylamine and carbon dioxide with a T1/2 of 7 min. But, BIC is an alkyl isocyanate and n-alkyl isocyanates are powerful active-site directors of serine proteases (i.e., trypsin and chymotrypsin).

Thus BIC will react instantaneously and irreversibly with the -OH group of serine, or fatty alcohol. Serine and threonine are requisite protein components (i.e., DNA, RNA, enzymes), and BIC has been reported to be a strong cutinase inhibitor, which was suggested as a possible protective mode of action of the fungicide benomyl because fungi that have a cutinase and penetrate into the host through the cuticle had a decreased infestation in benomyl-treated leaves.

Phosphatidylserine (PS) is a requisite membrane lipid, has a serine functional group, and is a constituent with a negative charge. Neutralization of the membrane negative charge by the positive charges on ruthenium red resulted in decreased 45 Ca^{2+} absorption by sorghum roots, which was explicable as an inhibition of H^+ -ATPase, Ca^{2+} -ATPase, and cation channels. Therefore, because BIC binds to serine and has a strong cationic charge, benomyl (and/or degradation products) might modify Ca^{2+} uptake by roots.

Calcium is a major metabolic "second messenger" in plants whose cytosolic concentration is very closely regulated. Modification of Ca^{2+} influx or efflux could have major implications to plant growth. Therefore, the influence of benomyl, two formulated benomyl products (i.e., DF and WP formulations), and the combined formulate for Benlate DF were evaluated for their influence on root absorption of 45 Ca^{2+} in sorghum and maize. B. Methods and Materials Untreated sorghum (GP-10, Funk G522DR) or maize (B73 × LH132) seeds (25/pot) were planted in sterile white quartz flintshot sand in 8 × 8 × 8 cm pots and watered with deionized water.

After 3 or 4 days, when the roots had elongated to about 6 cm, plants were washed from the sand. Ten seedlings were taped to a 1.25-cm diameter rigid plastic pipe and 1-cm root tips were immersed in 1N ammonium chloride (NH_4Cl) for 5 min to dissolve the root cap mucigel. The plants were transferred to 10 × 10 cm polyethylene refrigerator cartons containing 100 mL of 0.01M sodium acetate (NaAc) (pH 5.5) plus 0.1 μCi 45 Ca2+ (11.16 mCi/mg $Ca2^+$) plus the fungicide treatments (benomyl, inert formulation of Benlate DF, Benlate DF, or Benlate WP).

After 1 hr, the roots were removed from the treatment solution, the 1-cm tips were excised and washed with 0.01M ethylenediaminetetracetic acid (EDTA) and inserted into scintillation vials. After the addition of scintillation fluid (Scintiverse BD, Fisher Chemical Co., Pittsburgh, PA), the vials were placed in the dark (>4 hr) to allow fluorescence to decay, and the Ca^{2+} was assayed by liquid scintillation spectrometer (Beckman LS 5801) for 20 min or 1% accuracy.

Background counts/min (CPM) were subtracted from each assay and actual disintegrations/min (DPM) were calculated by dividing DPM by the LS counter efficiency. Because it is impossible to deliver exactly the same Ca^{2+} DPM in the treatment solutions, a 1-mL aliquot was taken of each treatment solution, and the DPM in the roots was adjusted to the equivalent of a 106 DPM exposure. Data from each set of treatments were subjected to analysis of variance and standard errors were calculated.

Fungicides and Benlate DF formulate concentrations were 0, 0.2, 2, 20, or 200 mg/L. C. Results and Discussion Benomyl induced a slight, nonsignificant increase in 45 Ca^{2+} absorption at benomyl concentrations below the water-solubility level of 3.8 mg/L. At concentrations greater than its water solubility, benomyl induced slight but statistically significant decreased 45 Ca^{2+} absorption by root tips of both sorghum and maize.

Many organic pesticides are rather insoluble in water, but the delivery system of choice utilizes water as a diluent. Therefore, various surfactants are added to the mixture to hold the active compound dissolved or suspended in the diluent during application.

The complex Benlate DF formulate (2 and 20 mg/L) induced significantly decreased Ca^{2+} uptake in root tips of sorghum and maize. But at 200 mg/L formulate, 45 Ca^{2+} uptake was significantly increased in both sorghum cultivars. The treatment solutions contained <"2×106 DPM/mL. If these surfactants functioned by PM disruption, the roots would have contained 45 Ca^{2+} in concentrations equivalent to those of the treatment solution.

These root tips contained <1% of the 45 Ca^{2+} DPM of equivalent volume treatment solution (<"3000 DPM). Therefore, this response cannot be due to membrane disruption. Rather, these data may be explicable as a partial influence on Ca^{2+} efflux. Differential responses by sorghum root PM of sorghum cultivars have been reported previously.

In Funk G522DR, Benlate DF (0.2, 2, and 20 mg/L) induced nonsignificantly increased Ca^{2+} adsorption but in all three cultivars the highest concentration (200 mg/L Benlate DF) induced significant increased accumulations of Ca^{2+}. These accumulations are explicable as an influence of Benlate DF on the external surface of the PM, where Ca^{2+} -ATPase mediated Ca^{2+} efflux was decreased. Benlate WP (0.2, 2, and 20 mg/L) significantly inhibited 45 Ca2+ accumulation in sorghum root tips, but 200 mg/L Benlate WP induced significantly increased accumulations of Ca^{2+} in both sorghum cultivars and maize.

These differences in response between maize and sorghum are similar to genetically determined differences between sorghum cultivars reported previously. Membranes have different enzymes and capacities to move substances through the membrane. One type of H^+ -ATPase is prevalent on tonoplasts while a second type is prevalent on plasma membranes, but both types are present in both membranes. Movement of ions (Ca^{2+}) through the plasma membrane is determined by the quantity of enzymes (or channels) present, and this is genetically determined.

These data show two basically different responses. At concentrations less than the water solubility, benomyl does not influence Ca^{2+} absorption. Nonsolubilized benomyl is highly adsorptive, and the only surface in these high concentrations available for benomyl to become attached to was the root. Therefore, adsorbed benomyl apparently induced Ca^{2+} accumulation. These evaluations were conducted without any other adsorptive surface in the system.

5

Ecological Processes in Forest

Ecological interactions have critical importance in the maintenance of biodiversity and ecological functions such as productivity and turnover. Mutualistic interactions are extremely common and include interactions between all major organismal groups, they have been largely neglected in the ecological literature, with greater emphasis placed on competition and predation. Many interactions may be quite unspecific with a great degree of ecological redundancy, such that the loss of a single species member of a mutualism results in little change in the overall outcome of the interaction. The extent of redundancy and the resistance of ecological interactions to anthropogenic disturbances are poorly known, yet of critical importance to forest managers in determining extractive mechanisms and limits. Vertebrate-plant interactions should be of interest to both forest managers and conservation biologists owing to the roles of vertebrates in plant recruitment and in regulating forest structure and composition through pollination, seed dispersal, and seed predation and herbivory.

Pollination

Pollination by vertebrates is almost non-existent in northern temperate forests where most species are wind-pollinated. Indeed there is a trend of increasing wind pollination with increasing latitude. In tropical forests, high tree diversity and wide spacing between conspecifics limit the efficiency of wind pollination and tree species in lowland tropical forests are almost all pollinated by animals (including insects). To attract vertebrate pollinators plants need to produce nectar in quantities much greater than that required for insect pollination. The energy costs of nectar production to plants can therefore be considerable. Thus nectar produced by vertebrate-pollinated plants tends to be relatively dilute. Vertebrate-pollinated plants are therefore most abundant in wet tropical climates where water does not limit nectar production, and are rarely found in dry forest or savannah habitats. Among vertebrates, bats, birds and a few non-flying mammals are the only known pollinators; although they pollinate only a minority of plants, they remain crucial for the successful reproduction of many large forest trees and a much greater variety of forest understorey plants.

Well-documented cases of non-flying mammal pollination involve 59 mammal species distributed among 19 families and six orders. The marsupials of Australia (12 species) and primates of Madagascar (9 species) and South America (10 species) are the best-known examples. However, the importance to plants of non-flying mammals as pollinators is debatable, as many of these plants are often served by other vertebrate and insect pollinators. Only in Madagascar do non-flying mammals (lemurs) act as sole pollinators of the plants they visit, and the precipitous decline of some lemur species may cause an associated decline of the plants they pollinate (*e.g.* the traveller's tree *Ravenala madagascarien-sis* pollinated by the endangered black-and-white ruffed lemur). Selective exclusion experiments have demonstrated that marsupials are at least as effective as birds in pollinating *Banksia* in Australia and *Protea* spp. in South Africa; indeed, declining small-mammal activity at *Banksia* inflorescences due to habitat fragmentation resulted in a sharp decrease in seed set of *Banksia goodii.*

However, documented cases of reduced seed set due to declines in mammal pollinators are rare. In most cases, evidence for effective pollination by non-flying mammals is largely circumstantial and, while non-flying mammals may feed at flowers and occasionally pollinate them, this service must be balanced with the damage they cause.

Bats pollinate species belonging to several tropical plant families including Bombacaceae *(Pseudobombax)*, Mimosaceae *(Parkia)*, Passi-floraceae *(Passiflora)* and Caesalpiniaceae *(Bauhinia);* on oceanic islands, such as Samoa, the majority of the dominant canopy tree species may be pollinated by bats. A number of economically important tropical trees rely on bats for pollination, including durian, banana, neem and timber species of *Eucalyptus* and several species of palm. Although it is energetically expensive to produce bat-attracting flowers rich in nectar, plants benefit from extensive pollen transfer as bats forage over large areas. Habitat change, hunting and the introduction of exotic species is causing the decline of bats across the tropics and several species are threatened with extinction. This is of particular concern on oceanic islands, where alternative pollinators for endemic tree species are rare or absent.

In the Neo-tropics hummingbird pollination is widespread among several plant families, while old-world pollinators include a much greater variety of birds, primarily sunbirds but also leafbirds, lorikeets, white-eyes and honey-eaters. However, birds are rarely the exclusive pollinators of plants and their importance relative to insect pollinators is not well resolved. Declines in fruit set due to temporary absence of hummingbirds have been noted, even where other invertebrate pollinators were present, but obligate pollinator dependency by plants on hummingbirds or sun-birds has not been documented. Rather, these birds may be important as biological 'insurance' where temporal fluctuation of invertebrate pollinator populations may be severe.

Loss of vertebrate pollinators resulting from forest conversion or fragmentation is only likely to affect plant seed production if the plant-pollinator interaction is highly specialized. Most plants are pollinated by a suite of mainly general-ist pollinators and are unlikely to suffer a large decline with the loss of one or a few closely related pollinator species. Nevertheless, in tropical floras specialist interactions among animals and plants do exist. On the small isolated Caribbean island of Tobago the absence of hermit hummingbirds resulted in reduced seed production of *Mandevilla hirsuta* (Apocynaceae) compared with the neighbouring island of Trinidad where the birds were present. In contrast, there was no difference across islands in seed production of *Justica secunda* (Acanthaceae) that is pollinated by a more general array of hummingbirds. In fact most hummingbirds appear to be quite plastic in their habitat requirements and regularly use edges and move between primary and secondary habitats to take advantage of a wide variety of floral resources; there is also evidence that sunbirds, which in the Palaeotropics fill a similar ecological niche to hummingbirds, are more abundant at flowering trees in disturbed secondary forests.

However, predicting the impacts of habitat and landscape modification on plant-pollinator interactions is difficult as both the behaviour and abundance of pollinators may change as a result of changing resource distribution. Pollinators may also depend on resources that are far from the plants they pollinate. In peninsular Malaysia, for example, the fruit bat *Eonycteris spelea* is the exclusive pollinator of durian trees but feeds primarily in coastal mangroves. The bats visit, and pollinate, durian *en route* to the mangroves from their limestone-cave roosts. Destruction of either the caves or the mangroves could affect the bat population and hence the pollination of durian.

Seed Predation

Predation of seeds by animals has been proposed as a mechanism for the maintenance of the high tree species diversity in tropical forests. This theory suggests that density-dependent consumption of seeds by mammalian seed predators prevents domination of the vegetation by species that have competitively superior seeds or greatest seed production. Terborgh (1988) suggested that vertebrate seed predators selectively prey upon the largest tree seeds, and where carnivores are eliminated following perturbations forest composition might shift to smaller-seeded species. There is some evidence to support this prediction from forests in Panama and Mexico. In Panama, high densities of small mammals on Barro Colorado Island due to an absence of large predators is thought to be the cause of recruitment failure among the large canopy tree *Dipteryx panamensis* due to the seed predation pressure exerted by the small mammals.

Some studies show seed predation by vertebrates (most often rodents) to be higher in mature forest compared with early successional forest, while other studies found the opposite. Rodents tend to avoid large areas of open forest or pasture probably due to the lack of protective cover and the scarcity of food resources. However, seed predation intensity under different disturbance regimes varies greatly with the species of seed plant making it difficult to draw generalizations to guide forest restoration programmes.

However, where seed predator densities are high, commercially available low-value grains might be used to satiate the seed predators in order to minimize mortality of the desired species. Use of these methods should be based on a sound knowledge of the factors that limit the population dynamics of the predator species, otherwise the availability of superabundant food resources leads to rapid population growth and subsequent heavy seed mortality in later years.

Seed Dispersal

Seed dispersal has been favoured by evolution because it decreases the probability of seed predation, which is often disproportionately high close to parent trees, and increases the probability that seeds find a suitable establishment site. Thus seeds have become adapted for dispersal by a variety of vectors, the most common of which are wind and animals, and the role of animals in the dispersal of seed and fruit has received much attention in the biological literature. Seeds carried by animals often have edible appendages (*e.g. Acacia* spp., *Anacardium* spp.) or are enclosed within fleshy fruits that are consumed and the seeds ejected later. In some cases the seeds themselves are harvested but dropped, or stored and later forgotten or abandoned.

In Neo-tropical forests, 50-90 per cent of the canopy trees and nearly all shrubs and subcanopy trees bear fruit adapted for animal dispersal, while a smaller but still substantial proportion of species in Palaeotropical forests are also dispersed by animals (35-48 per cent and 70-80 per cent, respectively). Birds, bats and scatter-hoarding rodents are the major dispersers of tropical tree seeds, while other seed dispersers include primates, fish in Amazonian forest, tortoises, some herbivorous lizards and even a frog.

In temperate coniferous and deciduous forests, seeds may be more often dispersed by wind or by cache-hoarding mammals and birds. However, this dichotomy between temperate and tropical forest dispersal mechanisms has been challenged by Wheelwright (1988), who asserts that interactions between plants and their fruit-eating bird dispersers are as complex and ecologically important in temperate regions as they are in the tropics. Howe and Smallwood (1982) state that more than 60 per cent of temperate trees have animal-dispersed seeds and record a significant negative correlation between annual precipitation and the percentage of wind dispersal. Nevertheless, there are more species of fruit-eating birds in the tropics and they comprise a larger fraction of the avian biomass. Only in the tropics are there bird species that rely exclusively on a diet of fruit (*e.g.* fruit pigeons *Ptilinopus* spp. in Australia and *Treron* spp. In South-East Asia), and most birds with a predominantly fruit diet are tropical species.

Seed dispersal syndromes are thought to reflect coevolutionary trends between plants and vertebrate (bird and mammal) seed dispersers. Bird-dispersed fruit are small and red, black, blue or purple, are conspicuous by sight rather than smell, and persist on the tree until removed by a disperser. Mammal-dispersed fleshy fruits are large, green or brown, emit odours, and frequently abscise shortly after ripening. However, the existence of clearly defined seed dispersal syndromes has recently been questioned and consumption of a particular type of fruit by an animal does not imply that the fruit is adapted for dispersal by that animal. The emerging view is that most interactions between plants and avian seed dispersers, in both tropical and temperate regions, are generalist, opportunistic and largely inefficient (from the plant's perspective), and there are few examples of tightly coupled coevolved mutu-alistic interactions. One well-documented exception is the commercially important brazilnut *Bertholletia excelsa,* which is entirely dependent on agoutis to gnaw open the seed capsules and release the seeds.

Animal behaviour can be crucial to the success of plant dispersal and recruitment. Animal seed dispersers often place seeds in sites suitable for germination, and seeds of some species (*e.g.* oak) will not germinate unless they are buried. Burial further reduces the probability that the seeds will be found by seed predators. Bats may reduce the suitability of fruit to insect seed predator attack, leading to increased survival of seeds dropped at a bat roost.

Animal digging, burrowing and tunnelling (by armadillos, coatis, porcupines, pigs, gophers) can bury seeds or unearth buried seeds. At Mount St Helens, for example, the activity of surviving gophers in bringing soil and propagules to the surface of the sterile ash deposits facilitated plant establishment and the start of forest regeneration (Andersen and Mac-Mahon 1985). Secondary dispersal of wind-dispersed seeds of *Pinus jeffieyi, Pinus ponderosa* and *Pinus contorta* by chipmunks and other rodents in the Sierra

Nevada is instrumental in moving seeds up to 69 m away from the parent tree compared with only 12 m by wind dispersal alone. Mockingbirds, doves and land iguanas have been essential in facilitating regeneration of the tree *Bursera graveolans* (Burseraceae) on the Galapagos Islands after the elimination of introduced goats. The *Bursera* seeds fail to germinate directly beneath adult trees, and recovery of the population to levels prior to the introduction of goats is entirely dependent on the native seed dispersers. Vertebrate dispersal agents may further benefit plants by dispersing mycorrhizal fungal spores in addition to seeds, as in the Pacific North-west where squirrels disperse the obligate symbiotic mycorrhizal fungi of conifer seedlings.

Dependence on animals for seed dispersal exposes the plants to the risk of dispersal failure should seed vectors become rare or extinct. The population structure of the tambalocoque tree *Sideroxylon sessiliflorum* (Sapotaceaea) on Mauritius is thought to have been affected by the extinction of the dodo, which dispersed the seeds and whose elimination doomed the tree to extinction as one of the 'living dead'. The likely cause of the dramatic decline of colonization rates of many fleshy fruited species in the remnant rain forests of the Mascarene Archipelago, in which Mauritius is located, is thought to be due to the extinction of over 50 per cent of its land vertebrates in recent decades. Cox *et al.* (1991) describe preliminary observations of pollination and seed dispersal failure for several bat-pollinated and -dispersed plants on the island of Guam where bats have suffered severe declines in recent years. Indeed, Fujita and Tuttle (1991) note that at least 289 plant species (according to current published information) depend to varying degrees on large populations of flying foxes for their propagation, and the fact that flying foxes are increasingly threatened is a cause for broad concern.

Selective logging and fragmentation of forest habitats have a large impact on vertebrate abundance and behaviour, which in turn is likely to affect seed dispersal of many animal-dispersed tree species. Forget and Sabatier (1997) reported that large frugivores avoid recently created gaps, and many bird species do not move into central regions of large gaps.

However the responses of species to fragmentation can be highly variable and the impact on forest tree regeneration is often difficult to predict. Frugivorous birds may decline sharply after fragmentation leading to decreased seed dispersal, while small mammal populations remain stable or even increase in abundance. However, the behaviour of small mammals may alter as the landscape is transformed into a primary and secondary forest mosaic. Terrestrial mammals readily move between primary and secondary forests and may promote regeneration by dispersing primary forest tree seeds into degraded secondary forest, although seeds can also be transported in the opposite direction and alter the nature of primary forest succession.

Management of animal seed-dispersers may be necessary to accelerate regeneration of degraded areas and to promote the establishment of native plant species. Availability of hollows, snags, perches and nest boxes increases the abundance and diversity of birds and bats, thereby preserving dispersal functions and accelerating forest regeneration. Where vertebrates choose to sit while processing seeds is critical to the reproductive success of plants and appropriate provision of perches and nest boxes can encourage frugivorous birds to process (and defecate) consumed seeds in degraded sites. However, if tightly coupled mutualisms exist between a plant and animal, then specific management strategies may be required to ensure the continued existence of both.

Herbivory

Vertebrate herbivores are instrumental in determining the vegetational composition of forest systems. The role of the African elephant in maintaining the balance between savannah and woodland in Africa is well documented and the impact of grazing and browsing mammals on temperate forests has been reviewed by Gill (1992a,b). The loss of large herbivores from Europe in the Pleistocene is thought to have led to the transformation of short grasslands to less productive forests with concomitant extinctions of many small mammals dependent on the more nutrient-rich vegetation. More recently, the elimination of rabbits by the disease myxomatosis in Britain has resulted in many grassland areas reverting to scrub woodland.

Overgrazing by deer in European and North American woodlands causes a decline in native woodland species, facilitates the spread of invasive weeds, prevents regeneration of woody species and may result in local extirpation of herbaceous plants. Moderate grazing can lead to plant species replacements. In North America, preferential feeding of white-tailed deer on pine *Pinus strobus* results in its replacement by birch *Betula papyrifera*, which has a greater resistance to browsing.

Moderate or low levels of grazing can also result in greater vegetational diversity than either overgrazing or an absence of grazing. Thus, in tropical Mexican forests the defaunation of large mammal herbivores such as tapirs, peccari and deer by hunting and illegal trading led to increased density but decreased diversity of seedlings and saplings. Grazing represents a nutritional drain on plants and the ability to survive sustained grazing pressure may depend on soil quality and efficiency of nutrient capture.

The response of *Colophosper-mum mopane* trees to high levels of elephant herbivory in *C mopane*-dominated woodland in Zambia was related to the availability of soil nutrients; poor soil quality combined with elephant herbivory increased plant species diversity and reduced dominance by *C. mopane*. Periodic large-scale diebacks were also suggested to be a function of soil nutrient depletion from sustained grazing by elephants in these woodlands.

By browsing and debarking seedlings, saplings and trees, large mammalian herbivores can influence forest plant diversity and abundance, which in turn affect the resource and habitat quality and quantity for a range of other plant and animal species. Woodland degradation in Botswana by African elephants resulted in substantial changes in bird species composition, although bird diversity was unchanged, while culling of hippopotamus in Uganda allowed regeneration of plant diversity and consequential increases in buffalo, elephant and waterbuck densities. In tropical wet forests, large mammal densities are considerably lower than in African savannah forests and vertebrate herbivores do not have a major impact on habitat structure or composition.

ECOLOGY AND THE POLITICS OF KNOWLEDGE

The paradigm of modern science has evolved in the last few centuries in an environment where all economic activities were aimed at maximising the productivity of man-made processes in individual sectors of the economy. This led to the development of modern technologies with highly negative externalities which remained invisible within the conceptual framework of modern science and economics. This shortcoming emanates from three basic fallacies of modern scientific knowledge:

1. It identifies development merely with sectoral growth, ignoring the underdevelopment introduced in related sectors through negative externalities and the related undermining of the productivity of the ecosystem.
2. It identifies economic value merely with exchange value of marketable resources. ignoring use values of more vital resources and ecological processes.
3. It identifies utilization merely with extraction. ignoring the productive and economic functions of conserved resources.

Development planning based on these false identifications tends to create severe ecological problems because of its inability to recognise ecosystem linkages and the ecological processes operative in the natural world. The ecological relationships between the sectors of natural resources contribute to essential ecological processes which are frequently found to be vital for human survival. Thus, the stability of ecological processes is not merely a matter of aesthetics. An incomplete understanding of the material and economic values of ecological processes leads to the destruction of the material conditions for economic development and eventually survival.

Since the availability of essential and vital resources for survival is dependent on the maintenance of essential ecological processes, economic activities which generate sectoral growth in the shortterm by destroying the essential ecological processes cannot lead to development in the long run. On the contrary, by decreasing the productivity and availability of vital resources, they initiate the process of underdevelopment.

When the natural world is viewed ecologically as a system of interrelated resources which maintain the material basis for human sustenance, economic values can no longer be perceived merely as exchange values in the market. Economic values in the ecological perspective are not always equivalent to their exchange value in the market, evaluated without any significance to their use value.

As a corollary, natural resources can have economic utility that cannot be quantified through the exchange value in the market. Such economic utility includes the maintenance of essential ecological processes that support human survival and, thus, all economic activities. The economic utilisation of resources through extraction may, under certain conditions, undermine and destroy vital ecological processes leading to heavy but hidden diseconomies. The nature of these diseconomies can be understood only through the understanding of ecological processes operating in nature.

The economics of sustenance and basic needs satisfaction is, therefore, linked with ecological perceptions of nature. The economics of sectoral growth on the other hand is related to reductionist science and resource wasteful technologies which are productive in the narrow context of sectoral and labour inputs, but may be counter-productive in the context of the overall economic base of natural resources.

The case studies are only representative of thousands of such cases seen everywhere. They reveal a certain pattern of contemporary economic development which can be identified thus:

1. Development has been equated only with the growth of manufacture in individual industrial sectors and with the increase in productivity of only man-made processes.
2. This sectoral growth of man-made processes has also led to ecological destruction of the natural resource base, affecting negatively other sectors of the economic system. This leads to the decay of systems productivity of all productive processes, man-made and natural.

As a result of this limitation of contemporary economics, economic development has, consequently, been taken to be synonymous with growth. The higher the rate of sectoral growth, the higher is the index of economic development. Possible ecological destruction caused by the resource intensity of sectoral growth that is guided purely by non-ecological economic considerations, has never been introduced in the processes of planning for economic development. The benefit-cost analysis of development projects has thus externalized those ecological changes and is incomplete in three important ways:

1. It deals with benefits and costs as profits and losses in financial ferms.
2. It deals with benefits and costs only in the narrow sectoral perspective and ignores costs generated by inter-sectoral linkages.
3. It deals with benefits that are largely available to more visible and economically powerful groups and ignores costs that are borne by the less visible and economically weaker groups. These costs and the associated underdevelopment are thus made invisible in modern economic analysis.

The utilisation and management of natural resources in India has so far been guided by the narrow and sectoral concept of productivity and restricted benefit-cost analysis. This narrow concept of productivity and benefit-cost analysis has blocked the conceptualization of the criteria of rationality of technology choice which maximizes needs satisfaction while minimising resource use, thus maximising systems productivity.

For example, the clear felling of natural forests in the catchments of rivers, and planting of industrial species of trees has been justified on the grounds of increasing productivity of forests. This concept of productivity is, however, only related to productivity of industrial timber, while forests produce other forms of biomass, like fodder and green mulch, or maintain productivity of soil and water resources. The direct impact of the clear felling of catchment forests on agricultural production through its destructive impact on soil and destabilisation of the hydrological balance is not taken into account in the calculations of the benefits and costs associated with forests. Regular floods and droughts, which are the consequences of irrational land and water management, are branded as natural disasters for which the whole nation pays heavily. Consequently, the poor and marginal groups which depend on agriculture for their livelihood face increasing impoverishment and poverty. This thrusting of negative externalities on the poor and marginal groups directly leads to the polarisation of society into two groups. One group gains from the process of narrow sectoral growth, while the poor and marginalised majority suffer because of the ecological destruction of natural resources on which they depend for survival.

The dialectical contradiction between the role of natural resources in production processes to generate growth and profits and their role in natural processes to generate stability is made visible by movements based on the politics of ecology.

These movements reveal that the perception, knowledge and value of natural resources vary for different interest groups in society. The politics of ecology is thus intimately linked with the politics of knowledge.

For subsistence farmers and forest dwellers a forest has the basic economic function of soil and water conservation, energy and food supplies, etc. For industries the same forest has only the function of being a mine of raw materials.

These conflicting uses of natural resources, based on their diverse functions, are dialectically related to conflicting perceptions and knowledge about natural resources. The knowledge of forestry developed by forest dwelling communities therefore evolves in response to the economic functions valued by them. In contrast, the knowledge of forestry developed by forest bureaucracies, which respond largely to industrial requirements, will be predominantly guided by the economic value of maximising raw material production.

The way nature is perceived is therefore related to the pattern of utilisation of resources. Modern scientific disciplines which provide the currently dominant perspectives of nature have generally been viewed es 'objective', 'neutral' and 'universally valid'. These disciplines are, however, particular responses to particular economic interests. This economic determination influences the content and structure of knowledge about natural resources which, in turn, reinforces particular forms of resource utilisation The economic and political values of resource use are thus built into the structure of natural science knowledge.

Partisan Science versus Public Interest Science

When the dominant resource use is guided by vested interests or special interest objectives, it generates a partisan science which tends to be reductionist in character. Two central assumptions underlie this reductionist perception of nature: (a) natural resources are isolated and non-interacting collections of individual resources, and (b) natural resources acquire economic value only when commercially exploited.

This approach to nature is reductionist on two counts. First, it reduces nature to its constituent parts, and takes no cognizance of the relationships between the parts, and the structure and functions of the whole system. Second, it reduces economic value to a man-made construct-something which is the product of technology and capital inputs for the market. Nature's work and the work of women or marginal communities which depend on nature s productivity is thus ignored and destroyed.

Partisan science tends to be epistemologically reductionist because maximisation of special, vested interest objectives focuses on single resource functions. Partisan science must be narrowly conceived-it is inherent in its logic to perceive nature in a way that maximises the special interest objective and to be blind to ecological and environmental costs that this perception entails. Environment movements that emerge as a protest against the violation of public interest through special interest groups must therefore not merely indicate the social and environmental consequences of narrow profit maximisation. A deep and sustained resolution of such conflicts in favour of the larger public interest must be based on the emergence of a different approach to nature in the creation of a public interest science. The characteristics of this public interest science are such that it must be ecological which means: (a) it must be based on the recognition of relationships and interdependence among the various material components of nature; (b) it must be able to see and assess nature's work and assign a value to it; and (c) relatedly, it must be able to locate how nature's processes support survival, not merely profitability.

Ecology provides an epistemological framework within which alternatives to reductionist science and technology are not merely possible, but preferable too, because reductionism fails to provide faithful accounts of nature. This cognitive failure of reductionist sciences stems from the incapability of reductionism to take into account properties that emerge from relationships in nature.

In this sense, the ecological foundations of an alternative science and technology differ from philosophies based on epistemological relativism. While epistemological relativism also includes the possibility of alternatives, it denies the existence of materialistic criteria of the rational choice of alternatives. This is the limitation of the Kuhnian model, as well as other models arguing for plurality from a purely sociological or physiological perspective, not from materialist foundations.

The ecological foundations for an alternative science and technology provide a materialist epistemology for evaluating the rationality of knowledge claims on the basis of their materialist adequacy in guiding action in the real and complex world. The rejection of the reductionist interpretation of materialism need not amount to an adoption of a materially vacuous philosophical position. The ecological perspective provides such a materialist alternative to reductionism. The distinction between reductionist materialism and ecology is the difference between mechanical materialism and dialectical materialism repeatedly articulated by Marx. Engels's analysis of this distinction in his critique of Duhring reads exactly like a contemporary ecological critique of reductionist science.

The analysis of nature into its constituent parts were the funda mental conditions for the gigantic strides made in our knowledge of nature during the last four hundred years.

But this method of investigation has also left us a legacy of the habit of observing natural objects and natural processes in their isolation, detached from the vast interconnection of things, and therefore not in their motion, but in their repose, not as essentially changing, but as fixed constants, not in their life but in their death, in contemplating their existence it forgets their coming into being and passing away, in looking at them at rest it leaves their motion out of account because it cannot see the wood for the trees. Dialectics grasps things and their concatenation, their motion, their coming into being and passing out of existence.

In a world where relationships are an actuality, the denial of such relationships and the multidimensional properties they give rise to, has created a reductionist world view and knowledge system which is inadequate in functioning in the real world. The materialist criteria provided by ecology allow for the perception of such a failure of knowledge systems through the ecological instabilities induced by them. Reductionist knowledge leads to unreliable claims about natural systems and processes on the basis of the ecological criteria of.materialist adequacy.

The cognitive failure of reductionism is due to the fact that reductionist science has created ecological instabilities which in turn threaten survival. In a materialist epistemology, systems of knowledge are simultaneously systems of action. Reductionist science leads to the human transformation of nature which is successful in creating artefacts and generating exchange value, but which fails to maintain the essential life-support systems on which human survival depends. Reductionism is not an epistemological accident.

It is a particular response to an economic need of a particular form of economic organization.

The reductionist world view, the industrial revolution and capitalist organisation are the philosophical, technological and economic components of the same process. Economic growth, the achievement of this economic organisation, is materially based on externalizing the real costs of production, and on commercialising hitherto common resources to provide inputs to the production process.

This entails a large withdrawal of industrial resources from the ecosystem in accordance with the demands of the market, not in accordance with the renewal capacity of resources or the needs of the people. Since it is the individual resource which generates exchange value through extraction, scientific knowledge of natural resources which is created as a response to this economic system must necessarily be reductionist. Properties of resources which stabilise ecological processes but are commercially valueless because they cannot be exchanged in the market place are ignored, and eventually destroyed. Profits and commercial exploitation shape the context in which properties of the natural systems will be perceived and known.

Scientific knowledge is not universal, objective and neutral as it is posited to be. It is always a particular response to a particular interest. When the interest is the commercial utilisation of resources for maximising exchange value, the type of knowledge system that is created is reductionist. Internalisation of profits and externalisation of costs is a normal consequence when nature is treated as if its individual components are isolated and unrelated, and the only components with economic value are those that can be transformed into commodities.

The basic terms, concepts and definitions have built into them the economic values of the interest to which the knowledge is a response. In contrast, when the interest is sustainable livelihood of the people and the satisfaction of basic needs, ecological knowledge is the response.

Ecology as a public interest science is central to a just resolution of environmental conflicts in the contemporary setting because it is science and not politics that is used as the explicit justification and legitimisation of destruction, in the name of progress. 'Science' is used as a final arbiter in all resource conflicts.

The term 'scientific' is viewed as synonymous to public interest. However, since dominant science is partisan, decisions based on it will serve the special interest groups. Public interest science is a tool which makes explicit the political nature of partisan science and makes it a factor located within environmental conflicts, not a source of independent and neutral judgements about conflicts.

Public interest science, however, does not merely have a critical role in the politics of knowledge and politics of the environment. It also has a constructive role in generating new paradigms of science and development based on ecological principles which ensure sustainability and justice.

Probably the exemplar of public interest science is Rachel Carson's Silent Spring (1962) which exposed the destruction caused by the use of poisons in pest control and laid the foundation for alternative non-chemical means of control. It was public interest science

Introduction because in substance it was ecological, and in form it was different from the work of entomologists which while being critical of pesticides had remained confined to debates among entomologists and had failed to inform public debate and public policy. Silent Spring as public interest science, as a technical critique of dominant partisan science supporting pesticides, helped the growth of the environment movement since the sixties. It strengthened the movement because while exposing the cognitive weakness of partisan entomology it gave congnitive strength to ecological pest control and to the right of the individual citizen not to be poisoned by another person's pesticides. Knowledge is power, and environment movements need the cognitive power derived from public interest science. The Narmada groups have shown how this power can be used to control powerful agencies like the World Bank. Doctors in the voluntary sector working in Bhopal have shown the power of public interest science in the rehabilitation and relief provided to the victims of the gas tragedy.

FORESTS AND CLIMATE CHANGE

The burning of fossil fuels is the most important source of greenhouse gases. Coal and petroleum are the principal fuels for power generation, industry, and transportation, accounting for about 75 percent of all emissions. As the global economy has grown, there has been a dramatic increase in the consumption of fossil fuels, witnessed most dramatically in the virtual revolution of the transportation sector. Cars and trucks have increased from a mere handful a hundred years ago to the tens of millions of vehicles currently on the road.

Airline travel has also gone up to thousands of flights per day. All of this change has been accompanied by a skyrocketing consumption of fossil fuels. Also, energy needs for heating and domestic cooking have not only increased with the growth in population, but also with the changes in technology. There has been a shift away from biomass fuels to more convenient, less expensive petroleum-based sources.

In addition to the burning of fossil fuels, other important sources of greenhouse gas emissions are activities related to land use, primarily tropical deforestation and forest fires. Greenhouse gases from deforestation are mostly carbon dioxide with lesser amounts of methane and carbon monoxide. Tropical deforestation is one of the most critical environmental problems facing the developing countries today in terms of its long-term and catastrophic impact on biodiversity, loss of economic opportunities, creation of social problems, and contribution to global climate change. Forests are both a source and a sink of carbon. Thus, managing forests for carbon storage will help to absorb atmospheric carbon dioxide. Like agricultural crops, forests sequester carbon from the atmosphere as a result of photosynthesis. As trees have a much longer lifespan, they act as long-term reservoirs that lock up the carbon for decades, even centuries, in the form of cellulose and lignin.

Forestry and Kyoto Protocol

Forestry has assumed greater significance after the inclusion of afforestation and reforestation activities under the Kyoto Protocol of the United Nations Framework Convention on Climate Change (UNFCCC). UNFCCC is an international environmental treaty formulated at the United Nations

Conference on Environment and Development (UNCED), informally known as the Earth Summit, held in Rio de Janeiro in 1992. The treaty aimed at reducing emissions of greenhouse gases, pursuant to its supporters' belief in the global warming hypothesis. The treaty as originally framed set no mandatory limits on greenhouse gas emissions for individual nations and contained no enforcement provisions; it is therefore considered legally non-binding.

The Kyoto Protocol was adopted in December 1997 and came into force in February 2005. The objective of this agreement is to stabilize greenhouse gas concentrations in the atmosphere at a level that would prevent dangerous anthropogenic interference with the climate system. Countries, which ratify this protocol, commit to reducing their emissions of carbon dioxide and five other greenhouse gases, or engage in emissions trading if they maintain or increase emissions of these gases.

The industrialized countries are required to reduce their collective emissions by 5.2 per cent compared to the year 1990. In addition to this the industrialized countries are also required to consider ways to minimize adverse affects of their greenhouse gas emissions on developing countries. The developing countries are not required by the Kyoto Protocol to reduce their greenhouse gas emissions, as the per-capita emission rates of the developing countries are a tiny fraction of those in the developed world. However, the capacity of the developing countries must be strengthened to enhance their contribution to fighting climate change. Capacity building and technology transfer needs to be a central part of the global approach to combating climate change.

Carbon mitigation in developing countries remains an area of minor priority as these countries have various other immediate problems to deal with and developmental needs to meet with. Many developing countries are of the view that taking up any obligation regarding carbon sequestration would reduce them to carbon colonies, and that they would be asked to compromise with their development to comply with the agreed terms of such projects. At the present stage of development, reducing energy consumption would mean compromising with the developmental potential of the country. What can be done at this stage is to ensure that the increased CO_2 emission due to continuous use of energy sources is mitigated continuously.

This can be achieved by afforestation and reforestation activities. So the implementation of carbon mitigation projects must be integrated within the general national economic policies. The Kyoto Protocol also includes three market-based instruments known as the Kyoto Mechanisms that allow countries to earn or buy credits outside their borders. They are Clean Development Mechanism (CDM), Joint Implementation (JI), and International Emissions Trading (IET). These mechanisms enable Parties to access cost-effective opportunities to reduce emissions or to remove carbon from the atmosphere in other countries. While the cost of limiting emissions varies considerably from region to region, the benefit for the atmosphere is the same, wherever the action is taken. The developing countries can participate in two of these mechanisms, directly in CDM activities and indirectly in IET through CDM activities.

The Clean Development Mechanism (CDM) is a way to earn credits by investing in emission reduction projects in developing countries. International Emissions Trading (IET) will permit developed countries that have taken on a Kyoto target to buy and sell credits among themselves. Forests and agricultural soils can remove and store carbon dioxide from the atmosphere. These carbon sequestration activities are called 'sinks'. Sinks can be enhanced through sustainable management practices in forestry and on farms. The Kyoto Protocol provides for inclusion of sinks as part of a country's strategy to meet its obligations. India signed and ratified the Protocol in August 2002. Since India is exempted from the framework of the Treaty, it is expected to gain from the Protocol in terms of transfer of technology and related foreign investments.

The best possible forestry scenario among the various options available needs to be identified such that the demand of wood and wood products is met optimally, besides mitigating carbon. After the energy sector, the focus of the Climate Convention and scientific literature is largely on the forestry sector for undertaking various projects under Land-Use, Land-Use Change and Forestry (LULUCF). Absorbing CO_2 from air and injecting it into the biomass is the only practical way of removing large volumes of GHGs from the atmosphere.

CLIMATE CHANGE IMPACTS ON FOREST HEALTH

The world's climate is changing. Increased temperatures and levels of atmospheric carbon dioxide as well as changes in precipitation and in the frequency and severity of extreme climatic events are just some of the changes occurring. These changes are having notable impacts on the world's forests and the forest sector through longer growing seasons, expansion of insect species ranges, and increased frequency of forest fires. Climate change can affect forest pests and the damage they cause by: directly impacting their development, survival, reproduction and spread; altering host defences and susceptibility; and indirectly impacting the relationships between pests, their environment and other species such as natural enemies, competitors and mutualists.

A deeper understanding of the complex relationships between a changing climate, forests and forest pests is vital to enable those in forest health protection and management to expect and prepare for changes in pest behaviours, outbreaks and invasions. This chapter investigates these relationships and the implications for forest health protection and management. Specific examples where insect and pathogen lifecycles or habits have been altered by local, national or regional climatic changes are discussed. For example, the mountain pine beetle (*Dendroctonus ponderosae*) has shown decreases in generation time and winter mortality resulting in exponential population growth and major range extension in western North America. Warmer temperatures have resulted in range expansions of pests such as the pine processionary caterpillar (*Thaumetopoea pityocampa*) and the oak processionary caterpillar (*T. processionea*) in Europe and the southern pine beetle (*D. frontalis*) and red band needle blight (*Mycosphaerella pini*) in the US. Similar patterns are expected for other pathogens such as *Armillaria mellea,* and *Phytophthora cinnamomi* in Europe.

In the Democratic Peoples Republic of Korea, decreased winter temperature and lighter snow cover have contributed to reduced mortality and early emergence of overwintering *Dendrolimus spectabilis* (pine moth) with resulting loss of native *Pinus densiflora.*

The purpose of this report is to compile and summarize the present knowledge on the impacts of climate change on forests and forest pests. Since limited research has been dedicated to determining such impacts on forest pests in particular, information on non-forest pests is provided throughout the report to enable a better understanding of the potential impacts of climate change on forest health.

Current Knowledge and Future Expectations

The world's climate is changing. While there are natural climate variations, the climate change we are most concerned about is in regards to the modifications to the greenhouse effect that human activities have caused. The Intergovernmental Panel on Climate Change (IPCC), in its Fourth Assessment Report, concluded with more certainty that global climate change is unequivocal and it is widely believed to result primarily from the effects of emissions of carbon dioxide (CO_2) and other greenhouse gases (GHGs) such as methane (CH_4) and nitrous oxide (N_2O), from human activities.

This conclusion was based on a number of observations about the Earth's climate including the following.

- Global surface temperature has increased by an estimated 0.74 degrees Celsius (°C) over the past century. Over a 50 year period from 1956 to 2005 the warming trend was nearly twice that for the 100 years from 1906 to 2005. Eleven of the 12 years from 1995 to 2006 rank among the 12 hottest years on record (since 1850, when sufficient worldwide temperature measurements began). Increases are widespread globally and are greater at higher northern latitudes. Over the last 50 years, cold days and nights as well as frosts have become less frequent over most land areas, while hot days and nights and heat waves have become more frequent.

- Consistent with warming, the extent of snow and ice has decreased. Mountain glaciers and snow cover have also declined on average worldwide. The maximum area of seasonally frozen ground in the Northern Hemisphere has decreased by about 7 percent since 1900, with decreases in the spring of up to 15 percent. Satellite data since 1978 show that the extent of Arctic sea ice during the summer has shrunk by more than 20 percent.
- Since 1961, the world's oceans have been absorbing more than 80 percent of the heat added to the climate, causing ocean water to expand thereby contributing to rising sea levels. This expansion was the largest contributor to sea level rise between 1993 and 2003. Melting glaciers and losses from the Greenland and Antarctic ice sheets have also contributed to recent sea level rise. The incidence of extreme high sea level has increased at a number of sites globally since 1975.
- From 1900 to 2005, significant increases in precipitation have been observed in eastern parts of North and South America, northern Europe and northern and central Asia. The frequency of heavy precipitation events has also increased over most areas. In contrast, precipitation has declined in the Sahel, the Mediterranean, southern Africa and parts of southern Asia. Droughts have become longer and more intense worldwide and have affected larger areas since the 1970s, particularly in the tropics and subtropics.
- Evidence of an increase in intense tropical cyclone activity in the North Atlantic has been observed since about 1970 and there are suggestions of similar increased activity in some other regions.

Predictions for the Future

The IPCC has made a number of predictions for future climate change. A warming of about 0.2°C per decade is projected for the next two decades; temperature projections beyond this period depend on specific emissions scenarios. Even if the concentrations of all GHGs and aerosols were kept constant at year 2000 levels, a further warming of about 0.1°C per decade would be expected.

The full range of projected temperature increase, based on six emission scenarios, is 1.1-6.4 °C by the end of the century. The best estimate range of projected temperature increase, which extends from the midpoint of the lowest emission scenario to the midpoint of the highest, is 1.8-4.0 °C by the end of the century. It is very likely that continued GHG emissions at or above current rates would cause further warming and induce many changes in the global climate system during the 21st century that would be larger than those observed during the 20th century. Geographically the predicted warming trends for the 21st century are believed to be similar to those observed over the past several decades whereby temperature increases are expected to be greatest over land and at most high northern latitudes, and least over the Southern Ocean (near Antarctica) and the northern North Atlantic. It is very likely that extreme heat, heat waves and heavy precipitation events will become more frequent. Increases in high latitude precipitation are very likely, while decreases are likely in most subtropical regions such as Egypt.

It is also likely that future tropical cyclones (typhoons and hurricanes) will become more intense, with higher peak wind speeds and heavier precipitation associated with warmer tropical seas. Snow cover area is projected to contract, widespread increases in thaw depth are projected over most permafrost regions and sea ice is projected to shrink in both the Arctic and Antarctic. In some projections, Arctic late-summer sea ice disappears almost entirely by the latter part of the 21st century. Climate change is impacting the world's ecosystems and it is expected that the magnitude of these impacts will increase along with temperatures over this century. Many species and ecosystems may not be able to adapt as the effects of global warming and associated disturbances, such as floods, drought, wildfire and insect outbreaks, are compounded by other stresses such as land use change, overexploitation of resources, pollution and fragmentation of natural systems. If the global average temperature increases more than 1.5-2.5 °C, it is believed likely that approximately 20-30 percent of plant and animal species assessed so far will be at an increased risk of extinction. Major changes in ecosystem structure and function, species' ecological interactions and species' geographical ranges, with predominantly negative consequences for biodiversity and ecosystem goods and services are also projected.

URBAN FORESTS AND TREES

Trees in the urban environment contribute significantly to the aesthetic appeal of cities, helping to maintain the psychological health of the inhabitants. Besides the aesthetic and environmental aspects, urban forestry is also of importance in helping populations poor in resources to meet basic needs. Urban plantings of fruit trees to provide firewood is one way of utilizing obvious benefits from the available natural resources, as done in Kampala, the capital of Uganda. Research has shown that urban trees benefit communities economically, socially and environmentally. The size, structure and condition of the urban forest directly affects the amount of benefits provided by the urban vegetation. Nevertheless, the social and environmental benefits provided by the urban forest are often largely ignored in land-use planning.

Economic Impact

Though trees are not usually thought of as economic resources, the presence of trees has an impact on different economic factors, including the level of real-estate prices, economic investments and employment. Results of recent Finnish studies show that the benefits provided by urban forests are reflected in property prices, and that environmental variables, such as proximity to wooded recreation areas and water courses as well as an increasing proportion of total forested area in the housing district, had a positive influence on apartment prices. The presence of trees may influence property values positively by as much as 20%, with an average increase of 5-10%.

Trees also provide different external environmental benefits. Costs for heating and cooling can be reduced by appropriate use of vegetation. Energy reductions for individual buildings have been shown to range from 5 to 15% for heating and 10-50% for cooling. Especially in areas with high summer temperatures, trees are important providers of shade. In areas with cool winters, it is of importance to use deciduous trees, as the loss of leaves in winter allows the sun to heat the house. Proper arrangements of vegetation around buildings can also reduce wind velocity and thereby reduce the heat loss from buildings.

Recreational use of Green Areas

Several studies have shown the importance of urban forests for participation in outdoor recreation activities. In a Danish national survey it was found that around two-thirds of all forest visits take place in the forest situated nearest the housing area. Danish and Swedish studies have also showed that the use of green areas by people is associated with three highly esteemed values: (i) a high degree of natural elements, (ii) fresh air and (iii) the possibility of solitude. In general, people use green areas less than they would like. According to Swedish studies, distance and the fear of assault are the most prevalent reasons for people not visiting green areas. When the distance to the park exceeds 300 m, one person in four postpones a daily visit. As many as 56% refrain from regular walks in the park when the distance increases to 500m. American studies indicate that the removal of vegetation at strategic points can reduce the risk of assault, although this should not be the reason for removing all the vegetation.

Psychological Aspects

City life is stressful but research shows that urban green areas have a beneficial influence on the health and well-being of the urban population.

Studies indicate that visits to green areas can counteract stress, renew vital energy and speed healing processes. In Sweden, Grahn (1989) conducted extensive studies on the significance of parks to different groups of the population. For instance, he persuaded 40 schools, hospitals, sports associations, cultural associations and day-care centres to keep diaries of their outdoor activities for 1 year. For example, the diaries show that periods spent outside had an actual medicinal value for patients and residents of hospitals, old people's homes and homes for the sick. People became happier, slept better, needed less medication, were less restless and far more talkative.

Ulrich (1984) showed that hospitalized patients recovered faster when they had a view through a window, allowing them to see trees. Ulrich *et al.* (1991) showed a gory film on industrial accidents to 120 people. Half the people were then shown a nature film, whereas the other half were shown a film on the city, with sequences of buildings and traffic. The subjects' heart beat, muscular tension and blood pressure were monitored throughout. All subjects exhibited strong signs of stress during the first film on industrial accidents. The stress levels of the subjects that then watched the nature film returned to a normal level after 4-6 min, whereas the half that watched the film on buildings and traffic continued to exhibit high stress levels. Kaplan and Kaplan (1989) have formulated a theory on the interaction between human attention and the surroundings. This theory distinguishes between spontaneous attention and conscious attention. Spontaneous attention demands no effort and occurs without premeditation.

Conscious attention demands energy and leads to psychological exhaustion in the long term. Rapid movements, strong colours, sudden noises and strong odours are typical stimuli that demand conscious attention. These signals have a powerful effect on our attention, consciously and unconsciously, because they are perceived as potential dangers to which we should react. This means that urban living, with fast vehicles, flashing neon signs and strong colours, causes constant stress. Kaplan and Kaplan's research indicates that vegetation and nature reinforce our spontaneous attention, allow our sensory apparatus to relax and infuse us with fresh energy. Visits to green areas bring relaxation and sharpen our concentration, since we only need to use our spontaneous attention. At the same time, we get fresh air and sunlight, which have significance for our diurnal and annual rhythms.

Environmental Education

The change and the continuity in nature provides not only a sense of time but also a sense of security and confidence, through the predictable change of seasons and the repetition of natural processes. The urban trees and forests play a role in educating young people and children in understanding the basic processes in nature and the complexities of the environment, either informally during play or as part of the school curriculum. Playing in nature or natural settings also helps children to develop their motoric senses and to regain and experience the human connection to nature through their imagination. Experiences with environmental education in the USA show that access to even a small area of the urban forest is of importance when learning about natural processes.

In England in 1985 a research project supported by the Department of Education and Science, the Countryside Commission and a consortium of local authorities resulted in the organization Learning through Landscapes (LTL). LTL was founded on the recognition of the impact that the physical surroundings has on children. LTL helps schools to design schoolyards that improve the quality of the environment and helps to create additional resources for the formal curriculum, such as the promotion of more effective teaching and learning in the outdoor classroom.

The English Community Forests are examples of integrated programmes in which environmental education is integrated in social programmes by well-coordinated planning. The forests are charged with running and coordinating social programmes, involving information, consultation, participation, art, education, sport, recreation and cultural activities.

Community Involvement

Other benefits of urban forestry are those provided by involving people in planning, planting and caring for the trees and urban forests in their own locality. By promoting social interaction and strengthening local pride and identity, local public engagement benefits management greatly, encouraging people to act protectively towards their local forests and providing a potentially huge volunteer workforce.

The possibilities for creating public awareness in any town are endless. In the USA there is a tradition of involving the public in all processes, from the policy-making to the care and maintenance of the urban forest. Through various types of tree programmes, public awareness has proved to be a valuable tool in the justification of tree activities because it develops a public interest group that helps to lobby for support. The projects that involve citizens have various aspects in common, such as planting, preserving, pruning, maintenance, public education, etc.. Examples of initiatives that enhance public awareness and engagement in a municipal tree programme are the Tree Boards, municipal non-profit groups with participants from a wide range of professions. The close cooperation between professionals and non-professionals provides direct communication of new ideas and research and helps to solve associated problems as experienced in a practical situation. Another way of involving the public is to encourage houseowners to adopt a tree, by taking part in the care and maintenance of a tree in their neighbourhood.

FORESTS AND COMMUNITY DEVELOPMENT

Because of their large number and wide distribution, the forest and wood-using industries influence the economic and social life of a great many communities. This influence is most keenly felt in the smaller cities and towns, particularly in wellforested regions, where they often constitute the dominant interest. In such situations, the prosperity of the community rises and falls to a very considerable extent with the prosperity of the forest-based industries.

These have a decidedly stabilizing influence wherever the forests are managed on a sustained-yield basis, with the average annual cut and average annual growth in balance. Ghost towns do not occur where sustained yields are obtained and where mill capacity is adjusted to the growing capacity of the forest. One of the important aspects of any industry is its influence on other industries and on service activities. The forest and wood-using industries purchase large quantities of axes, saws, tractors, trucks, planers, lathes, digesters, paper machines and other items of equipment; and they sell lumber, veneer, plywood, boxes, pulp, paper and similar items to other industries for use in the manufacture and marketing of their products. Railroads in some regions depend for their very existence on the freight revenue derived first from bringing raw materials, equipment and general supplies to communities dominated by one or more wood-using industries and secondly from transporting the products of these industries from mill to market.

Industry in general also supports many services, such as those supplied by grocers, druggists, clothiers, doctors, lawyers, ministers and teachers. The wood-using industries do not differ in this respect from other industries, except that in many rural districts they provide the sole or the main reason for the existence of a community. Where this is the case, they create the demand for such services; and where other industries are also present, they intensify that demand. One further item of community concern is the relation of the forest and its dependent industries to the small landowners and especially to the farmer. The existence of a nearby wood-using industry provides a market, which in turn should encourage thrifty management of the wood lot. The additional income thus available can have a stabilizing effect both on the farmer and on the community of which he is a part. Forestry is a key to permanence.

Community Forestry

In 1976, the National Commission on Agriculture in India introduced the concept of Social Forestry to encourage those who were dependent on fuelwood, fodder and other forest products, to meet their own needs through various activities, in order to reduce the burden on the Forests. This concept was further refined by FAO in 1978, by defining community forestry as the programme which intimately involved local people in afforestation, irrespective of the pattern of land ownership. While the traditional forestry covered the protection and production roles, social forestry was intended to play the social role.

Thus community forestry programmes included a wide range of activities such as growing trees on farm bunds and roadsides, developing woodlots on common properties and collection, processing and management of forest products by involving local communities. Realising the problems of poverty and unemployment closely linked with denudation of natural resources, scarcity of fuel, fodder and timber, the Government of India in their Sixth Five Year Plan (1980-85) aimed at generating rural employment through social forestry and thereby reducing poverty from 48% to 30%, which was further intended to be brought down to 10% during the Seventh Five Year Plan (1985-90). It was also intended to produce adequate fodder and fuel to meet the needs of the poor, particularly in forest deficit areas. The major focus was on the extension of forestry programme to non-forest lands with the active involvement of local communities. This was essential because only about 40% of the 5 million villages had access to forests, while the rest had to look for alternate sources of woodfuel. It was also an opportunity to develop 175 million ha of degraded lands. Subsequently, in the 1980s, the scope of social forestry was enlarged to cover the protection of reserved forests and establish tree species on vacant sites in urban areas. However, the programme did not include large-scale industrial forestry.

In 1985, the National Wastelands Development Board was established by the Government of India to promote the production of fodder, fuel and minor timber on wastelands, by involving local communities and voluntary agencies. Important social forestry models formulated to achieve these goals were - rehabilitation on degraded lands, strip plantations, village woodlots, farm forestry, agroforestry, homestead plantations and decentralised nurseries. Newly established State Social Forestry Departments were confident of implementing this programme, in view of their strong technical expertise and adequate resources. However, in the absence of social mobilisation, involvement of the local people was confined only to wage earning on community woodlots, while the implementation of these schemes was carried out by the Forest Officials.

Community Forestry Schemes in 1980's

By 1990, the drawbacks of various social forestry schemes launched in different parts of the country became apparent. The Social Forestry Departments had great difficulty in mobilising local participation. There was a wide gap between the assumed problems and actual realities in the field. As the work plans were not based on specific ground data and ecological conditions, the proposed models of social forestry were often found to be inappropriate. However, modifications in the project designs and implementation plans could not be carried out because of rigid rules and regulations. These schemes could not register the anticipated success because of the following reasons :

Community Woodlots: Development of fuelwood plantations on community wastelands was a major programme to generate employment for the local poor and the landless, while augmenting the fuel and forage shortfall faced by the community. However, this scheme could cover only 9% of the villages either due to non-availability of wastelands or unwillingness of the Village Panchayats and public institutions to spare their wastelands for community plantations. Many of these projects had failed to progress in terms of plant survival, growth and income generation. In the absence of effective local organisations, the programme heavily depended on the Village Panchayats, who had bare minimum staff to manage these plantations. As the area available for plantations was very small, the supply of fuel and fodder was also inadequate to meet the local demands. It was also realised that the problems of fuelwood and fodder shortages could not be solved simply by promoting the cultivation of these species, as these commodities were of least value as compared to timber wood. Therefore, despite the shortage of fuelwood, the farmers preferred to grow timber and fruit species.

In some successful community plantations, inspite of the offer to collect grass free of cost, the response from farmers was very poor. The villagers felt that feeding such fodder to poor quality animals would not improve the productivity except in a few locations where they had maintained livestock of improved breeds. As the community plantation activities could not motivate the local people, most of these plantations were destroyed within a short period after completion of the project.

Strip Plantations: Saplings of tall growing tree species were established in multiple lines along the railway tracks, canal bunds and roadsides and the landless families were involved in protecting them. This was fairly successful but the incentives offered by the project implementing agency were not adequate for the beneficiaries to devote sufficient time for protection. Thus some of these trees were stolen. In the absence of clear directives from the government regarding the sharing of benefits, the participants were not allowed to cut the trees.

Farm Forestry: It was the most successful scheme wherein farmers established plantations of eucalyptus, casuarina, poplar, teak, etc., on their agricultural lands using necessary inputs like irrigation and fertilisers with the hope of finding a suitable market and attractive price for the produce. Many of these farmers located near the wood based industries could sell wood at remunerative prices. However in the absence of any marketing infrastructure it was difficult for them to find attractive buyers in remote areas. Obsolete Tree Acts imposed by the government created further obstacles in felling, transporting and sawing of timber by the growers. This forced them to either sell it to the middlemen or delay the harvest. The community forestry programme also included a component of planting fruit species on marginal lands owned by poor families belonging to scheduled castes and scheduled tribes. However, the project could not get adequate response at the initial stage as most of the illiterate target families feared that the government would acquire their lands, after the establishment of trees. Subsequently, even the limited number of participants in the programme could not maintain the plants due to inadequate resources to provide irrigation and protection.

It was also observed that while promoting farm forestry, farmers were not informed about the profitability of various tree species which could be grown under local agro-climatic conditions. As a result, the farmers preferred only a few species such as eucalyptus, which they thought to be most profitable, while many other fruit and non-timber forest product species which could have provided higher income were neglected.

Decentralised nurseries: The primary objective was to build up the local capacity for assured supply of planting materials of popular tree species. As the focus was on fodder and fuelwood plantations, the participants were advised to raise those saplings which were of no interest to them. In the absence of well planned marketing arrangements, the nurserymen were totally dependent on the Social Forestry Department for selling their seedlings. As a result, farmers had to discontinue their activities immediately after completion of the project.

Energy Conservation: Several energy conservation measures like promotion of improved wood stoves and biogas plants did not achieve the expected results due to poor publicity and awareness. The poor response was also because of unsuitable designs of smokeless wood stoves which failed to save wood.

Lessons Learnt

No doubt the community forestry programmes in 1980s could not prove to be people-oriented, but they did generate a lot of awareness among the local people. Many success stories were recorded at micro-level which were good for replication and motivation of the rural people on a larger scale. Several lessons were learnt by the Project Implementing Agencies. Although biomass was the major source of fuel for cooking, the supply was not critical. Contrary to the earlier belief, it has now been understood that only 30 - 40% of biofuel was in the form of wood and only 10 - 15% of it was from natural forests. The rest of the biofuel was from crop residues, animal dung, shrubs and bushes grown on non-forest lands. However, as the demand for woodfuel will increase at 1.5 - 2.0% per annum, the estimated consumption of woodfuel in 2010 will be 226 million tons against the supply of 256 million tons. Apart from the wood for fuel, the annual demand for wood from industries, housing and agricultural sectors is 125 million tons, leading to further pressure on forest resources.

Compared to other sources of energy, woodfuel has several advantages. Firstly, wood can be easily regenerated through the establishment of energy plantations on marginal and wastelands. With its tropical climate, fairly good quality soil and well distributed rainfall, India presents an ideal condition to produce 10-15 tons of biomass per ha/year. Woodfuel production and distribution can also provide employment for rural people at various levels. The woodfuel business can provide employment for about 10% of the rural households and contribute to about 40% of their total earning. Inspite of huge involvement of labour, energy from wood is cheaper than fossil fuels.

Woodfuel is also environment friendly, when the rate of biomass harvest is equivalent to the rate of regrowth. In such a situation, CO_2 released from wood while burning will be absorbed by the greenery without any burden on the environment.

The use of woodfuel in the Asia Pacific Region in 1994 has resulted in saving 278 million tons of CO_2, which otherwise would have been released into the global atmosphere. With continued use of wood as a hypothetical replacement for LPG, the annual CO_2 saved will be 349 million tons in 2010. The estimated cost avoided by recapturing the CO_2 is estimated at US $ 14 billion in 1994 and US $ 17.5 billion in 2010. Thus, biomass production deserves high priority in community forestry.

Realising this need, emphasis was laid on Joint Forest Management which involved people's organisations to launch tree plantations both on forest and non-forest lands. This programme emphasized on the formation of Village Forest Committees and capacity building of the committee members to take suitable decisions on afforestation and its protection without any interference from the donor agencies and Forest Department.

Inspite of its good intentions, the success of the Joint Forest Management Programmes was also dependent on other factors such as productivity of the plantations based on soil fertility and composition of the tree species, demand for the produce, political support and transparency of the project implementing agency. In some states where the government had issued clear directives on the sharing of benefits between the government and local people, the latter had shown greater enthusiasm, resulting in a higher degree of success.

The success of the community forestry programme was also influenced by political commitment, correct assessment of local needs, appropriate technology, system of providing incentives, suitable local organisations and support services for finance, management, research and extension. Inspite of major setbacks, the Government of India has emphasized that those community forestry programmes which aim at conserving the natural resources should address the problem of poverty.

It was realised that the community forestry could not solve all the problems of the rural communities, although it had good potential to support the rural economy. There was a need to involve the local communities for planning the programme till they developed suitable interventions to fulfill the goals.

The key task for successful implementation of the programme in the future was to understand the socio-economic aspects of the local population and design a suitable technical programme to ensure sustainable development. The programme should have a strong component of extension for motivating the participants. The extension programme should highlight the benefits of various schemes through effective media, such as radio, TV, documentary films and newspapers. However, as most of the farmers were illiterate, involvement of local leaders, members of the village *Panchayats*, progressive farmers, school teachers and voluntary agencies was most effective in ensuring better people's participation and adoption of new technologies.

Programme Priorities for the Future

The community forestry programmes during the next two decades should focus on the following aspects.

- Enhancing the productivity of natural resources, while augmenting the basic needs of the community;
- Empowering the local communities to initiate the process of planning and programme implementation at the microlevel to promote afforestation for income generation and ecological conservation.

The programme during the next two decades may be divided into two phases. During the first phase of 10 years, emphasis should be given to enhance the productivity, while conserving biodiversity and the environment. The second phase should consolidate the programme by promoting micro and macro-level enterprises, involving the local people and the business interests to sustain the development and optimise the opportunities for employment and income generation.

Agroforestry for Improving Productivity of Private Lands

As over 70% of the agricultural lands in India are dependent on rainfall, the crop yields are comparatively low. In such a situation, promotion of tree based farming system has good potential to improve the Land Equivalent Ratio (LER) as well as crop yields. The system of combining horticultural crops with fodder, fuel, NWFP and agricultural crops can ensure the supply of essential commodities while generating cash surplus. Among these tree species, the income from fruit and NWFP plantation are generally higher than timber and industrial wood plantation, because of substantial annual income without cutting the trees.

Development of tree based farming systems on the watershed basis has the potential to improve water supply, food production, employment generation apart from supplying fuel and forage. Water conservation can be facilitated through contour bunding, gully plugging, formation of farm ponds and percolation tanks. This programme can help in recharging the ground water table to provide water for human beings, livestock and crops. The selection of a suitable farming system will be based on the soil fertility and moisture availability. As the Government of India has already launched a massive programme of watershed development, linkage of agroforestry as an integral part of this programme will not only provide an opportunity to enhance biomass production, but also improve the profitability.

While fruit orchards are ideal for deep soils having some water resources to protect the plants in the initial stages, farm forestry and agri-silviculture are suitable for marginal lands. With introduction of fruit species, farmers can be motivated to intensify their farming operations and improve the soil productivity. Through soil and water conservation, green manuring vermi-composting, agroforestry and integrated crop protection, the yields of intercrops can be substantially high, atleast for the next 10-15 years, till the intercrops are affected by the shade, although the LER will remain significantly high to maintain the orchards. Such tree based farming systems have been highly effective in preventing migration of rural families and supporting livestock husbandry to enhance their income by 35-40%.

Wood Production and Conservation

Commercial Plantations: Wood production should continue to be the priority under community forestry. However, fuelwood being a low value commodity, farmers prefer to grow superior quality wood suitable for timber and industrial use. Therefore the priority should be to promote cultivation of timber and industrial wood on degraded agricultural lands and community wastelands, which are not suitable for cultivation of fruit and NWFP species. The wood based industrial and housing sectors which are dependent on natural forests can associate with farmers to procure their raw materials. This programme can be managed with least financial support from the government, as commercial banks and industries are prepared to provide necessary finance.

Mixed Plantations: While the industries utilise the wood of a certain minimum diameter, almost 40-50% biomass in the form of branches and twigs can be available for fodder, manure and fuel, almost free of cost. Apart from producing fuelwood as a byproduct in commercial plantations, fast growing fuelwood species of short gestation can be introduced on field bunds and as mixed crops with commercial wood species. This will augment the fuelwood supply to a great extent.

Wood Saving Devices: Efforts are also needed to introduce various energy conservation measures. These may include the development of fuel efficient, low cost wood stoves, promotion of improved cooking vessels and introduction of efficient models of biogas to substitute woodfuel for cooking. Biomass being a renewable form of energy, it can be an excellent source for generating electricity in wood surplus countries. However, it is necessary to develop efficient gasifiers to take advantage of this technology in the future.

ECOSYSTEM OF TROPICAL RAINFOREST

A tropical rainforest is an ecosystem type that occurs roughly within the latitudes 28 degrees north or south of the equator (in the equatorial zone between the Tropic of Cancer and Tropic of Capricorn). This ecosystem experiences high average temperatures and a significant amount of rainfall. Rainforests can be found in Asia, Australia, Africa, South America, Central America, Mexico and on many of the Pacific, Caribbean, and Indian Ocean islands.

Within the World Wildlife Fund's biome classification, tropical rainforests are thought to be a type of tropical wet forest (or tropical moist broadleaf forest) and may also be referred to as *lowland equatorial evergreen rainforest*.Tropical rainforests can be characterized in two words: warm and wet. Mean monthly temperatures exceed 18 °C (64 °F) during all months of the year. Average annual rainfall is no less than 168 cm (66 in) and can exceed 1,000 cm (390 in) although it typically lies between 175 cm (69 in) and 200 cm (79 in). This high level of precipitation often results in poor soils due to leaching of soluble nutrients.

Tropical rainforests are unique in the high levels of biodiversity they exhibit. Around 40 per cent to 75 per cent of all biotic species are indigenousto the rainforests. Rainforests are home to half of all the living animal and plant species on the planet. Two-thirds of all flowering plants can be found in rainforests.

A single hectare of rainforest may contain 42,000 different species of insect, up to 807 trees of 313 species and 1,500 species of higher plants. Tropical rainforests have been called the "jewels of the Earth" and the "world's largest pharmacy", because over one quarter of natural medicines have been discovered within them. It is likely that there may be many millions of species of plants, insects andmicroorganisms still undiscovered in tropical rainforests.

Tropical rainforests are among the most threatened ecosystems globally due to large-scale fragmentation due to human activity. Habitat fragmentation caused by geological processes such as volcanism and climate change occurred in the past, and have been identified as important drivers of speciation.

However, fast human driven habitat destruction is suspected to be one of the major causes of species extinction. Tropical rain forests have been subjected to heavy logging and agricultural clearance throughout the 20th century, and the area covered by rainforests around the world is rapidly shrinking.

History

Tropical rainforests have existed on Earth for hundreds of millions of years. Most tropical rainforests today are on fragments of the Mesozoic era supercontinent of Gondwana. The separation of the landmass resulted in a great loss of amphibian diversity while at the same time the drier climate spurred the diversification of reptiles. The division left tropical rainforests located in five major regions of the world: tropical America, Africa, Southeast Asia, Madagascar, and New Guinea, with smaller outliers in Australia. However, the specifics of the origin of rainforests remain uncertain due to an incomplete fossil record.

Types of Tropical Rainforest

Several types of forest comprise the general tropical rainforest biome:

- Lowland equatorial evergreen rain forests are forests which receive high rainfall (more than 2000 mm, or 80 inches, annually) throughout the year. These forests occur in a belt around the equator, with the largest areas in the Amazon Basin of South America, the Congo Basin of Central Africa, Indonesia, and New Guinea.
- Moist deciduous and semi-evergreen seasonal forests, receive high overall rainfall with a warm summer wet season and a cooler winter dry season. Some trees in these forests drop some or all of their leaves during the winter dry season. These forests are found in parts of South America, in Central America and around the Caribbean, in coastal West Africa, parts of the Indian subcontinent, and across much of Indochina.
- Montane rain forests, some of which are known as cloud forests, are found in cooler-climate mountain areas. Depending on latitude, the lower limit of montane rainforests on large mountains is generally between 1500 and 2500 m while the upper limit is usually from 2400 to 3300 m.

- Flooded forests, seven types of flooded forest are recognized for Tambopata Reserve in Amazonian Peru:
- *Permanently waterlogged swamp forest*—Former oxbow lakes still flooded but covered in forest.
- *Seasonally waterlogged swamp forest*—Oxbow lakes in the process of filling in.
- *Lower floodplain forest*—Lowest floodplain locations with a recognizable forest.
- *Middle floodplain forest*—Tall forest, flooded occasionally.
- *Upper floodplain forest*—Tall forest, rarely flooded.
- *Old floodplain forest*—Subjected to flooding within the last two hundred years.
- *Previous floodplain*—Now *terra firme,* but historically ancient floodplain of Tambopata River.

Forest Structure

Rainforests are divided into different strata, or layers, with vegetation organized into a vertical pattern from the top of the soil to the canopy Each layer is a unique biotic community containing different plants and animals adapted for life in that particular strata. Only the emergent layer is unique to tropical rainforests, while the others are also found in temperate rainforests.

Forest Floor

The forest floor, the bottom-most layer, receives only 2 per cent of the sunlight. Only plants adapted to low light can grow in this region. Away from riverbanks, swamps and clearings, where dense undergrowth is found, the forest floor is relatively clear of vegetation because of the low sunlight penetration. This more open quality permits the easy movement of larger animals such as: ungulates like the okapi (*Okapia johnstoni*), tapir (*Tapirus* sp.), Sumatran rhinoceros (*Dicerorhinus sumatrensis*), and apes like the western lowland gorilla (*Gorilla gorilla*), as well as many species of reptiles, amphibians, and insects. The understory also contains decaying plant and animal matter, which disappears quickly, because the warm, humid conditions promote rapid decay. Many forms of fungi growing here help decay the animal and plant waste.

Understory Layer

The understory layer lies between the canopy and the forest floor. The understory is home to a number of birds, small mammals, insects, reptiles, and predators. Examples include leopard(*Panthera pardus*), poison dart frogs (*Dendrobates* sp.), ring-tailed coati (*Nasua nasua*), boa constrictor (*Boa constrictor*), and many species of Coleoptera. The vegetation at this layer generally consists of shade-tolerant shrubs, herbs, small trees, and large woody vines which climb into the trees to capture sunlight. Only about 5 per cent of sunlight breaches the canopy to arrive at the understory causing true understory plants to seldom grow to 3 m (10 feet). As an adaptation to these low light levels, understory plants have often evolved much larger leaves. Many seedlings that will grow to the canopy level are in the understory.

Canopy Layer

The canopy is the primary layer of the forest forming a roof over the two remaining layers. It contains the majority of the largest trees, typically 30–45 m in height. Tall, broad-leaved evergreen trees are the dominant plants. The densest areas of biodiversity are found in the forest canopy, as it often supports a rich flora of epiphytes, including orchids, bromeliads, mosses and lichens.

These epiphytic plants attach to trunks and branches and obtain water and minerals from rain and debris that collects on the supporting plants. The fauna is similar to that found in the emergent layer, but more diverse. It is suggested that the total arthropod species richness of the tropical canopy might be as high as 20 million. Other species habituating this layer include many avian species such as the yellow-casqued wattled hornbill (*Ceratogymna elata*), collared sunbird (*Anthreptes collaris*), African gray parrot(*Psitacus erithacus*), keel-billed toucan (*Ramphastos sulfuratus*), scarlet macaw (*Ara macao*) as well as other animals like the spider monkey (*Ateles*sp.), African giant swallowtail (*Papilio antimachus*), three-toed sloth (*Bradypus tridactylus*), kinkajou (*Potos flavus*), and tamandua (*Tamandua tetradactyla*).

Emergent Layer

The emergent layer contains a small number of very large trees, called emergents, which grow above the general canopy, reaching heights of 45–55 m, although on occasion a few species will grow to 70–80 m tall. Some examples of emergents include: *Balizia elegans, Dipteryx panamensis, Hieronyma alchorneoides, Hymenolobium mesoamericanum, Lecythis ampla* and*Terminalia oblonga*. These trees need to be able to withstand the hot temperatures and strong winds that occur above the canopy in some areas. Several unique faunal species inhabit this layer such as the crowned eagle (*Stephanoaetus coronatus*), the king colobus (*Colobus polykomos*), and the large flying fox (*Pteropus vampyrus*). However, stratification is not always clear. Rainforests are dynamic and many changes affect the structure of the forest. Emergent or canopy trees collapse, for example, causing gaps to form. Openings in the forest canopy are widely recognized as important for the establishment and growth of rainforest trees. It's estimated that perhaps 75 per cent of the tree species at La Selva

Biological Station, Costa Rica are dependent on canopy opening for seed germination or for growth beyond sapling size, for example.

Ecology and Climate

Most tropical rainforests are located around and near the equator, therefore having what is called an equatorial climate characterized by three major climatic parameters: temperature, rainfall, and dry season intensity Other parameters that affect tropical rainforests are carbon dioxide concentrations, solar radiation, and nitrogen availability. In general, climatic patterns consist of warm temperatures and high annual rainfall. However, the abundance of rainfall changes throughout the year creating distinct wet and dry seasons. Rainforests are classified by the amount of rainfall received each year, which has allowed ecologists to define differences in these forests that look so similar in structure.

According to Holdridge's classification of tropical ecosystems, true tropical rainforests have an annual rainfall greater than 800 cm and annual temperature greater than 24 degrees Celsius. However, most lowland tropical rainforests can be classified as tropical moist or wet forests, which differ in regards to rainfall. Tropical rainforest ecology- dynamics, composition, and function- are sensitive to changes in climate especially changes in rainfall. The climate of these forests is controlled by a band of clouds called the Intertropical Convergence Zone located near the equator and created by the convergence of the trade winds from the northern and southern hemispheres.

The position of the band varies seasonally, moving north in the northern summer and south in the northern winter, and ultimately controlling the wet and dry seasons in the tropics. These regions have experienced strong warming at a mean rate of 0.26 degrees Celsius per decade which coincides with a global rise in temperature resulting from the anthropogenic inputs of greenhouse gases into the atmosphere. Studies have also found that precipitation has declined and tropical Asia has experienced an increase in dry season intensity whereas Amazonia has no significant pattern change in precipitation or dry season. Additionally, El Niño-Southern Oscillation events drive the interannual climatic variability in temperature and precipitation and result in drought and increased intensity of the dry season.

As anthropogenic warming increases the intensity and frequency of ENSO will increase, leaving tropical rainforest regions susceptible to stress and increased mortality of trees.

Soil Types

Soil types are highly variable in the tropics and are the result of a combination of several variables such as climate, vegetation, topographic position, parent material, and soil age Most tropical soils are characterized by significant leaching and poor nutrients; however there are some areas that contain fertile soils. Soils throughout the tropical rainforests fall into two classifications which include the ultisols and oxisols.

Ultisols are known as well weathered, acidic red clay soils, deficient in major nutrients such as calcium and potassium. Similarly, oxisols are acidic, old, typically reddish, highly weathered and leached, however are well drained compared to ultisols. The clay content of ultisols is high, making it difficult for water to penetrate and flow through. The reddish colour of both soils is the result of heavy heat and moisture forming oxides of iron and aluminum, which are insoluble in water and not taken up readily by plants. Soil chemical and physical characteristics are strongly related to above ground productivity and forest structure and dynamics. The physical properties of soil control the tree turnover rates whereas chemical properties such as available nitrogen and phosphorus control forest growth rates.

The soils of the eastern and central Amazon as well as the Southeast Asian Rainforest are old and mineral poor whereas the soils of the western Amazon (Ecuador and Peru) and volcanic areas of Costa Rica are young and mineral rich. Primary productivity or wood production is highest in western Amazon and lowest in eastern Amazon which contains heavily weathered soils classified as oxisols. Additionally, Amazonian soils greatly weathered, making them devoid of minerals like phosphorus, potassium, calcium, and magnesium, which come from rock sources.

However, not all tropical rainforests occur on nutrient poor soils, but on nutrient rich floodplains and volcanic soils located in the Andean foothills, and volcanic areas of Southeast Asia, Africa, and Central America. Oxisols, infertile, deeply weathered and severely leached, have developed on the ancient Gondwanan shields. Rapid bacterial decay prevents the accumulation of humus. The concentration of iron and aluminum oxides by the laterization pro cess gives the oxisols a bright red colour and sometimes produces minable deposits. On younger substrates, especially of volcanic origin, tropical soils may be quite fertile.

Nutrient Recycling

This high rate of decomposition is the result of phosphorus levels in the soils, precipitation, high temperatures and the extensive microorganism communities. In addition to the bacteria and other microorganisms, there are an abundance of other decomposers such as fungi and termites that aid in the process as well. Nutrient recycling is important because below ground resource availability controls the above ground biomass and community structure of tropical rainforests. These soils are typically phosphorus limited, which inhibits net primary productivity or the uptake of carbon. The soil contains tiny microbial organisms such as bacteria, which break down leaf litter and other organic matter into inorganic forms of carbon usable by plants through a process called decomposition. During the decomposition process the microbial community is respiring, taking up oxygen and releasing carbon dioxide. The decomposition rate can be evaluated by measuring the uptake of oxygen. High temperatures and precipitation increase decomposition rate, which allows plant litter to rapidly decay in tropical regions, releasing nutrients that are immediately taken up by plants through surface or ground waters. The seasonal patterns in respiration are controlled by leaf litter fall and precipitation, the driving force moving the decomposable carbon from the litter to the soil. Respiration rates are highest early in the wet season because the recent dry season results in a large percentage of leaf litter and thus a higher percentage of organic matter being leached into the soil.

Buttress Roots

A common feature of many tropical rainforests is the distinct buttress roots of trees. Instead of penetrating to deeper soil layers, buttress roots create a wide spread root network at the surface for more efficient uptake of nutrients in a very nutrient poor and competitive environment.

Most of the nutrients within the soil of a tropical rainforest occur near the surface because of the rapid turnover time and decomposition of organisms and leaves. Because of this, the buttress roots occur at the surface so the trees can maximize uptake and actively compete with the rapid uptake of other trees. These roots also aid in water uptake and storage, increase surface area for gas exchange, and collect leaf litter for added nutrition. Additionally, these roots reduce soil erosion and maximize nutrient acquisition during heavy rains by diverting nutrient rich water flowing down the trunk into several smaller flows while also acting as a barrier to ground flow. Also, the large surface areas these roots create provide support and stability to rainforests trees, which commonly grow to significant heights. This added stability allows these trees to withstand the impacts of severe storms, thus reducing the occurrence of fallen trees.

6

Plant Adaptations to Variation in the Environment

Species adapted to high light intensity are called shade intolerant. Those adapted to shade environments are called shade tolerant. Shade tolerant species show little difference in their survival and growth rates under shaded or sun. Shade intolerant species were, however, greatly impaired when growing in shaded conditions. This is due to the difference in light compensation point between and carbon allocation between the two species: Shade tolerant plants can maintain a positive carbon uptake under limited light. Shade intolerant plants continue high rate of photosynthesis under low light intensity thus affecting their ability to survive, due to a deficit in carbon uptake.

In aquatic environments, light intensity decrease rapidly with depth. Phytoplankton is inhibited under high intensity light, so they move to deeper zones where the light intensity is optimum. As light intensity changes, they move up or down the water column. Phytoplankton and macrophytes are adapted to different wavelength of visible light.

RESPONSE TO ULTRAVIOLET RADIATION

Laboratory experiments show that UV-B radiation can damage DNA, partially inhibit photosynthesis, alter the growth form of plants, and reduce yield. Plants defend themselves against UV damage by having anthocyanins, colourless flavonoids and other phenols that absorb UV-B radiation but transmit PAR to the interior of the leaf. Plants have a wide range in their ability to screen UV-B radiation. *e.g.* in a group of Rocky Mountain plants growing at high elevations, conifers were the most effective in absorbing UV radiation and herbaceous dicots were the least effective; woody dicots and grass were in between. Conifer leaves are long lived and have evolved mechanism to protect themselves during their long life; herbaceous dicots are short lived and are exposed to UV less time.

PERIODICITY AND PLANT PROCESSES

Light serves as timing mechanism to keep plant activity in tune with the daily and seasonal changes in their environment. Photoperiod is the length of daylight in a 24-hour day, e. g. 10 hours of light in 24-hour day: the photoperiod is 10 hours. A physiological response to a photoperiod is called photoperiodism. Critical daylength: when the duration of sunlight promotes or inhibits a response to changing photoperiod. The length of the night or continuous darkness controls flowering and other responses to photoperiod. Phytochrome detects the varying periods of day length. Some plants measure the length of the night very accurately, not flowering if the night is one minute shorter than the critical length. Some plant flower after a single exposure to the photoperiod required. Others require several days of exposure. Others still require a previous exposure to another environmental stimulus before they respond to the photoperiod. The photoreceptor is a phytochrome. It consists of a protein covalently bonded to a nonprotein part that functions as chromophore, the light absorbing part of the molecule.

How it works: Phytochrome occurs in two forms: one form, P_r, absorbs red light at 660 nm and the other form, P_{fr}, absorbs far-red light at 730 nm. P_{fr} absorbs some red light, so in red light, there is a balance of 85% P_{fr} and 15% P_r. P_r absorbs very little far red light, so in far red light, there is a balance of 97% Pr to 3% P_{fr}. When either form absorbs its preferred wavelength, it changes to the other form. They called this phenomenon photoreversibility. P_{fr} was considered to be the active form and P_r the inactive form of the phytochrome. If a plant is kept in the dark, P_r remains in that form and all the Pfr is converted to P_r. At sunset, the plant converts the P_{fr} to P_r. P_{fr} absorbs in the far-red, almost the infrared.

At sunrise, the plant converts the P_r to P_{fr}. Pr absorbs in the visible range, the red. Short-day plants (long-night plants) flower when the night length is equal to or greater than some critical period. They require certain number of hours of darkness before they flower. Plant detects the shortening of the day or lengthening of the night. Minimum critical night length varies with the species. Fall flowers like poinsettias and chrysanthemums.

The P_{fr} inhibits flowering, They need long nights in order to flower; long nights lower the concentration of the inhibitor P_{fr}. Long-day plants (short-night plants) flower when the night length is equal to or less than some critical period. Plant detects the lengthening of the day and shortening of the night. Maximum critical night length varies with the species. Spring flowers, The P_{fr} induces flowering, They need short nights in order to flower; short nights maintain a high concentration of the inducer, P_{fr}. Day-neutral plants do not respond to photoperiod. Many originated in the tropics where there is little difference in day length throughout the year. Tomato, beans, corn, cucumber, etc. Phytochromes monitor the amount of shade a plant receives. Seasonality: changes in light, temperature and moisture due to the change of seasons. Phenology: recurring biological events due to seasonality. Plant budding, bird migration, insect larva appearing, flowering, fruiting, etc. are all phenology events.

In the spring events occur about four days later for every degree of latitude northward. Spring moves northward at an approximate rate of 17 miles/day. Events occur about a day later for every 100 feet of elevation. Hopkin's microclimatic law is a rule of thumb: events occur about four days later for every degree (~68 miles; ~108.8 km) of latitude north. for every 400 feet (122 meters) of altitude higher. for every 5° of longitude eastward in the spring. The process is reversed in autumn, *e.g.* leaves change colour four days later as we move south, or fall arrives four days earlier as we move north. Phenology is greatly affected by microclimate. *E.g.* spring flowers will bloom earlier in warm microhabitats.

MINERAL AND ENVIRONMENTAL STRESSES

Poor plant growth often can be attributed to inadequate levels of essential plant nutrients. Nitrogen, phosphorous, and potassium are used by the plant in relatively large amounts, and therefore are the nutrients that are most commonly deficient. However, micronutrient deficiencies can occur as well. Many minerals in the soil is too high. The buildup of salts in the soil, insufficient water, extreme temperatures, and poor application of pesticides also can affect the growth and yield of a crop.

Nitrogen, Phosphorus, and Potassium Deficiencies

Nitrogen deficient wheat appears pale green and lower leaves become yellow, usually from the tip to the sheath, followed by necrosis if the deficiency persists. Nitrogen deficiency is the most common and widespread nutrient deficiency in small grains.

Phosphorus deficiency usually results in stunted plants with fewer shoots, if the deficiency is mild. Severe deficiency often causes pale to yellowish red leaves, starting with the lower leaves and moving from the leaf tips inward. Affected tissue may turn brown and, with severe deficiency, eventually dies. Green portions of the leaves may be bluish-green and the base of the culms purple. The development of small heads is also a common symptom.

Potassium deficiency can be difficult to detect, and yield losses can occur long before visual symptoms appear. A severe deficiency will cause the shortening of internodes, and the tips and margins of the lower leaves will become dry and scorched.

Minor Element Deficiencies

Maganese deficiency causes grayish necrotic spots or streaks to appear on the basal portion of the newest leaves. The necrotic spots may extend across the blade causing the upper portion of the leaf to kink or twist. Deficiency of manganese occurs most commonly in soils that matter. Oats are more sensitive than other small grain species. Foliar applications of manganese sulfate can alleviate this deficiency. Copper deficiency symptoms include the discoloration of young leaf tips, followed by breaking and curling of the leaves. The plant may also produce bleached and sterile spikes. Often the spike does not emerge properly from the culm.

Aluminium Toxicity

Symptoms: High concentration of aluminium will first reduce development of the roots, giving them a stubby appearance. They will often have a brownish colour. Typical symptoms in the above ground portion of the plant are small leaves, and shortened and thickened internodes. It also is common for leaf tips to die and for old leaves to become yellow and brittle.

Development: This toxicity is associated with low soil pH, and it can be reduced by limiting.

Hosts/Distribution: Though many minerals can be toxic to plants, the most common toxicity affecting wheat is caused by an excess of free aluminium. Generic variability exists for aluminium tolerance within bread wheats and triticales.

Salt Stress

Symptoms: Salt concentrations within a field are rarely uniform; therefore, one of the first symptome indicating a salt problem is variability in crop growth within the field (barren spots are not uncommon). Plants suffering from salt stress are stunted and dark blue-green in colour, with tip burn and firing on the leaf margins. A soil test can rapidly confirm whether levels of salt in the soil are excessive.

Hosts/Distribution: All small grains are affected, but barley is more tolerant to high levels of salt than other small grain species.

Importance: In some areas, salt levels in the soil have limited yields for a long time; some poorly drained irrigated wheat areas are experiencing a buildup of salt that will eventually limit yields.

Moisture Stress

Symptoms: Moisture stress early in the crop cycle will stunt plants and reduce tillering and root development. Curling and rolling of leaves during midday also are symptoms of moisture stress. Moisture stress during the development of the spike can reduce the number of spikelets and florets, and severe stress may result in grain shrivelling. Other critical periods occur during late booting and during seed set. Severe water stress during these periods can cause complete or partial sterility.

Distribution: Moisture stress occurs to some extent each year in most rainfed environments.

Importance: Yield is often reduced without the appearance of obvious visual symptoms.

Heat Stress

Symptoms: The effects of high temperatures often are associated with the effects of moisture stress, and the symptoms are difficult to separate.

Moderately high temperatures increase the rate of plant development and reduce its rate of growth.

The number and formation of spikelets and florets, as well as grain filling, are reduced, resulting in lower yields. The late-boot and seed-set stages are especially vulnerable and, in many areas, high temperatures are more likely to occur during these later stages of plant development. Very high temperatures will kill plants by denaturing proteins.

Importance: In many areas, the flowering to maturity period in wheat coincides with the beginning of hot, dry weather. If desiccating winds occur along with high temperatures, major reductions in yield may be experienced.

Herbicide Damage

Symptoms: Phytotoxicity can result from the poor application of most pesticides. The application of such hormonal herbicides as 2,4-D too early in the crop cycle can cause leaf curling and deformed spikes; application near anthesis can cause sterility. Residues from the application of triazines (such as atrazine) to the crop preceeding wheat can adversely affect wheat growth; symptoms are bleaching of the leaves followed by necrosis.

Development: Damage results when chemicals are applied in excessive amounts, at the wrong growth stage, or to the wrong species.

Importance: In small grain cereals, damage is generally limited; deformations seldom cause significant losses.

ENVIRONMENTAL FEATURES OF COASTAL ZONE

The Natural and Human Setting

The principal settled areas are uniquely dependent on sound environmental management. The coastal plain occupies approximately 7 per cent of the total area of the country and extends along the entire 430 km. of the

Atlantic coast, varying in width from 26 to 77 km. Five major wetland systems are distinguished in the coastal plain: the marine ecosystem of the sea coast, the estuarine ecosystems of tidal wetlands of the river mouths, and the riverain, palustrine and lacustrine ecosystems. The fertile plain consists of surface clays underlain by clays of the Demerara and Coropina formations. Extending for as much as five miles inland, much of the coastal plain lies between 0.5 metres and 1.0 metres below high tide levels. The shore zone consists of coastal works, mud banks, a mangrove belt and sand flats, all of which serve to protect the plain from flooding.

Ninety per cent of the estimated population of 751,000 resides in the coastal zone. Georgetown has a population of approximately 200,000 in its greater metropolitan area. Agriculture is still the major economic activity, accounting for 24 per cent of GDP and 35-40 per cent of employment. Except for forestry, all agricultural products (sugarcane, rice, other crops, livestock, and fishing) come from the coastal area. Most of the industry is found in Georgetown and along the remaining coast, with only a small concentration in Linden and north of Linden along the Demerara river. Other major economic activities and investments outside Georgetown and the coast consist mainly of large and small scale mining, mostly on major rivers. Groundwater provides 90 per cent of the potable water supply and is extracted mainly from the coastal artisan basin.

Complex interlinked erosion and flooding issues threaten the viability of the intensely concentrated economic base. Sea level rise and possible coastal subsidence add to the pressures on the sea defences and, inevitably, lead to greater coastal erosion and flooding. The shorezone, which serves as the natural line of defence against coastal erosion, is subject to erosion from floating mud shoals in the Atlantic that originate in the Amazon, exacerbated by destruction of mangroves and by removal of sand for construction on shore. The system of water conservancies and drainage and irrigation works in the coastal plain, which have also suffered from lack of maintenance, cause periodic fresh water flooding.

Coastal Erosion

Coastal erosion has been taking place at a relatively rapid rate. A comparison of the 1783 and 1970 coastlines around Liliendall shows a regression of almost 1 kilometre (erosion rates of -4 to -5 metres annually). Evidence of this retreat can be seen all along the coast — old sluice gates form isles far out to sea, and old shorelines and sand ridges run parallel to the present shoreline. Coastal erosion has many causes, some natural and some man-made, and distinguishing between the effects of each is difficult given the paucity of baseline data.

Mud shoals have had and continue to have an unquantifiable impact on coastal erosion. These shoals move along the Brazil, Suriname, Guyana coast from east to west in a series of waves and macro ripples at an approximate speed of 1.3 km per year. They are in constant motion and the refraction and concentration of wave energy between ripples greatly increases the capacity of the shoals to erode the coastal area. On the eastern side of the shoal, the coast accumulates the mud that is colonized by mangroves. However, as the mud shoal moves westward, the mangroves are unable to survive the wave attack and erosion takes place.

Mangroves are a first line of defence against wave action and storms on the coast and also provide a habitat for juvenile fish and shrimp. The construction of drainage systems for agricultural production projects in the coastal zone may have adversely impacted mangroves, as was evident once the MMA-ADA drainage and irrigation scheme was in operation. Mangroves are also plundered for fuelwood and for use in construction and tanning. No clear picture of the extent of the degradation of the mangroves is available, but prudence dictates that they should be protected from further destruction to help prevent further erosion of the coastline and also to preserve the breeding grounds for some marine species.

Sea level rise is another possible cause of coastal erosion. Tide gauge readings in Georgetown from 1960 to 1981 showed a rise of 9 cm. in the relative level of the sea. Engineers in the Hydraulics Division have observed water levels reaching higher up the sea walls. The observed rise in water levels, however, may be partly attributable to subsidence of the coastal zone, caused by the extraction of fresh water from the coastal aquifers. At present the data are inadequate to determine how much of the observed water level rise might be due to subsidence and how much is due to actual sea level rise.

Flooding and its Costs

The coastal plain is subject to flooding from both sea water intrusion and from fresh water overflows. Flooding destroys the value of the country's physical capital and its productivity, e.g., agricultural lands normally remain out of production for at least a year once flooded by saline water. Floods also have serious public health consequences in coastal areas. In Georgetown, sewage is discharged untreated through an outfall into the mouth of the Demerara river and during high tides and flooding this sewage is returned inland. Other areas use septic tanks and pit latrines, which may contribute to pollution of groundwater and, during flooding, surface waters.

For the past two decades, lack of maintenance, mainly because of budgetary constraints, has seriously weakened the sea defences. In 1991 more than 25 breaches of the sea wall flooded agricultural and residential areas. One breach at Cornelia on Leguan Island resulted in more than 1,000 acres of rice land being flooded. Since 1993 responsibility for maintenance of the sea defences was transferred from regional authorities to the Hydraulics Division, but the pervasive lack of funding and staff affects this Division too, and maintenance of these critical defence works is not yet at the desired standard. However, a new maintenance and rehabilitation programme is in place and so this concern should abate in coming years. The problem of contamination of groundwater, however, is still not being addressed systematically.

An intricate system of water conservancies and drainage and irrigation has been constructed to control flooding and overcome the seasonality of rainfall for coastal agriculture. However, for lack of maintenance, drainage ditches are often silted up or clogged with garbage, the mechanical pumps fail and sluice gates that control the flow of water often do not function properly, leading to frequent fresh water flooding. At high tides the flooding is exacerbated because gravity drainage seaward has to be blocked. The drainage and irrigation systems have profoundly altered the natural surface water regime, which is likely to have significant environmental repercussions. Nevertheless, no structured monitoring of such effects is conducted, except in the MMA-ADA Project.

Integrated Coastal Zone Management

Even though the coastal zone supports the majority of the population and the main economic activities, there is no formal coastal zone management plan or strategy for the multiple uses to which these resources may be put. Many agencies have shorezone management responsibilities, including the Environment Unit, the Hydraulics Division, the Hydro-Meteorology Department and Fisheries Department, and the Central Planning and Housing Department. This last agency is responsible for planning and zoning in urban and rural settlements, the implementation of standards and regulations and development control. Government has recognised that improved coastal zone management depends on an integrated approach. In 1991 Government established a subcommittee on coastal zone management, formed by representatives from the major agencies dealing with the coastal zone. The next step should be more complete incorporation of coastal communities into the process of developing plans for the coastal zone and implementing them.

THE EMERGING SCIENCE OF ENVIRONMENTAL APPLICATIONS

The science of earth and environment has matured through two major phases and is entering a third. In the first phase, which ended two decades ago, Earth and environmental science was largely discipline oriented and focused on developing knowledge in geology, atmospheric chemistry, ecosystems, and other aspects of the Earth system. In the 1980s, the scientific community recognized the close coupling of these disciplines and began to study them as interacting elements of a single system.

During this second phase, the paradigm of Earth system science emerged. With it came the ability to understand complex, system-oriented phenomena such as climate change, which links concepts from atmospheric sciences, biology, and human behavior. Essential to the study of Earth's interacting systems was the ability to acquire, manage, and make available data from satellite observations; in parallel, new models were developed to express our growing understanding of the complex processes in the dynamic Earth system.

In the emerging third phase, knowledge developed primarily for the purpose of scientific understanding is being complemented by knowledge created to target practical decisions and action. This new knowledge endeavor can be referred to as the science of environmental applications. Climate change provides the most prominent example of the importance of this shift. Until now, the climate science community has focused on critical questions involving basic knowledge, from measuring the amount of change to determining the causes.

With the basic understanding now well established, the demand for climate applications knowledge is emerging. How do we quantify and monitor total forest biomass so that carbon markets can characterize supply? What are the implications of regional shifts in water resources for demographic trends, agricultural output, and energy production?

To what extent will seawalls and other adaptations to rising sea level impact coasts? These questions are informed by basic science, but they raise additional issues that can be addressed only by a new science discipline focused specifically on applications- a discipline that integrates physical, biogeochemical, engineering, and human processes. Its principal questions reflect a fundamental curiosity about the nature of the world we live in, tempered by the awareness that a question's importance scales with its relevance to a societal imperative. As Nobel laureate and U.S.

Secretary of Energy Steven Chu has remarked, "We seek solutions. We don't seek- dare I say this?-just scientific papers anymore". To illustrate the relationships between basic science and applications, consider the role of snowmelt runoff in water supplies. Worldwide, 1 billion people depend on snow or glacier melt for their water resources. Design and operations of water systems have traditionally relied on historical measurements in a stationary climate, along with empirical relationships and models. As climates and land use change, populations grow and relocate, and our built systems age and decay, these empirical methods of managing our water become inaccurate-a conundrum characterized as "stationarity is dead".

Snowmelt commonly provides water for competing uses: urban and agricultural supply, hydropower, recreation, and ecosystems. In many areas, both rainfall and snowfall occur, raising the concern that a future warmer climate will lead to a greater fraction of precipitation as rain, with the water arriving months before agricultural demand peaks and with more rapid runoff leading to more floods. In these mixed rain and snow systems, the societal need is: How do we sustain flood control and the benefits that water provides to humans and ecosystems when changes in the timing and magnitude of runoff are likely to render existing infrastructure inadequate?

The solution to the societal need requires a more fundamental, process-based understanding of the water cycle. Currently, historical data drive practices and decisions for flood control and water supply systems. Flood operations and reservoir flood capacity are predetermined by regulatory orders that are static, regardless of the type of water year, current state of the snowpack, or risk of flood. In many years, early snowmelt is not stored because statistically based projections anticipate floods that better information might suggest cannot materialize because of the absence of snow. The more we experience warming, the more frequently this occurrence will impact the water supply.

The related science challenges are:

- The statistical methods in use do not try to estimate the basin's water balance, and with the current measurement networks even in the U.S., we lack adequate knowledge of the amount of snow in the basins;
- We are unable to partition the input between rain and snow, or to partition that rain or snow between evapotranspiration and runoff;
- We lack the knowledge to manage the relationship between snow cover, forests, and carbon stocks;
- Runoff forecasts that are not based on physical principles relating to snowmelt are often inaccurate;
- We do not know what incentives and institutional arrangements would lead to better management of the watershed for ecosystem services.

Generally, models do not consider these kinds of interactions; hence the need for a *science of environmental applications.*

Its core characteristics differentiate it from the basic science of Earth and environment:

- *Need driven versus curiosity driven*: Basic science is question driven; in contrast, the new applications science is guided more by societal needs than scientific curiosity. Rather than seeking answers to questions, it focuses on creating the ability to seek courses of action and determine their consequences.
- *Externally constrained*: External circumstances often dictate when and how applications knowledge is needed. The creation of carbon trading

markets will not wait until we fully quantify forest carbon content. It will happen on a schedule dictated by policy and economics. Construction and repair of the urban water infrastructure will not wait for an understanding of evolving rainfall patterns. Applications science must be prepared to inform actions subject to these external drivers, not according to academic schedules based on when and how the best knowledge can be obtained.

- *Consequential and recursive*: Actions arising from our knowledge of the Earth often change the Earth, creating the need for new knowledge about what we have changed. For example, the more we knew in the past about locations of fish populations, the more the populations were overfished; our original knowledge about them became rapidly outdated through our own actions. Applications science seeks to understand not just those aspects of the Earth addressed by a particular use scenario, but also the consequences and externalities that result from that use scenario. A recent example is the shift of agricultural land to corn-for ethanol production—an effort to reduce climate change that we now recognize as significantly stressing scarce water resources.
- *Useful even when incomplete*: As the snowpack example illustrates, actions are often needed despite incomplete data or partial knowledge. The difficulty of establishing confidence in the quality of our knowledge is particularly disconcerting given the loss of stationarity associated with climate change. New means of making effective use of partial knowledge must be developed, including robust inference engines and statistical interpretation.
- *Scalable*: Basic science knowledge does not always scale to support applications needs. The example of carbon trading presents an excellent illustration. Basic science tells us how to relate carbon content to measurements of vegetation type and density, but it does not give us the tools that scale this to a global inventory. New knowledge tools must be built to accurately create and update this inventory through cost-effective remote sensing or other means.
- *Robust*: The decision makers who apply applications knowledge typically have limited comprehension of how the knowledge was developed and in what situations it is applicable. To avoid misuse, the knowledge must be characterized in highly robust terms. It must be stable over time and insensitive to individual interpretations, changing context, and special conditions.
- *Data intensive*: Basic science is data intensive in its own right, but data sources that support basic science are often insufficient to support

applications. Localized impacts with global extent, such as intrusion of invasive species, are often difficult for centralized projects with small numbers of researchers to ascertain.

New applications-appropriate sources must be identified, and new ways of observing (including the use of communities as data gatherers) must be developed. Each of these characteristics implies development of *new knowledge types* and *new tools for acquiring that knowledge.* The snowpack example illustrates what this requirement means for a specific application area. Four elements have recently come together that make deployment of a measurement and information system that can support decisions at a scale of a large river basin feasible:

1. Accurate, sustained satellite estimates of snow-covered area across an entire mountain range;
2. Reliable, low-cost sensors and telemetry systems for snow and soil moisture;
3. Social science data that complement natural and engineered systems data to enable analysis of human decision making;
4. Cyberinfrastructure advances to integrate data and deliver them in near real time.

For snow-dominated drainage basins, the highest-priority scientific challenge is to estimate the spatial distribution and heterogeneity of the *snow water equivalent*— i.e., the amount of water that would result if the snow were to melt. Because of wind redistribution of snow after it falls, snow on the ground is far more heterogeneous than rainfall, with several meters of differences within a 10 to 100 m distance. Heterogeneity in snow depth smoothes the daily runoff because of the variability of the duration of meltwater in the snowpack; seasonally, it produces quasi-riparian zones of increased soil moisture well into the summer.

The approach to estimating the snow water equivalent involves several tasks using improved data:

- Extensive validation of the satellite estimates of snow cover and its reflectivity;
- Using results from an energy balance reconstruction of snow cover to improve interpolation from more extensive ground measurements and satellite data;
- Development of innovative ways to characterize heterogeneity;
- Testing the interpolated estimates with a spatially distributed runoff model. The measurements would also help clarify the accuracy in precipitation estimates from regional climate models. This third phase of Earth and environmental science will evolve over the next decade as

the scientific community begins to pursue it. Weather science has already built substantial capability in applications science; the larger field of Earth science will need to learn from and extend those efforts. The need for basic science and further discovery will not diminish, but instead will be augmented and extended by this new phase. The questions to address are both practically important and intellectually captivating. Will our hydrologic forecasting skill decline as changes in precipitation diminish the value of statistics obtained from historic patterns? Where will the next big climate change issue arise, and what policy actions taken today could allow us to anticipate it? Equally important is improving how we apply this knowledge in our daily lives. The Internet and mobile telephones, with their global reach, provide new ways to disseminate information rapidly and widely. Information was available to avoid much of the devastation from the Asian tsunami and Hurricane Katrina, but we lacked the tools for rapid decision making and communication of needed actions. Applications science is therefore integrative; it couples understanding of physical phenomena and research into the ways that people and organizations can use better knowledge to make decisions. The public as a whole can also become an important contributor to localized Earth observation, augmenting our limited satellite and sensor networks through devices as simple as mobile phone cameras. The ability to leverage this emerging data-gathering capability will be an important challenge for the new phase of environmental science. The security and prosperity of nearly 7 billion people depend increasingly on our ability to gather and apply information about the world around us. Basic environmental science has established an excellent starting point. We must now develop this into a robust science of environmental applications.

The Limits of Global Environmental Management

Although steps have been taken between Rio 1992 and New York 1997 in the direction of the globalization of environmental protection, the world seems to be further away from sustainability today than it was then. With environmental globalization and the consensual concept of sustainable development, the perception of an ecological crisis, or at least of ecological limits to development, appears to have vanished: acting for environmental protection increasingly tends to be seen as a technical problem, the task of increasing efficiency and of better using resources such as science, technology, information, capital, and institutions. The cause of environmental problems is no longer perceived as linked to industrial development and ever-increasing material accumulation, but it has become the very existence of human beings.

Environmental problems are understood as unavoidable, as side effects of human activities, and efforts are then directed at solving these problems.

Indeed, global environmental management and sustainable development can be seen as "problem solving" concepts, in Robert Cox's terminology, as they only represent a strategy to allow the pursuit of present lifestyles and standards.

Following Strange's call for a critical International Political Economy and the need to address the question of "who gets what, how and why," the analysis of the evolution of the system of global environmental management has revealed that it tends to strengthen the mechanisms of exclusion and inequality (Strange 1988). Global environmental management and sustainable development tend to be uneven concepts, as they do not aim at promoting the correction of global disparities. They attempt to offer a universal framework in which the global society is the unit of analysis and a large share of the blame for environmental degradation rests on the Third World. Instead of stressing affluence, over-production and over-consumption in advanced countries as the main causes of environmental degradation, it tends to suggest that problems arise from poverty. Environmental degradation is transformed from a problem of affluence into a problem of poverty. The responsibility is shifted from major polluters and industrialized countries' abuses to all inhabitants of the planet. For Chatterjee and Finger (1994), the only different element in this approach is that development is now looked at from a global perspective, making the development discourse universal.

And the New York Summit represented a step further in that direction, asserting the desirability of the globalization process and underlining its beneficial aspects. It also consolidated the role of business and industry as privileged partners of the United Nations, establishing permanent contact and consultation on environmental issues. The regulatory situation relating to TNCs and business in general has worsened greatly in the past five years (Khor 1997).

Already in 1992, the US government successfully pressured for downsizing the UN Center on Transnational Corporations (UNCTC), which had been set up to monitor the social, economic and environmental impacts of corporate investment in developing countries. Today, the UN is considering cutting a sub-group of the UN Human Rights Commission which addresses the impacts of corporations on a broad spectrum on rights issues. The main international initiatives and institution for establishing guidelines for the behavior of corporations, which could together lay down a code of obligations and rights of TNCs and states, have disappeared.

In their place has come a strong and growing opposite trend to reduce and remove regulations that governments have over corporations, to grant them increased rights and powers, and to reduce the authority of states to control their behavior and operations. The Uruguay Round for example has already granted far higher standards of intellectual property rights protection to corporations, thus facilitating further their global monopolization of technology and ability to make profit through higher prices. There are also strong pressures from Northern governments at the World Trade Organization to grant foreign companies the right of entry, establishment and national treatment in all WTO member states (Khor 1997).

In addition, the partnership between the UN and global corporations seems to have been further strengthened in the past two years. In part due to the difficult financial and political situation in which the UN finds itself as a result of the US government's refusal to pay the US $1.6 billion it owes, the UN is now openly seeking political and economic support from corporations. At the last Davos Economic Forum in Switzerland, UN Secretary General Kofi Annan called for a human face to the global market and challenged business leaders to adhere to universal values defined by the UN and contribute to global environmental protection, indicating a broader trend of growing UN collaboration with transnational corporations.

Recently, the United Nations Development Program (UNDP) has solicited funds from global corporations with poor records on human rights, labor and the environment, such as Dow Chemical, Citibank and Rio Tinto Plc, in exchange of special UNDP sanctioned logos for use by corporate sponsors. Called the "Global Sustainable Development Facility (GSDF)," the plan calls for corporate sponsors to funnel donations to a separate entity which they will manage. In the words of the UNDP, the GSDF "brings together leading global corporations and the UNDP, to jointly define and implement a new facility to eradicate poverty, create sustainable economic growth and allow the private sector to prosper through the inclusion of two billion new people in the global market economy."

According to the internal memo, sponsors will benefit from the advice and support of UNDP through a special relationship, allowing corporations unprecedented access to UNDP's network of offices, high level governmental contacts and the knock-on effects of its reputation. The plan, revealed through a leaked internal UNDP memo, has been heavily criticized by observers and NGOs, who warn that the interests of global corporations are often at odds with the basic economic and social needs of the world's poor and the values of human rights and environmental protection the UN is meant to protect.

According to Ward Morehouse, President of the US Council on International and Public Affairs, the UN should be monitoring the human rights and environmental impacts of corporations in developing and industrialized nations, not granting special favors... Increasing collaboration will lead to a reluctance to criticize corporations which are central players in the human rights, environmental and developmental dramas unfolding every day across the globe.

To conclude, the UN and international organizations in general seem to be moving towards the adoption of a market-oriented global model of environmental governance, which sees economic globalization as a positive and integrative process. The key actors of economic globalization, transnational corporations, are taking the leading role and consolidating their influence on the system of international environmental governance. With the adoption of this project of global environmental management, one particular understanding of the world, the one promoted by business and large corporations in Western affluent societies, becomes hegemonic and appears to be universal (Shiva 1993).

Environmental concerns have been incorporated as a mere dimension of the "globalization project," understood in McMichael's definition as "an emerging vision of the world and its resources as a globally organized and managed free trade/free enterprise economy pursued by a largely unaccountable political and economic elite" (McMichael 1996, 300). This project advocates a universalized model of production, of consumption, and thus of dealing with problems of environmental protection resulting from these activities.

By assuming its universality, it tends to marginalize other knowledge and other solutions to problems of environmental protection. Interestingly enough, it was unanimously recognized that the most positive result and follow-up of UNCED was without doubt realized at the micro-level, within the Local Agenda 21 framework. In an effort to implement Agenda 21 locally, social groups have worked together with local authorities to make sustainable development a reality at the local level, often on a truly participatory basis and reflecting grassroots concern and involvement.

From a critical point of view, global management's failure, exemplified at the New York Summit, was not entirely unexpected. Indeed, the global management approach inspired by business perspectives and propagated by the international development establishment tends to strengthen the globalization process at work today, failing to counter its effects in terms of social exclusion and environmental destruction. It tends to weaken social protection and environmental protection in the name of economic efficiency (McMichael 1996).

It stands at odds with the commitment to social change and to equity that lies at the root of a critical, political economy view of global environmental politics as inserted within the dynamics of economic accumulation and social structures. The question of the ownership of natural resources, for example, is not addressed. However, environmental problems in the South are often linked to problems of resource ownership and equity.

Sustainable Development as defined in Rio and reasserted in New York has been practically translated into technocratic responses to what are in reality political problems.

Conclusion

The purpose of this article was to analyze and evaluate the process of "mainstreaming" of environmental concerns. Recalling the radical and transformative origins of the ecological project, it has provided evidence that environmental concerns have been remodeled by the joint action of technocratic environmentalists, the international UN-related development establishment and business and industry sectors. Examining the results of international cooperation, the article has questioned the nature of the sustainable development consensus, a consensus deeply marked by the growing access and influence of global corporations on UN activities. Today, market-oriented perspectives to environmental problems seem to be prevailing over more transformative views, especially at the international level, within the framework of international organizations and institutional agreements.

The article has suggested that the mainstream approach to sustainable development tends to reduce ecology to a set of managerial practices aiming at resource efficiency and risk management. In doing so, it tends to address a civilizational impasse as a mere technical problem (Sachs 1993). The mainstream approach proposes that environmentalists should operate using the language and the worldview of Western economics in approaching ecological concerns.

Instead of designing cultural and political limits to development, the project of "global environmental management" tends to become part of a technocratic effort to sustain industrial development in the age of economic globalization. Environmental protection, together with democracy, human rights and free market economics, becomes a universal consensus, a universal consensus which, as Baudrillard remarks, arouses suspicion, since it is about values that have become devalued, values becoming emptied at the very moment of their hegemony (Huysmans 1995). Environmental concerns become just another element in a process leading to global uniformity, a uniformity of cultures, lifestyles, mentalities, but also of relationships with nature (Sachs 1993; Latouche 1996).

This market-oriented agenda may provide a starting point for dealing with global environmental problems. The documents, which emerged from international environmental negotiations from Rio to New York, replete with inconsistencies, represent a complex mix of disagreements, hopes and compromises. One may concede that conventions and obligations reflect the need for government negotiators to find the minimum agreeable grounds to initiate a large open-ended process on major environmental issues.

In this sense, they only produced a general framework for negotiations, steps on the way to building international regimes. They do not form a series of real commitments representing an effective consensus on how to deal with global environmental issues. Yet considering the amount of time, energy and resources invested in this process of international environmental regime building, one might have hoped for more concrete, positive results. The failure of the present framework to effectively promote sustainability, which became evident in the 1997 New York summit, is recognized even by one of the major promoters of this path, Maurice Strong, ex-secretary general of UNCED, today President of the Earth Council. For Strong, unfortunately, the economic, social and demographical forces that lead to unsustainable development still prevail. Strong sees the lack of political will'from governments as the main cause of this failure.

The present framework appears to contain many contradictions that limit the ability of the international and national communities to solve satisfactorily environmental problems. Adopting an international political economy perspective, this article has argued that the main problem that international efforts to protect the environment have to address is the issue of the impact of economic globalization. Economic globalization has in a sense helped to create conditions for the development of policy mechanisms and institutions that will universalize and promote the concept of "sustainable development." Global change is exerting a structuring influence on the redefinition of environmental politics.

However, the kind of sustainable development being promoted seems to represent more the consolidation of a global project of "environmental management" than a real shift away from destructive practices. Globalization is consolidating a market-friendly view of sustainable development, a view that gives priority to the sustainability of "global growth" and to the correction of environmental damage. This tends to be carried out at the expense of the competing alternatives and participative view of sustainable development as stressing not only development but also social equity and decentralized participation. The "globalization project" has shaped and redefined both the content of environmentalism and environmental policies and structured the international political economy in a way that makes sustainability more difficult to achieve.

7

Ecological Geography and Conservation

In the mid-nineteenth century, the field of ecological geography became established through the writings of George Perkins Marsh. One book published in 1864, *Man and Nature, or, Physical Geography as Modified by Human Action,* laid the foundation of ecological geography and conservation. As Stewart Udall pointed out in *The Quiet Crisis,* this book marked "the beginning of land wisdom in this country." Lewis Mumford described *Man and Nature* as "the fountainhead of the conservation movement."

Marsh's basic theme in *Man and Nature* was that man's economic progress has often disrupted the balance of nature to his own detriment. He clarified the reciprocal interaction of man and environment. Marsh traced the history of civilizations, particularly those in the Mediterranean area, in terms of physical geography, natural resources and land changes induced by man. He first called attention to the striking effects of deforestation and land scarring on erosion, agriculture, and water resources. He forced his readers to look upon man in a different light—not as a conqueeor but as a despoiler.

Marsh's greatest achievements were in scholarly fields. He became an accomplished linguist, a master of twenty languages, and he wrote several books of historical and linguistic scholarship. His Vermont background fostered a keen interest in landscape and nature, and he became intensely aware of man's influence on his environment. During his Mediterranean travels from 1848 to 1851, and his subsequent tenure in Italy beginning in 1861, he viewed the rocky and arid landscapes of the Middle East and the Mediterranean countries with an alarming new insight. He undertook historical investigations of former vegetation and water resources, and he documented carefully his conclusions on the role of man in shaping once fertile lands into present-day deserts.

Although *Man and Nature* was a financial success and was widely read upon publication in 1864, its influence on the conservation movement in the

United States was slow in coming. In fact, the period of the 1870's and 1880's in this country witnessed unprecedented environmental exploitation. Forests were cut at a tremendous rate without regard for conservation, lands were cleared, plowed and abandoned with increasing speed. Devastation of animal resources accelerated, resulting in the decline of the American bison from more than 60 million prior to 1850 to a total United States population of less than 600 by 1890. The passenger pigeon was so ruthlessly hunted and its nesting habitat so effectively destroyed that it was virtually extinct by the end of the nineteenth century and the last zoo specimen died in Cincinnati in 1914.

Not for almost 40 years, in fact, were the conservation concerns expressed in *Man and Nature* turned into political realities through the activism of Gifford Pinchotand Theodore Roosevelt. Pinchot, later governor of Pennsylvania, was one of the first persons to advocate planned forest conservation in the United States. He became a member of the new National Forest Commission in 1896 and Chief of the Division of Forestry in 1898. Pinchot served as Chief of the Forest Service of the U.S. Department of Agriculture from 1905 to 1910 when he became president of the National Conservation Committee. In the same year he published an influential book entitled, *The Fight for Conservation*.

The greatest political momentum to the conservation movement in the United States came through the forceful efforts of Theodore Roosevelt. As a Dakota rancher from 1884 to 1886, Roosevelt became intensely interested in wildlife and natural habitat. He wrote profusely throughout this period, centering his writings on the history of the West and the benefits of wilderness. Twenty years later, as President of the United States, he emphasized environmental conservation as one of the country's most important domestic problems He added more acreage to the national forests than all presidents before and after. He regulated grazing and lumbering on national lands, and in 1908 he called the first White House conference on conservation. He worked closely with Pinchot in establishing the National Conservation Commission.

IMPORTANCE IN ECOLOGY

Microbes are critical to the processes of decomposition required to cycle nitrogen and other elements back to the natural world.

Hygiene

Hygiene is the avoidance of infection or food spoiling by eliminating microorganisms from the surroundings. As microorganisms, particularly bacteria, are found practically everywhere, this means in most cases the reduction of harmful microorganisms to acceptable levels. However, in some cases it is required that an object or substance be completely sterile, i.e. devoid of all living entities and viruses. A good example of this is a hypodermic needle.

In food preparation microorganisms are reduced by preservation methods (such as the addition of vinegar), clean utensils used in preparation, short storage periods or by cool temperatures. If complete sterility is needed, the two most common methods are irradiation and the use of an autoclave, which resembles a pressure cooker.

There are several methods for investigating the level of hygiene in a sample of food, drinking water, equipment etc. Water samples can be filtrated through an extremely fine filter. This filter is then placed in a nutrient medium. Microorganisms on the filter then grow to form a visible colony. Harmful microorganisms can be detected in food by placing a sample in a nutrient broth designed to enrich the organisms in question. Various methods, such as selective media or PCR, can then be used for detection. The hygiene of hard surfaces, such as cooking pots, can be tested by touching them with a solid piece of nutrient medium and then allowing the microorganisms to grow on it.

There are no conditions where all microorganisms would grow, and therefore often several different methods are needed. For example, a food sample might be analyzed on three different nutrient mediums designed to indicate the presence of "total" bacteria (conditions where many, but not all, bacteria grow), molds (conditions where the growth of bacteria is prevented by e.g. antibiotics) and coliform bacteria (these indicate a sewage contamination).

Metallurgy

Metallurgy, science and technology of metals, including the extraction of metals from ores, the preparation of metals for use, and the study of the relationship between structures and properties of metals.

Metallurgical processes consist of two operations: concentration, separating a metal or metallic compound from the useless waste rock material, or gangue, which accompanies it in the ore; and refining, producing the metal in a pure or nearly pure state suitable for use. Three types of processes are employed both for concentration and refining: mechanical, chemical, and electrical. In most cases a combination of these methods is used.

One of the simplest methods of mechanical separation is gravity separation. This process is based on the difference in specific gravity between native metals and metallic minerals, and the other rock materials with which they are mixed. When crushed ore or ore concentrates are suspended either in water or an air blast, the heavier metal or metallic mineral particles fall to the bottom of the processing chamber, and the lighter gangue is blown or washed away. The prospector's technique of panning gold from gold-bearing sand, for example, is a small-scale gravity-separation process. Similarly, by virtue of its higher specific gravity, magnetite, a mineral of iron, may be separated from the gangue rock in which it occurs. Flotation is the most important present-day method of mechanical concentration. In its simplest form, flotation is a modified gravity process in which finely ground ore is mixed, usually with a liquid.

The metal or metallic mineral floats while the gangue sinks, although the reverse is true in some instances. In most modern flotation processes, the floating of either the metal or gangue is aided by an oil or other surface-active agent. By this means, comparatively heavy substances can be made to float on water. In one typical process, a finely ground ore containing copper sulfide is mixed with water, to which small amounts of oil, acid, or other so-called flotation reagents are added. When air is blown through this mixture, a froth is formed on the surface that has the property of mixing with the sulfide but not with the gangue.

The latter material settles, and the sulfide is collected from the froth. Use of the flotation process has made possible the exploitation of many ore deposits of low concentration, and even of the wastes from processing plants that used less efficient techniques. In some cases, by means of differential flotation, different minerals can be concentrated from one complex ore in a single process.

Ores, such as magnetite, that have marked magnetic properties are concentrated by means of electromagnets that attract the metal but do not attract the gangue. Electrostatic separation employs an electric field to separate minerals of different electrical properties by exploiting the attraction between unlike charges and the repulsion between like charges.

Chemical separation methods are, in general, the most important from the economic point of view. In present-day practice chemical separation often is used as a second stage after mechanical concentration. A greater tonnage of refined metal is obtained by smelting than by any other process. In smelting, the ore, or the concentrate from a mechanical separation process, is heated with a reducing agent and a flux to a high temperature.

The reducing agent combines with the oxygen in a metallic oxide, leaving pure metal; and the flux combines with the gangue to form a slag that is liquid at the smelting temperature and thus can be skimmed off or poured away from the metal. The production of pig iron in blast furnaces is an example of smelting, and the process is also used to extract copper, lead, nickel, and many other metals from their ores.

Amalgamation is a metallurgical process that utilizes mercury to dissolve silver or gold to form an amalgam. This process has been largely supplanted by the cyanide process, in which gold or silver is dissolved in solutions of sodium or potassium cyanide. Various types of aqueous solutions are employed in different leaching, or percolating, processes to dissolve metals from ores.

Metallic carbonates and sulfides are treated by roasting, heating to a temperature below the melting point of the metal. In the case of carbonates, carbon dioxide is driven off in the process, leaving a metallic oxide. When sulfides are roasted, the sulfur combines with the oxygen of the air to form gaseous sulfur dioxide, leaving metallic oxides, which are subsequently reduced by smelting.

Agglomeration of ore fines (fine particles) is accomplished by sintering or pelletizing. In the sintering process, fuel, water, air, and heat are used to fuse the ore fine into a porous mass. In pelletizing, moistened fine is formed into small pellets in the presence of limestone flux and then fired.

A number of other processes, of which pyrometallurgy (high-temperature metallurgy) and distillation are the most important, are employed in further refinement stages of a variety of metals. In the process of electrolysis the metal is deposited at the cathode from aqueous solutions or in an electrolytic furnace.

Copper, nickel, zinc, silver, and gold are several examples of metals that are refined by deposition from aqueous solutions. Aluminum, barium, calcium, magnesium, beryllium, potassium, and sodium are metals that are processed in electrolytic furnaces.

General Sequence of Operations

Occasionally, but rarely, metallic ores occur as practically pure compact masses, from which the accompanying matrix or "gangue" can be detached by hand and hammer. In most cases the "ore", as it comes out of the mine or quarry, is simply a mixture of ore proper and gangue, in which the latter not unfrequently predominates.

Hence it is generally necessary to purify the ore before the liberation of the metal is attempted. Most metallic ores are specifically heavier than the accompanying impurities and their purification is generally effected by reducing the crude ore to a fine enough powder to detach the metallic from the earthy part, and then washing away the latter by a current of water, as far as possible.

The majority of ores being chemical compounds, the extraction of their metals demands chemical treatment. The chemical operations involved may be classified as follows: I. *Fiery Operations. - The* ore, generally with some "flux," is exposed to the action of fire. The fire in most cases has a chemical, in addition to its physical, function. Moreover the furnace is designed so as to facilitate the action of the heat and furnace gases in the desired direction.

It is intended either to burn away certain components of the ore - in which case it must be so regulated as to contain a sufficient excess of unburned oxygen; or it is meant to deoxidize ("reduce") the ore,when the draught must be restricted so as to keep the ore constantly wrapped up in combustible flame gases (carbon monoxide, hydrogen, marsh-gas, &c.).

The majority of the chemical operations of metallurgy fall into this category, and in these processes other metal-reducing agents than those naturally contained in the fire (or blast) are only exceptionally employed.

Amalgamation

The ore by itself (if it is a reguline one), or with certain reagents (if it is not), is worked up with mercury so that the metal is obtained as an amalgam, which can be separated mechanically from the dross. The purified amalgam is distilled, when the mercury is recovered as a distillate while the metal remains.

Wet Processes

Strictly speaking, certain amalgamation methods fall under this head; but, in its ordinary acceptance, the term refers to processes in which the metal is extracted either from the natural ore, or from the ore after roasting or other preliminary treatment, by an acid or salt solution, and from this solution precipitated - generally in the reguline form - by some suitable reagent.

Few methods of metal extraction at once yield a pure product. What as a rule is obtained is a more or less impure metal, which requires to be "refined" to become fit for the market.

Chemical Operations

Amalgamation and wet-way processes have limited applications, being practically confined to copper, gold and silver. We therefore here confine ourselves, in the main, to pyro-chemical operations.

The method to be adopted for the extraction of a metal from its ore is determined chiefly, though not entirely, by the nature of the non-metallic component with which the metal is combined. The simplest case is that of the reguline ores where there is no nonmetallic element. The important case is that of gold.

Oxides, Hydrates, Carbonates and Silicates

All iron and tin ores proper fall under this heading, which, besides, comprises certain ores of copper, of lead and of zinc. The first step consists in subjecting the crude ore to a roasting or calcining process, the object of which is to remove the water and carbon dioxide, and burn away, to some extent at least, the sulphur, arsenic or organic matter.

The residue consists of an impure oxide of the respective metal, which in all cases is reduced by treatment with fuel at a high temperature. Should the metal be present as a silicate, lime must be added in the smelting to remove the silica and liberate the oxide. The temperature required for the reduction of zinc lies above the boiling point of the metal; hence the mixture of ore and reducing agent (charcoal is generally used) must be heated in a retort combined with condensing apparatus. In all the other cases the reduction is effected in the fire itself, a tower-shaped blast furnace being preferably used.

The furnace is charged with alternate layers of fuel and ore and the whole kindled from below. The metallic oxide, partly by the direct action of the carbon with which it is in contact, but principally by that of the carbon monoxide produced in the lower strata from the oxygen of the blast and the hot carbon there, is reduced to the metallic state; the metal fuses and runs down, with the slag, to the bottom of the furnace, whence both are withdrawn by opening plug-holes.

Sulphides

Iron, copper, lead, zinc, mercury, silver and antimony very frequently present themselves in this state of combination, as components of a family of ores which may be divided into two sections:

- Such as substantially consist of simple sulphides, as iron pyrites (FeS_2), galena (PbS), zinc blende (ZnS), cinnabar (HgS); and
- Complex sulphides, such as the various kinds of sulphureous copper ores (all substantially compounds or mixtures of sulphides of copper and iron); bournonite, a complex sulphide of lead, antimony and copper; rothgiltigerz, sulphide of silver, antimony and arsenic; fahlerz, sulphides of arsenic and antimony, combined with sulphides of copper, silver, iron, zinc, mercury, silver; and mixtures of these and other sulphides with one another.

In treating a sulphureous ore, the first step as a rule is to subject it to oxidation by roasting it in a reverberatory or other furnace, which leads to the burning away of at least part of the arsenic and part of the sulphur.

The effect on the several individual metallic sulphides (supposing only one of these to be present) is as follows:

- Those of silver (Ag_2S) and mercury (HgS) yield sulphur dioxide gas and metal; in the case of silver, sulphate is formed at low temperatures. Metallic mercury, in the circumstances, goes off as a vapour, which is collected and condensed; silver remains as a regulus, but pure sulphide of silver is hardly ever worked.
- Sulphides of iron and zinc yield the oxides Fe_2O_3 and ZnO as final products, some basic sulphate being formed at the earlier stages, especially in the case of zinc. The oxides can be reduced by carbon.
- The sulphides of lead and copper yield, the former a mixture of oxide and normal sulphate, the latter one of oxide and basic sulphate. Sulphate of lead is stable at a red heat; sulphate of copper breaks up into oxide,

sulphur dioxide and oxygen. In practice, neither oxidation process is ever pushed to the end; it is stopped as soon as the mixture of roasting-product and unchanged sulphide contains oxygen and sulphur in the ratio of 0 2: S. The access of air is then stopped and the whole heated to a higher temperature, when the whole of the sulphur and oxygen is eliminated. This method is largely utilized in the smelting of lead from galena and of copper from copper pyrites.

- Sulphide of antimony, when roasted in air, is converted into a kind of alloy of sulphide and oxide; the same holds for iron, only its oxysulphide is quite readily converted into the pure oxide Fe_2O_3 by further roasting. Oxysulphide of antimony, by suitable processes can be reduced to metal, but these processes are rarely used, because the same end is far more easily obtained by "precipitation," *i.e.* withdrawing the sulphur by fusion with metallic iron, forming metallic antimony and sulphide of iron. Both products fuse, but readily part, because fused antimony is far heavier than fused sulphide of iron. A precisely similar method is used occasionally for the reduction of lead from galena. Sulphide of lead, when fused together with metallic iron in the proportion of 2Fe: I PbS yields a regulus (= I Pb) and a "mat" Fe_2S, which, however, on cooling, decomposes into the ordinary sulphide FeS, and finely divided iron. What we have been explaining are special cases of a more general metallurgic proposition: Any one of the metals, copper, iron, tin, zinc, lead, silver, antimony, arsenic, in general, is capable of desulphurizing (at least partially) any of the others that follows it in the series just given, and it does so the more readily and completely the greater the number of intervening terms. Hence, supposing a complete mixture of these metals to be melted down under circumstances admitting of only a partial sulphuration of the whole, the copper has the best chance of passing into the "mat," while the arsenic is the first to be eliminated as such, or, in the presence of oxidants, as oxide.

SCIENTIFIC METHODS IN ECOLOGY

Systems analysis is an important techniqve of ecosystem research and environmental management. Watt has pointed out that ecological systems are characteristically dynamic and complex, usually involving interactions between many variables, and often displaying lag effects, cumulative effects, thresholds, and nonlinear causal relationships. Such complex phenomena cannot always be studied by traditional techniques of individual research and scholarship. Computer analysis and team research are often necessary.

Systems analysis is a logical scientific method which approaches complex phenomena in several stages of operation: (1) *systems measurement*, in which the objectives of the problems are outlined and accurate data are obtained on important variables which relate to these objectives; (2) *data analysis,* in which the relationships between variables are explored through appropriate statistical procedures, and those variables most important in regulating the system are determined, (3) *systems modelling,* in which functional or mathematical models are composed to provide a theor,etical basis for relating the variables, (4) *systems simulation,* in which variables are anipulated mathematically to evaluate the consequences of changes within the system, and (5) *systems optimization,* in which the best strategies for achieving the objectives are evaluated and selected.

This approach is basically similar to standard scientific procedure which involves description, classification, hypothesis formation, experimentation, and clinical tests or field trials. The particular characteristic of systems analysis, however, is that it can operate in very complex systems which require computerized data handling and do not lend themselves to direct experimentation. One can —a city, an ocean, or a range of mountains. Thus, mathematical modelling and computer simulation is sometimes the only feasible experimental approach in large-scale ecological research. Team research is also a usual component of systems analysis, for rarely can a single person possess all the skills necessary for the complete systems approach.

Systems analysis can be illustrated with the common problem of improving water quality in a badly polluted river. *Systems measurement* would first involve a statement of the objectives in water quality and river characteristics which are desired. These would be expressed in terms of physical characteristics (temperature, clarity, dissolved oxygen, nutrient levels, trace element concentrations, etc.), and biological characteristics (bacterial, algal, crustacean, insect, fish pop ulations, etc.) which are desired in the river. Systems measurement would then involve making a detailed inventory of existing conditions, so that accurate data would be obtained on the major physical and biotic features of the river in its present polluted condition. Systems measurement would finally involve the identification of the major influences on the stream. This would require knowledge of its watershed, weather patterns, land-use patterns, geologic formations, domestic inputs, industrial operations, and stream flow characteristics. Hence, the enormity of just stage one, systems measurement, becomes apparent. This stage in a relatively small river could easily take a team of 5 to 10 scientists several years to get baseline data and understand the prevailing situation in specific terms.

Stage two, *data analysis,* would involve computer and statistical analysis of relationships between variables. How do land-use patterns, industrial operations, and domestic inputs interact with topography, weather, and stream flow characteristics to influence the physical and biotic qualities of the'river? Some specific questions in this area would be: What are the sources of the nutrients? How do the nutrient levels influence the biotic communities? Are oxygen and temperature levels within satisfactory ranges If not, why not? Are toxic chemicals present in the stream. If so, what are their origins, their effects, and their fates? A great many questions of this type can be asked, and it is apparent that multivariate analyses, as well as other statistical procedures, must be utilized.

The third stage, *systems modelling,* would be undertaken when the investigators felt they had a lead on the origins and relationships of the important variables within the system. They could then propose a mathematical relationship between various factors influencing the prevailing conditions within the river. Data analyses might suggest, for example, that pesticide run-off from agricultural operations was poisoning the river and responsible for the absence of certain organisms. The analyses might also suggest that excessive nutrients from domestic sewage were creating high bacterial populations which reduced dissolved oxygen below satisfactory levels.

The fourth stage, *systems simulation,* would consist of computer runs with different variables modified. The model would then predict changes in other variables. For example, systems simulation would estimate and predict changes in the river if agricultural practices were altered, if sewage treatment plants were installed, or if industrial operations were curtailed. It becomes apparent that modern computer techniques are essential at several stages in systems analysis, especially in data analysis and in systems simulation. Ideally, an integrated computer technology program should be utilized throughout the entire systems research if possible, from data collection to systems optimization.

8

Forest Ecology

The crisis in tropical forest resources is today recognised as the world's most severe ecological and economic crisis. This is primarily because of the linkages between the genetic resources and diversity of tropical forests and food security of the entire world, and the linkages between the ecological stability of tropical forests and the economic well-being of the majority of the world's people who live in the tropics, in what is called the Third World.

These Third World countries, the erstwhile colonies of the industrialized coun tries, provided natural resources on which the industrialization of the latter was based. Both industrialisation and economic growth in the colonial and post-colonial periods have been based on the reckless exploitation of tropical forests. Today, the cumulative impact of this over-exploitation has led to critical and almost irreversible ecological degradation.

The famine in Africa and other arid regions has shifted the world's attention to the high ecological and social costs of tropical deforestation. It has become the central concern of governments, development agencies and ecology movements. Yet the focus on tropical deforestation and its reversal is not automatically translated into the protection of tropical forests and those who depend on them for survival. As long as misconceptions about the nature of tropical forest ecosystems prevail, as long as conflicting demands are ignored and as long as the causes of tropical deforestation are inaccurately located, this degradation cannot be arrested. As a result, tropical ecosystems will continue to be degraded, the survival of people of the Third World will continue to be threatened, and forest conflicts will continue to grow. Normally, forests are identified only with the economy associated with the commercial-industrial use of forests. lowever, the crisis of tropical forestry needs to be understood in the light of the conflicting demands for forest biomass, by the three fundamental economies associated with forests:

1. Nature's economy of essential ecological processes.
2. The survival economy of basic needs satisfaction of the people.

3. The market economy of industrial-commercial demands.

Nature's economy of essential ecological processes generates a demand on the products of the forest in terms of the maintenance of the stability of soil systems and the hydrological balance of the forest ecosystems. In ecologically sensitive ecosystems like upland watersheds, this economy becomes the most crucial one and should be given the necessary attention in forest management. Neglecting this economy in upland watersheds will imply tremendous negative externalities to the national exchequer as relief for regular floods and drought, which are easily described as loss due to nature's fury. The survival economy of basic needs satisfaction reflects the requirement of forest biomass of the people living in and in the vicinity of forests in terms of fuelwood, fodder, fruits, nuts, green manure, small timber, etc. In forest areas where human settlements have either existed or are in the vicinity, the requirements of the survival economy have been satisfied all along without any major ecological damage. However, under certain situations, the pressure of the survival economy can be substantial and its neglect can lead to the unexpected and rapid degradation of forest resources.'

The market economy of industrial-commercial demands coastitutes the forest biomass demand of the total market system in the formal market economy. It includes the demand for pulpwood. plywood. furniture, house construction, etc., as well as fuelwood for the urban market. The demand for biomass from the urban industrial sector as well as the survival requirements of people have increased dramatically in the last century in India. There are many examples which illustrate that the growth of forest based industries is disproportionately beyond the ecological limit of the renewable productivity of nature. under the present system of management. The growth in population adds another significant demand for biomass for domestic purposes. It has, however, not been recognised, quantified and internalized in formal forest management. In the perspective of the increasing demand from survival and market economies, the biomass requirement for nature's economy are systematically sacrificed and nature's needs remain totally unfulfilled. In due course, this leads to the ecological destabilisation of the forest ecosystems.

Again, the conflict between survival and market economies assumes large proportions when most of the biomass produced is cornered by the economically powerful groups through the formal official mechanisms while the basic needs of fuel, fodder and small timber of the economically weak remain unsatisfied due to their weak political and economic status. Obviously, these three diverse economies push for the satisfaction of their demands either silently or loudly, resulting in both overt and covert conflicts over forest resources. The tacit and invisible nature of these conflicts combined with a mistaken or incomplete understanding of these diverse economies can result in the lack of perception of conflicts between them. The failure to perceive conflicts in forest use can only aggravate the forestry crisis. It is thus absolutely essential to understand and perceive the covert as well as explicit demands on forest resources to evolve a forest policy that is ecologically sensitive and socially just, so that our forest and land resources can be used for the overall satisfaction of the needs of the nation and the people in an equitable and sustainable manner.

The conceptual framework based on the three economies adopted here differs from the conventional categories related to forest resources. We do not use the dichotomy between quantity/quality as categories of forest use that Hallsworth, for example, has used. According to him, Human demands on the forest fall into two categories. First a demand for forest quantities; for the actual things a forest can produce: for timber, for food and for space for cultivation or for grazing; secondly, a demand for forest qualities; for the effects that forests have on the environment of man-to protect supplies of water, provide havens for wild-life and maintain the pool of genetic resources, to protect the soil against erosion, and to provide space for recreations.

The dichotomy between quantity and quality, as between tangible and intangible, fails to capture the reality of those village women in Garhwal who launched the Chipko movement because for them water from the forest is a more significant product than wood and timber. For them water is not an 'intangible' produce or a mere quality. It is more tangible and basic in their sustenance economy than the commercial wood extracted and exported from their forests.

For similar reasons we have not adopted the local-national dichotomy between local and national interests to understand conflicts over natural resources, because the local subsumes the national interest. The national interest is or should be the integration of all local interests, not just another interest acting over and against local interests. The demands of nature's economy and survival economy are national demands, seen throughout the country, and are not peculiar to a particular region. What has usually passed as the 'national interest' are the large scale demands of the commercial industrial sector, operating through the government. The emergence of ecology movements at the.national level are indicative of the fact that these are demands of a socially narrow sector which come into conflict with socially broader sets of demands that are more appropriately termed the national interest.

We have also avoided the categories of private versus public demands because they fail to show adequately that what are called individual or private needs at the local level are located in the public context of a village community, and what usually passes as public policy in forestry is a government policy which is totally subservient to commercial/industrial interests. The 'privatisation' inherent in a commercially-oriented forest policy is What has been challenged by movements like Chipko which demand a more effective social and public control over forest resources. The official management of forest resources in the name of 'national' or 'public' interest has, in reality, privatised people's 'common resources. This privatization trend which was rooted in the colonial period has survived to the present day. As Chhattarpati Singh observes, 'The class or "public" which more often than not benefits from such acquisitions is the rich. This is patently true in the acquisition of common land, especially forests. The public of the "public purpose" for which forests have been acquired constitutes all but the forest dwellers.

We have therefore preferred to distinguish human demands on the basis of use for survival and use for commerce and industry, and have included nature's demands to avoid an anthropocentric bias as well as to have a context to locate forest movements like Chipko which struggle for forest conservation to respect nature's rights, and not just to assert their own rights to forest resources.

ECOLOGY MOVEMENTS AND CONFLICTS OVER FOREST NATURAL RESOURCES

The recent period in human history contrasts with all the earlier ones in its strikingly high rate of resource utilization. Ever expanding and intensifying industrial and agricultural production has generated increasing demands on the world's total stock and flow of resources. These demands are mostly generated from the industrially advanced countries of the North and the industrial enclaves in the underdeveloped countries of the South. Paradoxically, the increasing dependence of the industrialised societies on natural resources, through the rapid spread of energy and resource-intensive production technologies, has been accompanied by the spread of the myth that increased dependence on modern technologies implies a decreased dependence on nature and natural resources This myth is supported by the introduction of a long and indirect chain of resource utilisation which leaves invisible the real material resource demands of the industrial processes.

Through this combination of resource intensity at the material level and resource indifference at the conceptual and political levels, conflicts over natural resources generated by the new pattern of resource utilisation are generally shrouded and overlooked. These conflicts become visible when resource and energy-intensive industrial technologies are challenged by communities whose survival depends on the conservation of resources threatened by destruction and overexploitation, or when the devastatingly destructive potential of some industrial technologies is demonstrated as in the Bhopal disaster.

For centuries, vital natural resources like land, water and forests had been controlled and used collectively by village communities thus ensuring a sustainable use of these renewable resources. The first radical change in resource control and the emergence of major conflicts over natural resources induced by non-local factors was associated with colonial domination of this part of the world. Colonial domination systematically transformed the common vital resources into commodities for generating profits and growth of revenues. The first industrial revolution was to a large extent supported by this transformation of commons into commodities which permitted European industries access to the resources of South Asia.

With the collapse of the international colonial structure and the establishment of sovereign countries in the region, this international conflict over natural resources was expected to be reduced and replaced by resource policies guided by comprehensive national interests. However, resource use policies continued along the colonial pattern and, in the recent past, a second drastic change in resource use has been initiated to meet the international requirements and the demands of the elites in the Third World, leading to yet another acute conflict among the diverse interests. The most seriously threatened interest, in this conflict, appears to be that of the politically weak and socially disorganised group whose resource requirements are minimal and whose survival is primarily dependent directly on the products of nature outside the market system. Recent changes in resource utilisation have almost wholly by-passed the survival needs of these groups. These changes are primarily guided by the requirements of the countries of the North and of the elites of the South.

This book analyses environmental conflicts in contemporary human society. In general it relates to societies all over the world, but in particular it addresses the most intense and emerging social contradictions in India related to conflicts over natural resources. Science and technology are central to these conflicts because while scientific knowledge has been used by contemporary societies to considerably enlarge man's access to natural resources, it has also allowed the utilisation natural resources at extremely high rates.

The contemporary period is characterised by the emergence of ecology movements in all parts of the world which are attempting to redesign the pattern and extent of natural resource utilisation to ensure social equality and ecological sustainability. Ecology movements emerging from conflicts over natural resources and the people's right to survival are spreading in regions like the Indian subcontinent where most natural resources are already being utilised to fulfil the basic survival needs of a large majority of people.

The introduction of resource and energy-intensive production technologies under such conditions leads to economic growth for a small minority while, at the same time, undermines the material basis for the survival of the large majority.

In this way, ecology movements have questioned the validity of the dominant concepts and indicators of economic development. The ideology of economic development, which remained almost monolithic in the post World War II period, is thus faced with a major foundational challenge.

In this chapter an attempt has been made to provide a systematic conceptual framework for analysing the processes and structures of modern economic development from an ecological -perspective. It attempts to analyse the relationship between economic development and conflicts over natural resources to trace the roots of ecological movements.

Further, in the light of the ecological perspective, it examines the fundamental assumptions and categories of modern development economics that are used to determine the objectives of economic development as well as the criteria for the choice of technologies that are used to achieve these objectives.

FOREST HYDROLOGY AND MANAGEMENT

Forest hydrology has built a strong foundation of general principles concerning the direct effects of forest management on hydrologic processes from plot studies, process studies, and watershed experiments. The challenge now is to apply these principles to predict how hydrologic processes will respond to many forms of change in forest landscapes. Forest hydrologists have long recognized the need to understand indirect and interacting effects of forest management at much larger spatial scales and longer temporal scales than is possible in plot studies, process studies, and watershed experiments. Indirect effects are responses to forest management that are displaced in time or space, such as fire suppression leading to insect outbreaks that affect forest hydrology. Interacting effects occur when two or more management practices coincide, such as when post-salvage logging and road building have a different collective effect on forest hydrology that differs from their individual effects.

This chapter examines the research challenges faced by forest hydrology as it moves from principles to prediction at larger spatial scales, at longer temporal scales, and in a changing social context. The chapter concludes by outlining the potential for improved cumulative watershed effects analysis that could provide the predictions needed by forest and water managers in the twenty-first century.

SPATIAL RESEARCH NEEDS

A key unresolved issue in forest hydrology is how to apply the findings of hydrological studies in one area to a different area or how to scale up the findings to large watersheds and landscapes. Although forest hydrologists have confidence in the general principles of hydrologic responses to forest management and disturbance, they cannot predict precisely how forest management will affect hydrologic processes in specific places other than those that have been intensively studied. Most forest hydrology studies are conducted in small watersheds that are instrumented to measure streamflow and other hydrologic properties. However, the sum total of the area studied by forest hydrology is only a tiny fraction of the watersheds in the United States, and hydrologists recognize the need to extend hydrologic knowledge from "gauged basins" (watersheds that have measured records) to ungauged basins. Predictions are most needed in ungauged places to better understand hydrologic effects where conflicts sometime arise: in water supply systems for agriculture and cities; rivers where endangered and threatened aquatic species occur; large water bodies such as the Chesapeake Bay; and many, many others.

Forest hydrology is adopting a landscape perspective to examine spatial patterns of forests and associated hydrologic processes and to link principles from plot- and small watershed scales to predictions at larger spatial scales (hundreds of square kilometers). Within a watershed, forests can be located in the headwaters, along riparian corridors, in woodlots in agriculture lands, and in urban or suburban areas. Based on its intra-basin position, a forest fulfills various water-related functions with respect to water quantity and quality. For example, forests in headwaters influence water yield and the quality of water delivered to downstream areas. Riparian forests located along streams throughout a watershed provide key functions for protecting streams from inputs of sediment, nutrients, and herbicides; provide wildlife habitat for terrestrial and aquatic organisms; and support a diversity of other functions. Riparian forests have been greatly altered by economic development, and they are the focus of many forest management guidelines designed to preserve water quantity and water quality.

Hydrologists use models to predict water quantity and quality in watersheds where there are no measured records. Since 2004, a working group for Prediction in Ungauged Basins (PUB) of the International Association of Hydrological Sciences has developed methodologies for assessing uncertainty in hydrologic predictions arising from uncertainties in landscape properties and climate inputs, choice of model structure, and methods of information transfer from gauged to ungauged watersheds. Most hydrological models are developed and tested for gauged basins and subsequently are validated and applied to ungauged areas.

However, models that have been fitted to data in small, gauged watersheds often provide inaccurate or imprecise predictions when they are (1) extrapolated to other small forested headwater basins, (2) extrapolated to future time periods, or (3) applied to large watersheds. This problem of prediction in ungauged basins has preoccupied hydrology researchers for several decades, and is compounded by a lack of information about how direct hydrologic effects interact under the multiple sets of specific conditions that occur in changing forest landscapes. By examining forest hydrologic processes under a wide range of conditions, landscape-scale studies could provide data and understanding to help extend basic forest hydrology principles to make predictions needed by water managers.

Road networks are a pervasive feature of forest landscapes. The location and density of roads in a watershed can influence the hydrologic effects of roads. In many forested areas, roads are concentrated in the valley bottoms immediately adjacent to streams, meadows, and wetlands. These roads have a particularly high potential for delivering runoff and sediment to streams, lakes, and aquatic ecosystems. The legacy of midslope roads from past logging practices is also of concern, because these have a high potential for subsurface flow interception, connectivity to the drainage network, and initiating shallow landslides. Considerable research effort has been devoted to modifying road design and management to mitigate erosion, and to developing techniques to decommission roads. The hydrologic effects of road networks at large scales, and the effects of road decommissioning are not widely studied.

TEMPORAL RESEARCH NEEDS

Water management systems have been designed and operated under the assumption that hydrologic variables such as annual water yield, while varying over time, can be predicted reliably based on instrument records. However, increased understanding of long-term variability and trends in climate has undermined this assumption. If precipitation and streamflow vary over the long term, future annual water yields may fall short of the levels that water supply systems—and attendant agricultural and urban development—were designed to provide. Given this context, it is critical for forest hydrologists to extend beyond general principles to make predictions of how forest management and disturbance affect hydrologic response on time scales that exceed those of most forest hydrology science.

Some forest and stream management plans now include the historical range of variability, which presupposes that (1) past conditions and processes provide context and guidance for managing ecological systems today; and (2) disturbance-driven spatial and temporal variability is a vital attribute of nearly all ecological systems. The historical range of variability helps characterize the variation in quantity, quality, and timing of streamflow from forests. It can also be used to establish baselines for assessing change in water from forests over time.

Forests and their associated hydrologic processes change on time scales ranging from decades to hundreds, or even thousands, of years. The temporal context for understanding forest hydrologic processes involves expanding the temporal scale into the past to consider the effects of past forest practices and into the future to project and anticipate changes in land use and climate. Many different kinds of legacies of past human activities affect forests in the United States. In some areas, native forests have been converted to agricultural and urban uses, and forests have regrown on abandoned agricultural lands in others. Roads and expansion of urban areas have fragmented forests into smaller, less-contiguous patches and created new drainage patterns. Fire suppression has changed the structure and community composition of many forests, especially in those with otherwise active fire regimes. Exotic species introductions, grazing by domestic animals, predator eradication, and timber harvesting methods have changed forest cover and species composition as well. Future urban and suburban development and climate change are expected to continue to alter forest cover and species composition. Human activities will modify forests in the future, and future legacies will reflect current, regional forest histories.

INVERTEBRATE SPECIES IN FOREST ECOSYSTEMS

The diversity and abundance of invertebrate species in forest ecosystems are determined by the interaction of complex ecological and environmental factors. Research into these factors is gradually providing data that can be incorporated into models, both descriptive and mathematical, of the processes involved. At the core of such models is the description of the availability of resources that enables a particular invertebrate species to reproduce, whereas the rate of reproduction is dependent on multiple factors, including temperature, competition, etc., that determine utilization of available resources. In relation to exploitation of resources within a forest ecosystem, the primary focus for forest managers is the potential of invertebrates to cause damage and to reduce yields of the trees themselves. This is certainly the case in managed forests where the primary aim is to grow trees for commercial gain, often with associated value from recreational, landscape or environmental considerations. Any invertebrates that feed directly on the trees, or have an influence of how the trees grow, may be classified as pests and hence may require some form of pest management to reduce the threat. But it is pertinent to consider how ecological theory and practice can be used both to understand why a pest problem has arisen and to provide guidance on how to combat that problem. The same principles can be applied to understanding and enhancing the biodiversity of forests, including conservation of rare and beneficial invertebrates. Indeed, the two extremes of pest outbreak and invertebrate rarity are part of the same continuum of interaction between invertebrates and their host trees.

In general, considering that trees are known to harbour the greatest numbers of insect species (diversity), it is surprising that serious pest status is reached only relatively infrequently. For example, although oak *(Quercus* spp.) is known to support at least 450 species of insect in Britain , Bevan (1987) lists only 35 species as pests, of which five were classified as important or severe (XXX-XXXXX on Bevan's scale). Wider listing of pest species has been noted for forest insects in continental Europe, although even here the number of consistently serious pests is small relative to the total diversity of insects present (Klimetzek 1993).

Naturally, the severity of a pest outbreak will be classified differently depending on the purposes of the forest manager, and thus it is not always possible to classify insects consistently as pests across geographical ranges or, indeed, between years. Further, an insect may normally be classified as uncommon or rare but, given an abundance of resources, may be described later as a pest. This was certainly the case for oak pinhole borer, *Platypus cylindrus* (Coleoptera: Platypodidae), which prior to the 1987 great storm in southern England was listed in the British Red Data Book as rare.

Winter (1988) warned that the great increase in availability of freshly dead oak following the storm could result in an increase in numbers of *P. cylindrus* and, subsequently, it has been noted that the insect is now causing damage to high-value oak logs as a result of its habit of boring directly into the heartwood. Therefore, consideration of why invertebrate abundance might increase above a given threshold level can provide a more consistent appraisal of status and also potential approaches for reducing populations below that threshold or indicating measures that can be taken to encourage rare or endangered species.

Among the many interacting processes that determine insect diversity and abundance, a few attributes that are particularly well linked to the environmental status of trees can be distinguished. These provide a means to describe intrinsic processes but also allow comparison with other plants, thus offering the potential for a more consistent approach to descriptive population ecology of invertebrates irrespective of the host plant being considered.

Longevity

Trees are the longest-lived components of an ecosystem and, in the majority of natural situations, approach or represent the climax stage of vegetation succession. This provides opportunities for continuity of insect population growth and over time this will give a particular set of insect associates for a given tree species. Continuing the theme of resource availability, the fact that trees may be present in the same location for tens or hundreds of years ensures that both migrant and, particularly, relatively sedentary invertebrates can exploit them at some stage during their growth. However, longevity *per se* is not a quantifiable attribute but does provide the means for the other components, to influence invertebrate diversity and abundance. Increasing stability in the environment, as represented under forest conditions, leads to stability in both microclimate and resource availability, particularly favouring exploitation by specialist insect feeders and their associates.

Biogeography

Tree species richness in a given region or locality varies considerably with geographical location and thus the climax community structure and longevity of individual species may vary accordingly. Although subject to uncertainty and lack of unequivocal evidence of the underlying processes, there is certainly a gradient of species richness of plant cover, especially trees, from the tropics to the poles. Not surprisingly, the same applies to a wide range of animals and plants; as an extreme example, the species richness of orchids ranges from 15 to 2500 in a latitudinal range from 0 to 66° S. Further examples are provided by Brown (1988). More specifically, in an analysis of species richness of deciduous forests both in the tropics and, latitudinally, within North America, Brown and Gibson (1983) contrasted the high diversity of tree species in the tropics (up to 100 ha^{-1}) with the low diversity from north to south within North America (1–30ha^{-1}). However, even within such a generalization there are exceptions, so that for example conifers are more diverse in temperate latitudes.

Geological Time

The ecological structure of forests and of their associated invertebrate faunas is determined by both present and recent characteristics, particularly area, and by their history in geological time. The latter characteristic is driven as much by *time per se* as by the history of major disturbances (glaciations, volcanic eruptions, land shifts, etc.) within geological time. Thus, present flora and fauna may well be determined by recolonization since the last major disturbance, the diversity of species being a reflection of both colonization and speciation relative to more recent ecological conditions. The gradient of species from polar to tropical regions could therefore be explained by the high level of disturbance closer to the polar masses compared with the relative stability of climate in the tropics. Evidence from habitats that have become isolated since the last major disturbance indicates that current species diversity may reflect the historical link to the original major habitat. For example, islands that were once joined by land bridges to the larger land masses of New Guinea have species diversities of birds greater than expected compared with other islands that were never connected. However, although local ecological communities can be explained by historical patterns, the gradients over wide geographical scales are not so easily attributed to time as the major determinant.

The concept that major disturbances drive change undoubtedly carries weight, but closer analysis of tropical rain forests reveals that they too have been subject to disturbances of various sorts and are, in many cases, much changed over geological time. Based on this knowledge Haffer proposed a theory that disturbances in the tropics during the Pleistocene (alternating wet and dry periods giving rise to forest blocks surrounded by grassland) gave rise to refugia in which high levels of speciation took place, ultimately leading to the current high diversity characteristic of the tropics. While this theory is plausible and has been invoked by other authors, tests of the hypothesis have cast doubt over its wide applicability.

Irrespective of the mechanistic bases for variation in species richness over wide latitudinal ranges, time is a significant determinant at a more local scale. Birks (1980) analysed the insect faunas of trees in Britain during the period since the last glaciation 13000 years ago and concluded that there was a significant correlation with the time that a given tree species had been continuously present in Britain during that period. Taking this further, Kennedy and Southwood (1984) included Birks' radiocarbon estimates of time in Britain as a variable in a multiple regression analysis of insects on British trees. They showed that time was a significant predictor, both in its own right and as a co-predictor with log abundance (area). This is logical considering that over time there will be a tendency for well-established tree genera to increase their abundance, despite the recent proliferation in areas arising from commercial afforestation.

Size

A consequence of basic structure and longevity is that trees tend to be the largest components of the phylloplane, thus providing a much wider number and range of ecological niches compared with herb and shrub layer plants. Such attributes enable more insect species to colonize the plants without facing competition, both interspecific and intraspecific. Size has many interrelated characteristics that help to explain the presence of both herbivores and their natural enemies.

- A larger physical presence is more easily detected and colonized by invertebrates. This concept, termed 'apparency', reflects a higher visual profile for colonizing adults or passively migrating immature life stages (*e.g.* mean height was a good predictor in models of the distribution of Scolytidae in Finland; Heliovaara & Vaisanen 1995) and a greater production of olfactory cues.
- Complex plant architecture is a consequence of greater size and for trees is particularly linked to the provision of many niches capable of supporting invertebrates with a wide range of feeding strategies (guilds). Although the concept of the guild is not always clearly defined , it is nevertheless a useful means of describing the trophic interactions of

invertebrates and trees without having to consider their precise taxonomic status. Thus, seed, bud, leaf, bark and wood feeders can be distinguished, each occupying a different part of the tree and therefore potentially avoiding competition.

- Increased biomass provides greater food resources per individual, thus encouraging growth and breeding success whilst reducing potential intraspecific competition. Price (1992) has reviewed the role of plant resources in insect population dynamics and concludes that, in part, the carrying capacity of an ecosystem depends on plant succession in time and space. Carrying capacity is therefore greater for trees, which generally appear late in succession, compared with herbs or shrubs. Thus biomass is available for longer and in greater quantities on trees compared with other plants.
- The concept of enemy-free space applies to the likelihood of herbivores being overlooked by searching parasitoids or predators. One aspect of size is that there is more opportunity for herbivores to occupy a part of the plant that offers protection against natural enemies (and competition from other herbivores). The complexity and number of niches present on a plant (plant architecture; Lawton 1983) therefore has an effect on enemy-free space. The greater the architectural complexity, the greater the time that natural enemies may have to spend in searching for prey, thus reducing their overall effectiveness and enhancing the survival probability of herbivores.

Area

Forests tend to occupy greater areas than other plants. There is evidence to support the view that the greater the area occupied by the host plant, the greater the number of insect species associated with that host. This is called the species-area relationship and was originally linked to the island biogeography theories of species isolation and colonization.

Species-area relationships have been demonstrated for many plants and animals, including both highly mobile and sedentary species. With regard to the numbers of insect species on trees, data on the British insect fauna, one of the best characterized in the world, have been analysed by a number of authors.

Arising from earlier tentative analyses , Kennedy and Southwood (1984) analysed the relationships between insect species and characteristics of tree species in Britain. They concluded that there was a significant relationship between the area occupied by British tree species and the numbers of insect species associated with them. The area occupancy data were based on county and subcounty information of plant records and were thus potentially overestimates of actual areas occupied.

Claridge and Evans (1990) reanalysed the species-area relationships using the same insect data as Kennedy and Southwood but employing actual area information derived from Forestry Commission census data. They concluded that area was not a good descriptor for insect species on deciduous trees but was just significant for conifers.

However, further unpublished analysis of the data broken down into numbers and areas of habitat patches occupied by the tree genera indicated that whereas total area was not a good descriptor, the degree of fragmentation of that area provided a better explanation for the observed insect species numbers. A similar conclusion, concentrating on Lepidoptera that have moved hosts to include conifers, was reached by Fraser and Lawton (1994) in an analysis of new associations on British trees. The overall finding that area provides a broad descriptor of insect diversity remains valid, although this does not explain the mechanisms that lead to these associations.

Taxonomic Relatedness

In a given ecosystem, the closer the taxonomic relatedness of host plants, the more similar the numbers of insect species associated with those plants. This has been documented for tree species that have a long history in a particular location and thus provide rich sources of invertebrate species that may subsequently colonize other tree species, especially if they are taxonomically related. A particularly good example of the process in action is the colonization of *Nothofagus,* a member of the Fagaceae newly introduced to Britain, which has been colonized rapidly by insects associated with closely related members of the native Fagaceae.

Geographical isolation as a critical factor in determining invertebrate diversity and implications for international movement of pest organisms. Geographic isolation drives the acceleration of speciation and provides the means to derive principles on the processes involved. In addition, the fact of isolation means that some invertebrates abundant in one region will be absent elsewhere, despite conditions being suitable for their establishment. In such situations, it is pertinent to examine the international plant health implications of geographical isolation and how modern patterns of trade influence the degree of isolation and later colonization by new insect species.

Geographical Isolation as a Factor in Determining Insect Diversity

In general, the basic principles apply across ecosystem boundaries and geographical zones extending from the poles to the tropics. In addition, the isolation afforded by relatively small islands provides further evidence of the principles of species colonization over space and time. Great Britain provides a particularly good example, because of its island position in the Atlantic

Offshore climatic zone and the fact that it has been subjected to glaciation in recent geological time.

Among the ecological characteristics that arise from this set of circumstances are a relatively depauperate mix of both animal and plant species that have arisen from the combination of losses resulting from the last ice age and the slow rate of recolonization arising from island status. British flora and fauna are therefore impoverished relative to continental Europe. Further influences arise from the preponderance of exotic tree species in commercial forestry in Britain, which although dominated by exotic conifer species also has increasing numbers of exotic broadleaved species.

Expanding on the principle that colonization of tree species is determined by the features, the ranges of numbers of insect species associated with trees in Britain reflect both the area (with provisos) and length of time that trees have been continuously present in Britain. However, there are exceptions, so that Sitka spruce in particular would appear to support far fewer species than predicted on the basis of area, although this probably also reflects the relatively short history of the species and recent expansions in areas planted in Britain.

Implications for International Movement of Pest Insects

Trading patterns between countries have had a considerable influence on both the flora and fauna of most of the countries in the world. This reflects deliberate introductions of plants and animals for agricultural, forestry and amenity purposes and also accidental introductions by association with other commodities. In the majority of cases, the introduced species have had a neutral to beneficial effect, reflecting their 'domesticity' within managed crop or animal husbandry systems.

However, there are many exceptions to this generalization and in most cases the results of introduction of new species were not foreseen, either through lack of knowledge of the potential impacts or because the introduction was accidental and undetected. The literature on international biological control is dominated by examples where attempts have been made to rectify the effects of new pest introductions (both animal and plant). A classic example is the control of the woodwasp *Sirex noctilio* (Hymenoptera: Siricidae) in exotic pine forests in Australia with the introduced nematode *Deladenus siricidicola* (Nematoda: Neotylenchidae) isolated from *Sirex* in New Zealand. This nematode has a life cycle that includes a free-living form that feeds on the fungus *Amylostereum areolatum* and a parasitic form that invades *S. noctilio* larvae and subsequently migrates to the reproductive organs of the female wasp, causing sterility. In this situation, all elements of the interaction are exotic to the new location, with little prospect of natural control being realized.

Bibliography

Akhil Baruah: *Advanced Morphology of Angiosperms*, Aavishkar, Delhi, 2008.

Bauer MW: *Biotechnology-the Making of a Global Controversy*, Cambridge, Cambridge University Press, 2002.

Bernauer, Thomas: *Genes, Trade, and Regulation: The Seeds of Conflict in Food Biotechnology*, Princeton, Princeton University. 2003.

Broach, J.R.: *The Molecular Biology of the Yeast*, Cold Spring Harbor, Cold Spring Harbor Laboratory, 1981.

Burch, William R. Jr.: *Human Ecology: An Environmental Approach*, Belmont, Duxbury Press, 1994.

Chrispeels, Maarten : *Plants, Genes and Crop Biotechnology*, Sudbury MA, Jones and Barlett Publishers, 2003.

Duckworth, W L H : *Morphology and Anthropology : A Handbook for Students*, Cosmo, Delhi, 2006.

Dusenbery, David B.: *Life at a Small Scale: the Behavior of Microbes*, New York, Scientific American Library, 1996.

Fransman M, Junne G, Roobeek A: *The Biotechnology Revolution?*, Oxford, Blackwell, 1995.

Fumento, Michael: *Bioevolution: How Biotechnology is Changing Our World*, San Francisco, Encounter Books, 2003.

Govind Prasad: *Environmental Geomorphology*, Discovery Publishing House, Delhi, 2008.

Gupta, O.P. : *Water in Relation to Soils and Plants : With Special Reference to Agriculture*, Agrobios, Delhi, 2002.

Hofrichter, Richard: *The Theory and Practice of Environmental Justice*, Philadelphia, New Society Publishers, 1993.

Jain, P.C. and M.C. Bhargava: *Entomology : Novel Approaches*, New India, Delhi, 2007.

Jameson, J. L.: *Principles of Molecular Medicine*, Totowa, Humana Press, 1998.

Kannaiyan, S. : *Rice Management Biotechnology*, Associated, Delhi, 1995.

Keshav Prasad Yadav: *Application of Morphometry in Geomorphology*, Radha Pub, Delhi, 2008.

Kruvant, W.J.: *People, Energy, and Pollution*, Cambridge, Ballinger Publishing, 1975.

Lodish, H.: *Molecular Cell Biology*, New York, Freeman, 2000.

Lorenzen, S.: *The Phylogenetic Systematics of Freeliving Nematodes*, London, The Ray Society, 1994.

Lynch, J.M., and Hobbie, J.E.: *Micro-organisms in Action: Concepts and Applications in Microbial Ecology*, Blackwell Scientific Publications, Oxford, 1988.

Maarten, C.: *Plants, Genes and Biodiversity*, Sudbury MA, Jones and Barlett Publishers, 2003.

Madan Lal Bagdi: *Physiology, Biochemistry and Biotechnology*, Manglam Pub, Delhi, 2007.

Menninger, Karl: *Number-Words and Number-Symbols*. London, MIT, 1969.

Nikolsky, G.V. : *The Ecology of Fishes*, Agrobios, Delhi, 2008.

Pilgrim R.: *Post Harvest Handling of Minor Exotics*, St. George's, Grenada, 1996.

Politycka, A.R. and C L Goswami: *Plant Physiology : Research Methods*, Scientific, Delhi, 2007.

Raff, K. Roberts, and J. Watson, *Molecular Biology of the Cell*, New York: Garland Publishing, 1989.

Ramann, E. : *The Evolution and Classification of Soils*, Asiatic Pub, Calcutta, 2006.

Rietman, Ed.: *Molecular Engineering of Nanosystems*, New York, Springer, 2001.

Robinson, D.H. ; *Entomology : Principles and Practices*, Agrobios, Delhi, 2001.

Saravanan, T. and K. Vanangamudi: *Principles and Methods of Plant Breeding*, International Book, Delhi, 2005.

Sayler, G.S., Fox, R., and Blackburn, J.W.: *Environmental Biotechnology for Waste Treatment*, Plenum Press, New York, 1991.

Sheldon, J.K.: *Practical Environmental Bioremediation*, Lewis Publishers, Boca Raton, 1992.

Shubhrata R. Mishra: *Morphology of Fungi*, Discovery Pub, Delhi, 2005.

Singh, S.K. and Seema Srivastava: *Plant Physiology and Biochemistry*, Campus Books, Delhi, 2009.

Sudharmai Devi, C.R. : *Analytical Procedures in Soil Science and Agricultural Chemistry*, Agrotech, Delhi, 2004.

Switzer, R.L.: *Experimental Biochemistry*, New York, W.H. Freeman and Company, 1977.

Tawde A. B.: *Propagation and Rootstocks of Mango*, New Delhi, Malhotra, 1993.

Teich, M.: *Fundamentals of Photonics*, New York: Wiley, 1991.

Trivedi, P C : *Plant Physiology : Current Trends*, Pointer, Delhi, 2007.

Wenz, Peter S.: *Environmental Justice*, Albany, State University of New York Press, 1988.

Wood, E.J. Ferguson: *Marine Microbial Ecology*, London, Chapman and Hall, 1965.

Yoshida T.: *Cultivation of Citrus Genetic Resources for Evaluation of Characteristics*, Tokyo, JICA, 1996.

Index

G

H

I

L

M

N

O

P

R

S

T

U

W

❑❑❑